SIGNLL Conference on Computational Natural Language Learning 2020

CoNLL 2020 Shared Task: Cross-Framework Meaning Representation Parsing

Online
19 - 20 November 2020

ISBN: 978-1-7138-1993-6

CoNLL 2020

The SIGNLL Conference on Computational Natural Language Learning

Proceedings of the CoNLL 2020 Shared Task: Cross-Framework Meaning Representation Parsing

November 19-20, 2020
Online

Preface

We are excited (and a little relieved) to present the proceedings from the 2020 Shared Task on *Cross-Framework and Cross-Lingual Meaning Representation Parsing* (MRP 2020) at the Conference for Computational Language Learning (CoNLL), colocated with EMNLP 2020. This is the second, extended edition of the MRP Shared Task, following on from the earlier MRP task at CoNLL 2019, adding, among other things, additional languages beyond English.

This volume provides linguistic, methodological, and technical background to the target representations, mode of operation, and participating systems in a 'system bake-off' for *data-driven parsing* into *graph-structured* representations of *sentence meaning*.

The task received submissions from seven teams and one 'reference' submission by one of the task co-organzers. Two teams declined the invitation to submit a system description for publication in the proceedings, such that the volume in total comprises an in-depth task overview, two additional background pieces by task co-organizers, and five system descriptions by participanting teams. All system descriptions (and the background papers) were reviewed by at least three experts, drawing from among the task participants and an external pool of colleagues working in meaning representation parsing.

We much look forward to the presentation of results and meeting with task participants, even if online, at CoNLL in late November 2020. The conference will be completely virtual, with talks prerecorded and with one live Q&A session for the shared task.

The MRP 2020 shared task has been an intensive experience for organizers and participants alike, with data preparation, definition of evaluation metrics, system development, submission of parser outputs, scoring and compilation of the task proceedings—running near-continuously between February and October 2020. We are deeply grateful to all participants (including several who in the end did not make a submission) for the time and effort they have invested in system development and documentation. With no less than five distinct linguistic frameworks for graph-based meaning representation, in several languages, combined for the first time in a uniform training and evaluation setting, this was not an easy competition to enter. As co-organizers of the MRP 2019 and 2020 competitions, we will continue to work on facilitating cross-framework meaning representation parsing and enabling participants to further build on their work. All MRP 2019 and 2020 data has been submitted for release through the Linguistic Data Consortium, and we are further preparing an open-source release of those parts of the data that are free of copyright constraints.

Oslo, Jerusalem, Utrecht, Groningen, Prague,
Copenhagen, Nanjing, Boulder, and Waltham;

October 2020

Stephan Oepen, Omri Abend, Lasha Abzianidze, Johan Bos, Jan Hajič,
Daniel Hershcovich, Bin Li, Tim O'Gorman, Nianwen Xue and Daniel Zeman

Organizers:

Stephan Oepen, University of Oslo
Omri Abend, The Hebrew University of Jerusalem
Lasha Abzianidze, Utrecht University
Johan Bos, University of Groningen
Jan Hajič, Charles University, Prague
Daniel Hershcovich, University of Copenhagen
Bin Li, Nanjing Normal University
Tim O'Gorman, University of Colorado Boulder
Nianwen Xue, Brandeis University, Waltham
Daniel Zeman, Charles University, Prague

Program Committee:

Lasha Abzianidze
Ofir Arviv
Wanxiang Che
Bo Chen
Jayeol Chun
Longxu Dou
Daniel Hershcovich
Matthias Lindemann
Gaku Morio
Stephan Oepen
Hiroaki Ozaki
David Samuel
Nathan Schneider

Table of Contents

Conference Program

MRP 2020: The Second Shared Task on Cross-Framework and Cross-Lingual Meaning Representation Parsing

Stephan Oepen♣, Omri Abend♠, Lasha Abzianidze♡, Johan Bos◇, Jan Hajič°,
Daniel Hershcovich⋆, Bin Li•, Tim O'Gorman◦, Nianwen Xue*, and Daniel Zeman°

♣ University of Oslo, Department of Informatics
♠ The Hebrew University of Jerusalem, School of Computer Science and Engineering
♡ Utrecht University, UiL OTS
◇ University of Groningen, Center for Language and Cognition
° Charles University, Prague, Faculty of Mathematics and Physics, Institute of Formal and Applied Linguistics
⋆ University of Copenhagen, Department of Computer Science
• Nanjing Normal University, School of Chinese Language and Literature
◦ University of Massachusetts at Amherst, College of Information and Computer Sciences
* Brandeis University, Department of Computer Science

`mrp-organizers@nlpl.eu`

Abstract

The 2020 Shared Task at the Conference for Computational Language Learning (CoNLL) was devoted to Meaning Representation Parsing (MRP) across frameworks and languages. Extending a similar setup from the previous year, five distinct approaches to the representation of sentence meaning in the form of directed graphs were represented in the English training and evaluation data for the task, packaged in a uniform graph abstraction and serialization; for four of these representation frameworks, additional training and evaluation data was provided for one additional language per framework. The task received submissions from eight teams, of which two do not participate in the official ranking because they arrived after the closing deadline or made use of additional training data. All technical information regarding the task, including system submissions, official results, and links to supporting resources and software are available from the task web site at:

`http://mrp.nlpl.eu`

1 Background and Motivation

The 2020 Conference on Computational Language Learning (CoNLL) hosts a shared task (or 'system bake-off') on Cross-Framework Meaning Representation Parsing (MRP 2020), which is a revised and extended re-run of a similar CoNLL shared task in the preceding year. The goal of these tasks is to advance data-driven parsing into *graph-structured* representations of *sentence meaning*. For the first time, the MRP task series combines *formally* and *linguistically* different approaches to meaning representation in graph form in a uniform training and evaluation setup.

Key differences in the 2020 edition of the task include the addition of a graph-based encoding of Discourse Representation Structures (dubbed DRG); a generalization of Prague Tectogrammatical Graphs (to include more information from the original annotations); and a separate cross-lingual track, introducing one extra language (beyond English) for four of the frameworks involved.[1]

Participants were invited to develop parsing systems that support five distinct semantic graph frameworks in four languages (see §3 below)— all encoding core predicate–argument structure, among other things—in the same implementation. Ideally, these parsers predict sentence-level meaning representations in all frameworks in parallel. Architectures utilizing complementary knowledge sources (e.g. via parameter sharing) were encouraged, though not required. Learning from multiple flavors of meaning representation in tandem has hardly been explored (with notable exceptions, e.g. the parsers of Peng et al., 2017; Hershcovich et al., 2018; Stanovsky and Dagan, 2018; or Lindemann et al., 2019).

The task design aims to reduce framework-specific 'balkanization' in the field of meaning representation parsing. Its contributions include

---

[1]To reduce the threshold to participation, two of the target frameworks represented in MRP 2019 are not in focus this year, viz. the purely bi-lexical DELPH-IN MRS Bi-Lexical Dependencies and Prague Semantic Dependencies (PSD). These graphs largely overlap with the corresponding (but richer) frameworks in 2020, EDS and PTG, respectively, and the original bi-lexical semantic dependency graphs remain independently available (Oepen et al., 2015).

Proceedings of the CoNLL 2020 Shared Task: Cross-Framework Meaning Representation Parsing, pages 1–22
Online, Nov. 19-20, 2020. ©2020 Association for Computational Linguistics

(a) a unifying formal model over different semantic graph banks (§2), (b) uniform representations and scoring (§4 and §6), (c) contrastive evaluation across frameworks (§5), and (d) increased cross-fertilization of parsing approaches (§7).

2   Definitions: Graphs and Flavors

Reflecting different traditions and communities, there is wide variation in how individual meaning representation frameworks think (and talk) about semantic graphs, down to the level of visual conventions used in rendering graph structures. Increased terminological uniformity and guidance in how to navigate this rich and diverse landscape are among the desirable side-effects of the MRP task series. The following paragraphs provide semi-formal definitions of core graph-theoretic concepts that can be meaningfully applied across the range of frameworks represented in the shared task.

Basic Terminology   Semantic graphs (across different frameworks) can be viewed as directed graphs or *digraphs*. A semantic digraph is a triple (T, N, E) where N is a set of *nodes* and $E \subseteq N \times N$ is a set of *edges*. The *in-* and *out-degree* of a node count the number of edges arriving at or leaving from the node, respectively. In contrast to the unique *root* node in trees, graphs can have multiple (structural) roots, which we define as nodes with in-degree zero. The majority of semantic graphs are structurally multi-rooted. Thus, we distinguish one or several nodes in each graph as *top* nodes, $T \subseteq N$; the top(s) correspond(s) to the most central semantic entities in the graph, usually the main predication(s).

In a tree, every node except the root has in-degree one. In semantic graphs, nodes can have in-degree two or higher (indicating shared arguments), which constitutes a *reentrancy* in the graph. In contrast to trees, general digraphs may contain *cycles*, i.e. a directed path leading from a node to itself. Another central property of trees is that they are *connected*, meaning that there exists an undirected path between any pair of nodes. In contrast, semantic graphs need not generally be connected.

Finally, in some semantic graph frameworks there is a (total) linear order on the nodes, typically (though not necessarily) induced by the surface order of corresponding tokens. Such graphs are conventionally called *bi-lexical dependencies* (probably deriving from a notion of lexicalization articulated by Eisner, 1997) and formally consti-

tute *ordered graphs*. A natural way to visualize a bi-lexical dependency graph is to draw its edges as semicircles in the halfplane above the sentence. An ordered graph is called *noncrossing* if in such a drawing, the semicircles intersect only at their endpoints (this property is a natural generalization of projectivity as it is known from dependency trees).

A natural generalization of the noncrossing property, where one is allowed to also use the halfplane below the sentence for drawing edges is a property called *pagenumber two*. Kuhlmann and Oepen (2016) provide additional definitions and a quantitative summary of various formal graph properties across frameworks.

Hierarchy of Formal Flavors   In the context of the MRP shared task series, we have previously defined different *flavors* of semantic graphs based on the nature of the relationship they assume between the linguistic surface signal (typically a written sentence, i.e. a string) and the nodes of the graph (Oepen et al., 2019). We refer to this relation as *anchoring* (of nodes onto sub-strings); other commonly used terms include alignment, correspondence, or lexicalization.

Flavor (0) is characterized by the strongest form of anchoring, obtained in bi-lexical dependency graphs, where graph nodes injectively correspond to surface lexical units (i.e. tokens or 'words'). In such graphs, each node is directly linked to one specific token (conversely, there may be semantically empty tokens), and the nodes inherit the linear order of their corresponding tokens.

Flavor (1) includes a more general form of anchored semantic graphs, characterized by relaxing the correspondence between nodes and tokens, allowing arbitrary parts of the sentence (e.g. sub-token or multi-token sequences) as node anchors, as well as unanchored nodes, or multiple nodes anchored to overlapping sub-strings. These graphs afford greater flexibility in the representation of meaning contributed by, for example, (derivational) affixes or phrasal constructions and facilitate lexical decomposition (e.g. of causatives or comparatives).

Finally, Flavor (2) semantic graphs do not consider the correspondence between nodes and the surface string as part of the representation of meaning (thus backgrounding notions of derivation and compositionality). Such semantic graphs are simply unanchored.

While different flavors refer to formally defined

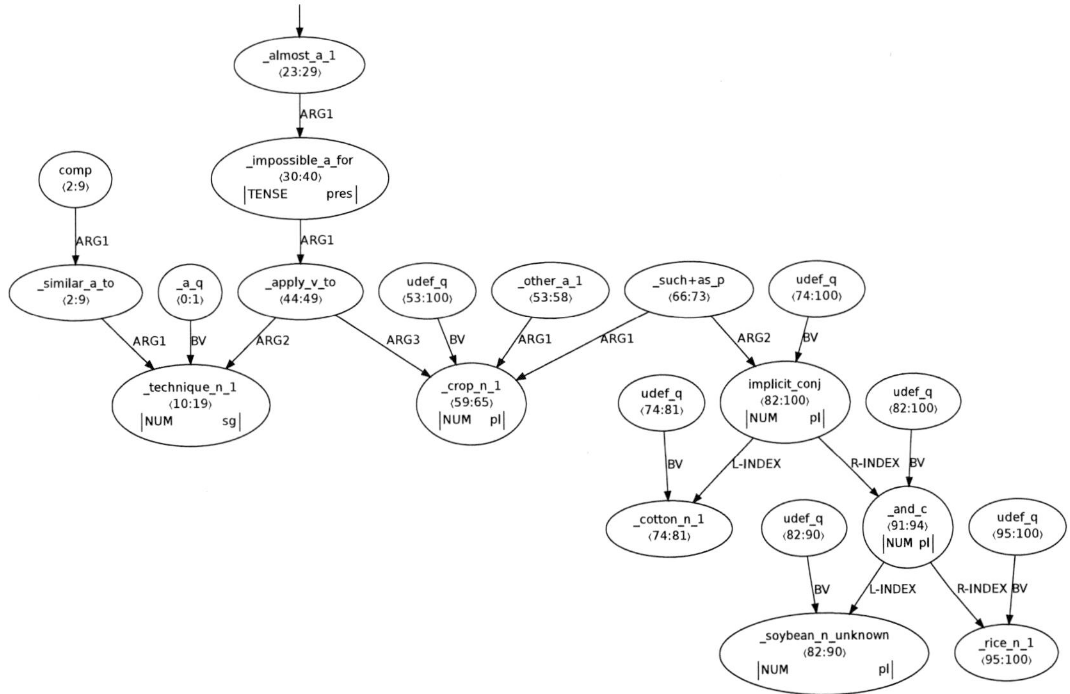

Figure 1: Semantic dependency graphs for the running example *A similar technique is almost impossible to apply to other crops, such as cotton, soybeans and rice*: Elementary Dependency Structures (EDS). Node properties are indicated as two-column records below the node labels.

sub-classes of semantic graphs, we reserve the term *framework* for specific linguistic approaches to graph-based meaning representation (typically encoded in a particular graph flavor, of course). However, the coarse classification into three distinct flavors does not fully account for the variability of anchoring relations observed across frameworks. For example, graphs can be partially anchored, meaning that only a subset of nodes are explicitly linked to the surface string; the anchoring relations that are present, can in turn stand in one-to-one correspondence to surface tokens, or allow overlapping and sub-token or phrasal relationships. At the same time, a framework may impose a total ordering of nodes independent (or possibly only partly dependent) on anchoring. We will interpret Flavors (0) and (2) strictly, as fully lexically anchored and wholly unanchored, respectively, leading to the categorization of mixed forms of anchoring as Flavor (1), and allow for the presence of ordered graphs, in principle at least, at all levels of the hierarchy.[2]

3 Meaning Representation Frameworks

The shared task combines five distinct frameworks for graph-based meaning representation, each with its specific formal and linguistic assumptions. This section reviews the frameworks and presents English example graphs for sentence #20209013 from the venerable Wall Street Journal (WSJ) Corpus from the Penn Treebank (PTB; Marcus et al., 1993):

(1) *A similar technique is almost impossible to apply to other crops, such as cotton, soybeans and rice.*

The example exhibits some interesting linguistic complexity, including what is called a tough adjective (*impossible*), a scopal adverb (*almost*), a tripartite coordinate structure, and apposition. The example graphs in Figures 1 through 4 are pre-

---

[2]Albeit in the realm of syntactic structure, the popular Universal Dependencies (UD; Nivre et al., 2020) initiative is currently exploring the introduction of 'enhanced' dependencies,

where unanchored nodes for unexpressed material beyond the surface string can be postulated (Schuster and Manning, 2016). Whether or not these nodes occupy a well-defined position in the otherwise total order of basic UD nodes remains an open question, but either way the presence of unanchored nodes will take enhanced UD graphs beyond the bi-lexical Flavor (0) graphs in our terminology.

3

sented in order of (arguably) increasing 'abstraction' from the surface string, i.e. ranging from fully anchored Flavor (1) to unanchored Flavor (2).

Elementary Dependency Structures The EDS graphs (Oepen and Lønning, 2006) originally derive from the underspecified logical forms computed by the English Resource Grammar (Flickinger et al., 2017; Copestake et al., 2005). These logical forms are not in and of themselves semantic graphs (in the sense of §2 above) and are often refered to as English Resource Semantics (ERS; Bender et al., 2015).[3] Elementary Dependency Structures (EDS; Oepen and Lønning, 2006) encode English Resource Semantics in a variable-free semantic dependency graph—not limited to bi-lexical dependencies—where graph nodes correspond to logical predications and edges to labeled argument positions. The EDS conversion from underspecified logical forms to directed graphs discards partial information on semantic scope from the full ERS, which makes these graphs abstractly—if not linguistically—similar to Abstract Meaning Representation (see below).

Nodes in EDS are in principle independent of surface lexical units, but for each node there is an explicit, many-to-many anchoring onto sub-strings of the underlying sentence. Thus, EDS instantiates Flavor (1) in our hierarchy of different formal types of semantic graphs and, more specfically, are fully anchored but unordered. Avoiding a one-to-one correspondence between graph nodes and surface lexical units enables EDS to adequately represent, among other things, lexical decomposition (e.g. of comparatives), sub-lexical or construction semantics (e.g. corresponding to morphological derivation or syntactic compounding, respectively), and covert (e.g. elided) meaning contributions. All nodes in the example EDS in Figure 1 make explicit their anchoring onto sub-strings of the underlying input, for example span $\langle 2 : 9 \rangle$ for *similar*.

In the EDS analysis for the running example, nodes representing covert quantifiers (e.g. on bare nominals, labeled udef_q[4]), the

two-place such+as_p relation, as well as the implicit_conj(unction) relation (which reflects recursive decomposition of the coordinate structure into binary predications) do not correspond to individual surface tokens (but are anchored on larger spans, overlapping with anchors from other nodes). Conversely, the two nodes associated with *similar* indicate lexical decomposition as a comparative predicate, where the second argument of the comp relation (the 'point of reference') remains unexpressed in Example (1).

Prague Tectogrammatical Graphs These graphs present a conversion from the multi-layered (and somewhat richer) annotations in the tradition of Prague Functional Generative Description (FGD; Sgall et al., 1986), as adopted (among others) in the Prague Czech–English Dependency Treebank (PCEDT; Hajič et al., 2012) and Prague Dependency Treebank (PDT; Böhmová et al., 2003). For more details on how the graphs are obtained from the original annotations, see Zeman and Hajič (2020).

The PTG structures essentially recast core predicate–argument structure in the form of mostly anchored dependency graphs, albeit introducing 'empty' (or *generated*, in FGD terminology) nodes, for which there is no corresponding surface token. Thus, these partially anchored representations instantiate Flavor (1) in our hierarchy of different formal types of semantic graphs, where anchoring relations can be discontinuous: For example, the *technique* node in Figure 2 is anchored to both the noun and its indefinite determiner *a*. PTG structures assume a total order of nodes, which provides the foundation for an underlying theory of topic–focus articulation, as proposed by Hajičová et al. (1998).

The PTG structure for our running example has many of the same dependency edges as the EDS graph (albeit using a different labeling scheme and inverse directionality in a few cases), but it analyzes the predicative copula as semantically contentful and does not treat *almost* as 'scoping' over the entire graph. In the example graph, there are two generated nodes to represent the unexpressed BEN(efactive) of the *impossible* relation as well as the unexpressed ACT(or) argument of the three-place *apply* relation, respectively; these nodes are related by an edge indicating grammatical coreference. In this graph, the indefinite determiner, infinitival to, and the vacuous preposition marking

---

[3]The underlying grammar is rooted in the general linguistic theory of Head-Driven Phrase Structure Grammar (HPSG; Pollard and Sag, 1994).

[4]In the EDS example in Figure 1, all nodes corresponding to instances of bare 'nominal' meanings are bound by a covert quantificational predicate, including the group-forming implicit_conj and _and_c nodes that represent the nested, binary-branching coordinate structure. This practice of uniform quantifier introduction in ERS is acknowledged as "particularly exuberant" by Steedman (2011, p. 21).

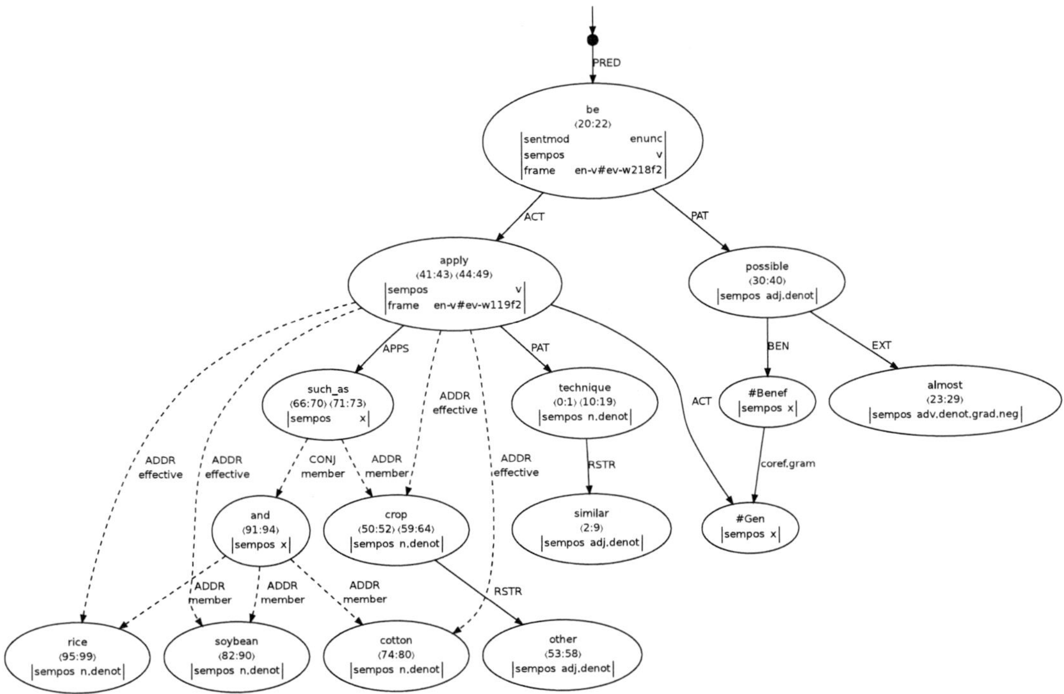

Figure 2: Semantic dependency graphs for the running example *A similar technique is almost impossible to apply to other crops, such as cotton, soybeans and rice*: Prague Tectogrammatical Graphs (PTG). In addition to node properties, visualized similarly to the EDS in Figure 1, boolean edge attributes are abbreviated below edge labels, for true values.

the deep object of apply can be argued to not have a semantic contribution of their own.

The ADDR argument relation to the *apply* predicate has been recursively propagated to both elements of the apposition and to all members of the coordinate structure. Accordingly, edge labels in PTG are not always functional, in the sense of allowing multiple outgoing edges from one node with the same label.

In FGD, role labels (called *functors*) ACT(or), PAT(ient), ADDR(essee), ORIG(in), and EFF(ect) indicate 'participant' positions in an underlying valency frame and, thus, correspond more closely to the numbered argument positions in other frameworks than their names might suggest.[5] The PTG annotations are grounded in a machine-readable valency lexicon (Urešová et al., 2016), and the `frame` values on verbal nodes in Figure 2 indicate specific verbal senses in the lexicon.

Universal Conceptual Cognitive Annotation
Universal Cognitive Conceptual Annotation (UCCA; Abend and Rappoport, 2013) is based on cognitive linguistic and typological theories, primarily Basic Linguistic Theory (Dixon, 2010/2012). The shared task targets the UCCA foundational layer, which focuses on argument structure phenomena (where predicates may be verbal, nominal, adjectival, or otherwise). This coarse-grained level of semantics has been shown to be preserved well across translations (Sulem et al., 2015). It has also been successfully used for improving text simplification (Sulem et al., 2018c), as well as to the evaluation of a number of text-to-text generation tasks (Birch et al., 2016; Sulem et al., 2018a; Choshen and Abend, 2018).

The basic unit of annotation is the *scene*, denoting a situation mentioned in the sentence, typically involving a predicate, participants, and potentially modifiers. Linguistically, UCCA adopts a notion of semantic constituency that transcends pure dependency graphs, in the sense of introducing separate, unlabeled nodes, called *units*. One or more labels are assigned to each edge. Formally, UCCA has a

---

[5]Accordingly, multiple instances of the same core participant role—as ADDR:member in Figure 2—will only occur with propagation of dependencies into paratactic constructions.

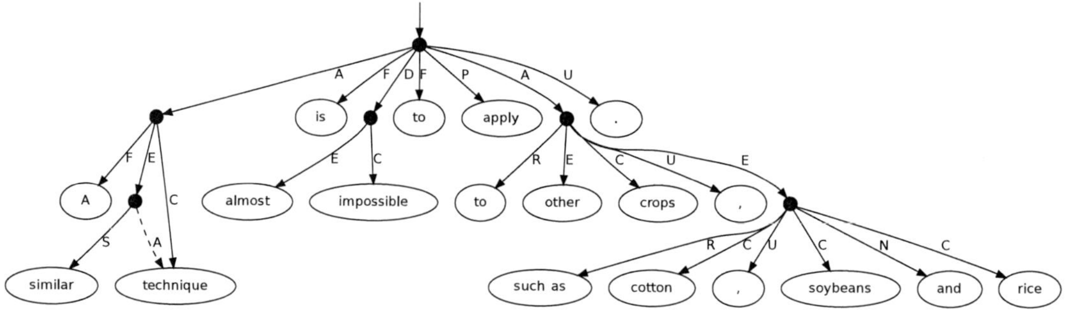

Figure 3: Universal Conceptual Cognitive Annotation (UCCA), foundational layer, for the running example *A similar technique is almost impossible to apply to other crops, such as cotton, soybeans and rice*. The dashed edge whose target is the node anchored to *technique* abbreviates a boolean remote edge attribute.

Type (1) flavor, where leaf (or terminal) nodes of the graph are anchored to possibly discontinuous sequences of surface sub-strings, while interior (or 'phrasal') graph nodes are formally unanchored.

The UCCA graph for the running example (see Figure 3) includes a single scene, whose main relation is the Process (P) evoked by *apply*. It also contains a secondary relation labeled Adverbial (D), *almost impossible*, which is broken down into its Center (C) and Elaborator (E); as well as two complex arguments, labeled as Participants (A). Unlike the other frameworks in the task, the UCCA foundational layer integrates all surface tokens into the graph, possibly as the targets of semantically bleached Function (F) and Punctuation (U) edges. UCCA graphs need not be rooted trees: Argument sharing across units will give rise to reentrant nodes much like in the other frameworks. For example, *technique* in Figure 3 is both a Participant in the scene evoked by *similar* and a Center in the parent unit. UCCA in principle also supports implicit (unexpressed) units which do not correspond to any tokens, but these are currently excluded from parsing evaluation and, thus, suppressed in the UCCA graphs distributed in the context of the shared task.

Abstract Meaning Representation The shared task includes Abstract Meaning Representation (AMR; Banarescu et al., 2013), which in the MRP hierarchy of different formal types of semantic graphs (see §2 above) is simply unanchored, i.e. represents Flavor (2). The AMR framework is independent of particular approaches to derivation and compositionality and, accordingly, does not make explicit how elements of the graph correspond to the surface utterance. Although most AMR parsing research presupposes a pre-processing step that

'aligns' graph nodes with (possibly discontinuous) sets of tokens in the underlying input, this anchoring is not part of the meaning representation proper.

At the same time, AMR frequently invokes lexical decomposition and normalization towards verbal senses, such that AMR graphs often appear to 'abstract' furthest from the surface signal. Since the first general release of an AMR graph bank in 2014, the framework has provided a popular target for data-driven meaning representation parsing and has been the subject of two consecutive tasks at SemEval 2016 and 2017 (May, 2016; May and Priyadarshi, 2017).

The AMR example graph in Figure 4 has a topo-

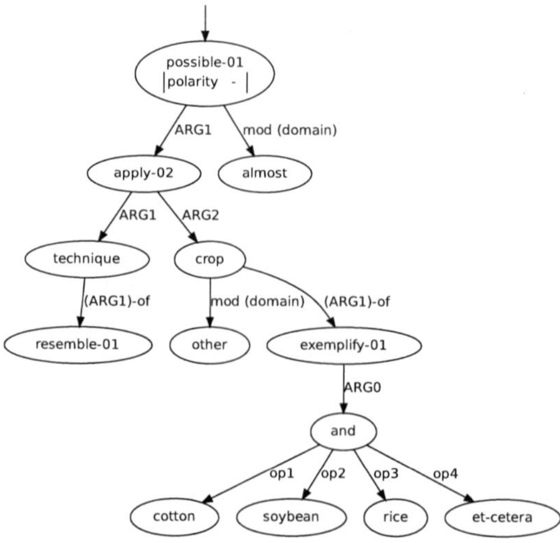

Figure 4: Abstract Meaning Representation (AMR) for the running example *A similar technique is almost impossible to apply to other crops, such as cotton, soybeans and rice*. Edge labels in parentheses indicate normalized (i.e. un-inverted) roles.

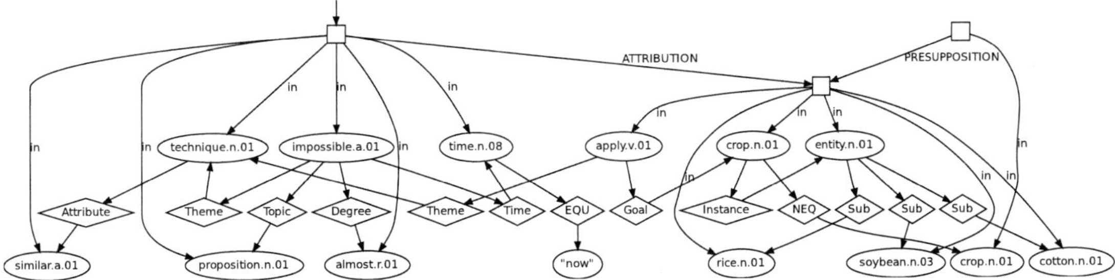

Figure 5: Discourse Representation Graph (DRG) for the running example *A similar technique is almost impossible to apply to other crops, such as cotton, soybeans and rice*. Different node shapes are not formally part of the graph but serve as a visual aid to distinguish different types of the underlying DRS elements.

logy broadly comparable to EDS, with some notable differences. Similar to the UCCA example graph (and unlike EDS), the AMR representation of the coordinate structure is flat. Although most lemmas are linked to derivationally related forms in the sense lexicon, this is not universal, as seen by the nodes corresponding to *similar* and *such as*, which are labeled as resemble-01 and exemplify-01, respectively. These sense distinctions (primarily for verbal predicates) are grounded in the inventory of predicates from the PropBank lexicon (Kingsbury and Palmer, 2002; Hovy et al., 2006).

Role labels in AMR encode semantic argument positions, with the particular roles defined according to each PropBank sense, though the counting in AMR is zero-based such that the ARG1 and ARG2 roles in Figure 4 often correspond to ARG2 and ARG3, respectively, in the EDS of Figure 1. PropBank distinguishes such numbered arguments from non-core roles labeled from a general semantic inventory, such as frequency, duration, or domain.

Figure 4 also shows the use of inverted edges in AMR, for example ARG1-of and mod. These serve to allow annotators (and in principle also parsing systems) to view the graph as a tree-like structure (with occasional reentrancies) but are formally merely considered notational variants. Therefore, the MRP rendering of the AMR example graph also provides an unambiguous indication of the underlying, normalized graph: Edges with a label component shown in parentheses are to be reversed in normalization, e.g. representing an actual ARG0 edge from resemble-01 to technique or a domain edge from other to crop.

Given the non-compositionality of AMR annotation, AMR allows the introduction of semantic concepts which have no explicit lexicalization in the text, for example the et-cetera element in the coordinate structure in Figure 4. Conversely, like in the other frameworks (except UCCA), some surface tokens are analyzed as semantically vacuous. For example, parallel to the PTG graph in Figure 2, there is no meaning contribution annotated for the determiner *a* (let alone for covert determiners in bare nominals, as made explicit in EDS).

Discourse Representation Graphs Finally, Discourse Representation Graphs (DRG) provide a graph encoding of Discourse Representation Structure (DRS), the meaning representations at the core of Discourse Representation Theory (DRT; Kamp and Reyle, 1993; Van der Sandt, 1992; Asher, 1993). DRSs can model many challenging semantic phenomena including quantifiers, negation, scope, pronoun resolution, presupposition accommodation, and discourse structure. Moreover, they are directly translatable into first-order logic formulas to account for logical inference.

DRG used in the shared task represents a type of graph encoding of DRS that makes the graphs structurally as close as possible to the structures found in other frameworks; Abzianidze et al. (2020) provide more details on the design choices in the DRG encoding. The source DRS annotations are taken from data release 3.0.0 of the Parallel Meaning Bank (PMB; Abzianidze et al., 2017; Bos et al., 2017).[6] Although the annotations in the PMB are compositionally derived from lexical semantics, anchoring information is not explicit in its DRSs; thus, (like AMR) the DRG framework formally instantiates Flavor (2) of meaning representations.

The DRG of the running example is given in Figure 5. The concepts (vissualized as oval shapes) are represented by WordNet 3.0 senses and semantic roles (in diamond shapes) by the adapted version

---

[6]https://pmb.let.rug.nl/data.php

		EDS	**PTG**	**UCCA**	**AMR**	**DRG**
	Flavor	1	1	1	2	2
TRAIN	Text Type	newspaper	newspaper	mixed	mixed	mixed
	Sentences	37,192	42,024	6,872	57,885	6,606
	Tokens	861,831	1,026,033	171,838	1,049,083	44,692
VALIDATE	Text Type	mixed	mixed	mixed	mixed	mixed
	Sentences	3,302	1,664	1,585	3,560	885
	Tokens	65,564	40,770	25,982	61,722	5,541
TEST	Text Type	mixed	newspaper	mixed	mixed	mixed
	Sentences	4,040	2,507	600	2,457	898
	Tokens	68,280	59,191	18,633	49,760	5,991

Table 1: Quantitative summary of English gold-standard training, validation, and evaluation data for the five frameworks in the cross-framework track; token counts reflect the morpho-syntactic companion parses, see §4.

of VerbNet roles. Nodes with quoted labels represent entities which semantically behave as constants. Such a node is used for the indexical "now", modelling the time of speech, which is part of the semantics of the present-tense copula *is*.

Explicit encoding of the scope is one of the main differences between DRG and the other frameworks. Scopes can be triggered by discourse segments, negation, universal quantification, clause embedding (e.g. *to apply* ...), and presuppositions (e.g. *other crops*). The scopes are represented as unlabeled (square-shaped) nodes in DRG (UCCA also has unlabeled nodes, albeit for a different reason). The node for the first discourse segment is treated as a root, which is connected to the scope of the embedded clause by the ATTRIBUTION discourse relation. The latter scope presupposes the scope containing a *crop* which is different (with NEQ inequality) from the group of crops consisting of (with the Sub semantic role) *rice, soybeans*, and *cotton*. Each concept, represented by a WordNet synset, has explicitly assigned its scope via in edges.[7]

Compared to the other frameworks, DRG structures are larger in size due to the number of semantic relations, explicit nodes for scope, scope membership edges, role reification, and information about the time (which usually introduces at least four additional nodes).

4   Task Setup

The following paragraphs summarize the 'logistics' of the MRP 2020 shared task. Except for the addition of the new cross-lingual track, the overall task setup mirrored that of the 2019 predecessor; please see Oepen et al. (2019) for additional background.

Cross-Framework Track   The English training, validation, and evaluation data are summarized in Table 1. For EDS, PTG, UCCA, and AMR the provenance of these gold-standard annotations is the same as in the MRP 2019 setup (Oepen et al., 2019).[8] The DRG target structures have been converted using the procedure sketched in §3 above. Unlike in the 2019 edition of the task, designated validation segments have been provided for all five frameworks in the cross-framework track; this data could be used during system development, e.g. for parameter tuning, but not for training the final system submission. For EDS, UCCA, and AMR, the 2020 validation data corresponds to the 2019 evaluation segments, thus allowing some comparability across the two editions of the MRP shared task.

As a common point of reference, the training data includes a sample of 89 WSJ sentences annotated in all five frameworks (twenty for DRG); for all frameworks but DRG, the evaluation data further includes parallel annotations over the same random selection of 100 sentences from the novel *The Little Prince* (by Antoine de Saint-Exupéry) as used in MRP 2019, dubbed LPPS. These parallel subsets of the gold-standard data are available for public download from the task site (see §9 below).

---

[7]Since in principle the scope of a semantic role cannot be uniquely determined by the scopes of its arguments, semantic roles are reified as nodes and can have ingoing in edges. But whenever the scopes of a role and its arguments coincide, the scope membership edge for the role is omitted and hence recoverable. This decision decreases the number of edges in DRG.

[8]There are slightly more EDS and PTG (compared to PSD in 2019) graphs this year, because the two underlying resources are no longer intersected; for UCCA, the 2020 release includes additional, recent gold-standard annotations.

			EDS	PTG	UCCA	AMR^{-1}	DRG
	(02)	Average Tokens per Graph	22.17	24.42	25.01	18.12	6.77
	(03)	Average Nodes per Token	1.26	0.74	1.33	0.64	2.09
	(04)	Distinct Edge Labels	10	72	15	101	16
PROPORTIONS	(05)	Percentage of top nodes	0.99	1.27	1.66	3.77	3.40
	(06)	Percentage of node labels	29.02	21.61	–	43.91	39.81
	(07)	Percentage of node properties	12.54	26.22	–	7.63	–
	(08)	Percentage of node anchors	29.02	19.63	38.80	–	–
	(09)	Percentage of (labeled) edges	28.43	26.10	56.88	44.69	56.79
	(10)	Percentage of edge attributes	–	5.17	2.66	–	–
TREENESS	(11)	$\%_g$ Rooted Trees	0.09	22.63	28.19	22.05	0.35
	(12)	$\%_g$ Treewidth One	68.60	22.67	34.17	49.91	0.35
	(13)	Average Treewidth	1.317	2.067	1.691	1.561	2.131
	(14)	Maximal Treewidth	3	7	4	5	5
	(15)	Average Edge Density	1.015	1.177	1.055	1.092	1.265
	(16)	$\%_n$ Reentrant	32.77	16.23	4.90	19.89	25.92
	(17)	$\%_g$ Cyclic	0.27	33.97	0.00	0.38	0.27
	(18)	$\%_g$ Not Connected	1.90	0.00	0.00	0.00	0.00
	(19)	$\%_g$ Multi-Rooted	99.93	0.00	0.00	71.64	32.32

Table 2: Contrastive graph statistics for the MRP 2020 English training data using a subset of the properties defined by Kuhlmann and Oepen (2016). Here, $\%_g$ and $\%_n$ indicate percentages of all graphs and nodes, respectively, in each framework; AMR^{-1} refers to the *normalized* form of the graphs, with inverted edges reversed, as discussed in §3. The second block of statistics indicates the proportional distribution of different formal types of information in the graphs, according to the categorization used in the MRP cross-framework evaluation metric (see §5).

Table 2 provides a quantitative side-by-side comparison of the training data, using some of the graph-theoretic properties discussed by Kuhlmann and Oepen (2016); see §2 for semi-formal definitions. The table indicates clear differences among the frameworks. The underlying input strings for AMR (where text selection is more varied), for example, are shorter, and much shorter in turn for DRG. EDS, UCCA, and DRG have many more nodes per token, on average, than the other frameworks—reflecting lexical decomposition, 'phrasal' grouping, and role reification, respectively, as evident in Figures 1, 3, and 5. In some respects, the PTG and UCCA graphs are more tree-like than graphs in the other frameworks, for example in their proportions of actual rooted trees, the frequencies of reentrant nodes, and the lack of multi-rooted structures. At the same time, PTG exhibits comparatively high average and maximal treewidth and is the only framework with a non-trivial percentage of cyclic graphs.

Cross-Lingual Track For four of the frameworks (excluding EDS), gold-standard training and evaluation data has been compiled in other languages than English: Mandarin Chinese for AMR, Czech for PTG, and German for UCCA and DRG. For UCCA and in particular DRG, however, available data is comparatively limited, as summarized in Table 3. These target representations constitute a separate *cross-lingual* track, which transcends the MRP 2019 task setup.

Additional Resources For reasons of comparability and fairness, the shared task constrained which additional data or pre-trained models (e.g. corpora, word embeddings, language models, lexica, or other annotations) can be legitimately used besides the resources distributed by the task organizers—such that all participants should in principle have access to the same range of data. However, to keep such constraints to the minimum required, a 'white-list' of legitimate resources was compiled from nominations by participants (with a cut-off date eight weeks before the end of the eval-

		PTG	UCCA	AMR	DRG
	Language	Czech	German	Chinese	German
	Flavor	1	1	1	2
TRAIN	Text Type	newspaper	mixed	mixed	mixed
	Sentences	43,955	4,125	18,365	1,575
	Tokens	740,466	95,634	428,054	9,088
TEST	Text Type	newspaper	mixed	mixed	mixed
	Sentences	5,476	444	1,713	403
	Tokens	92,643	10,585	39,228	2,384

Table 3: Quantitative summary of gold-standard data for the four frameworks in the cross-lingual track.

uation period).[9] Thus, the task design reflects what is at times called a *closed track*, where participants are constrained in which additional data and pre-trained models can be used in system development.

Companion Syntactic Parses At a technical level, training (and evaluation) data were distributed in two formats, (a) as sequences of 'raw' sentence strings and (b) in pre-tokenized, part-of-speech–tagged, lemmatized, and syntactically parsed form. For the latter, premium-quality morpho-syntactic dependency analyses were provided to participants, called the MRP 2020 companion parses. These parses were obtained using a pre-release of the 'future' UDPipe architecture (Straka, 2018; Straka and Straková, 2020), trained on available gold-standard UD 2.x treebanks, for English augmented with conversions from PTB-style annotations in the WSJ and OntoNotes corpora (Hovy et al., 2006), using the UD-style CoreNLP 4.0 tokenizer (Manning et al., 2014) and jack-knifing where appropriate (to avoid overlap with the texts underlying the MRP semantic graphs).

Rules of Participation While the various meaning representation frameworks and graph banks represented in the shared task inevitably present considerable linguistic variation, all MRP 2020 data was repackaged in a uniform and normalized abstract representation with a common serialization, the same JSON Lines format as used in the previous year (Oepen et al., 2019). Because some of the semantic graph banks involved in the shared task had originally been released by the Linguistic Data Consortium (LDC), the training data was made available to task participants by the LDC under no-cost evaluation licenses. All task data (including system submissions and evaluation results) is being prepared for general release through the LDC, while subsets that are copyright-free will also become available for direct, open-source download.

The shared task was first announced in March 2020, the initial release of the cross-framework training data became available in late April, and the evaluation period ran between July 27 and August 10, 2020; during this period, teams obtained the unannotated input strings for the evaluation data and had available a little more than two weeks to prepare and submit parser outputs. Submission of semantic graphs for evaluation was through the

	EDS	PTG	UCCA	AMR	DRG
Top Nodes	✓	✓	✓	✓	✓
Node Labels	✓	✓	✗	✓	✓
Node Properties	✓	✓	✗	✓	✗
Node Anchors	✓	✓	✓	✗	✗
Labeled Edges	✓	✓	✓	✓	✓
Edge Attributes	✗	✓	✓	✗	✗

Table 4: Different tuple types per framework.

on-line CodaLab infrastructure. Teams were allowed to make repeated submissions, but only the most recent successful upload to CodaLab within the evaluation period was considered for the official, primary ranking of submissions. Task participants were encouraged to process all inputs using the same general parsing system, but—owing to inevitable fuzziness about what constitutes 'one' parser—this constraint was not formally enforced.

5 Evaluation

Following the previous edition of the shared task, the official MRP metric for the task is the micro-average F_1 score across frameworks over all tuple types that encode 'atoms' of information in MRP graphs. The cross-framework metric uniformly evaluates graphs of different flavors, regardless of a specific framework exhibiting (a) labeled or unlabeled nodes or edges, (b) nodes with or without anchors, and (c) nodes and edges with optional properties and attributes, respectively (see Table 4).

The MRP metric generalizes earlier framework-specific metrics (Dridan and Oepen, 2011; Cai and Knight, 2013; Hershcovich et al., 2019a) in terms of decomposing each graph into sets of typed tuples, as indicated in Figure 6. To quantify graph similarity in terms of tuple overlap, a correspondence relation between the nodes of the gold-standard and system graphs must be determined. Adapting a search procedure for the NP-hard maximum common edge subgraph (MCES) isomorphism problem, the MRP scorer will search for the node-to-node correspondence that maximizes the intersection of tuples between two graphs, where node identifiers (m and n in Figure 6) act like variables that can be equated across the gold-standard and system graphs.[10] This means that during evaluation all information in the MRP graphs is con-

---

[9]See http://svn.nlpl.eu/mrp/2020/public/resources.txt for the list of legitimate extra resources.

[10]Conceptually, the search expands both graphs into larger structures with 'lightly labeled' nodes and edges, e.g. treating node properties much like 'pseudo-edges' with globally unique constant-valued target nodes.

Teams	Cross-Framework					Cross-Lingual				Reference
	AMR	DRG	EDS	PTG	UCCA	AMR	DRG	PTG	UCCA	
Hitachi	✓	✓	✓	✓	✓	✓	✓	✓	✓	Ozaki et al. (2020)
ÚFAL	✓	✓	✓	✓	✓	✓	✓	✓	✓	Samuel and Straka (2020)
HIT-SCIR	✓	✓	✓	✓	✓	✓	✓	✓	✓	Dou et al. (2020)
HUJI-KU	✓	✓	✓	✓	✓	✓	✓	✓	✓	Arviv et al. (2020)
ISCAS	✓	✓	✓	✓	✓	✗	✗	✗	✗	
TJU-BLCU	✓	✓	✓	✓	✓	✓	✓	✓	✗	
JBNU	✓	✗	✗	✗	✗	✗	✗	✗	✗	Na and Min (2020)
ÚFAL	✓	✓	✓	✓	✓	✓	✓	✓	✓	Samuel and Straka (2020)
ERG	✗	✗	✓	✗	✗	✗	✗	✗	✗	Oepen and Flickinger (2019)

Table 5: Overview of participating teams and the tracks they participated in. Columns correspond to tracks and frameworks, and rows correspond to teams. The top block represents 'official' submissions, which participated in the competition. The middle block represents 'unofficial' submissions, which were submitted after the closing deadline. The bottom row represents the ERG baseline.

sidered with equal weight, i.e. tops, node and edge labels, properties and attributes, and anchors.

MRP scoring is carried out using the open-source `mtool` software—the Swiss Army Knife of Meaning Representation[11]—which implements a refinement of the MCES algorithm by McGregor (1982). Based on pre-computed per-node rewards and upper bounds on adjacent edge correspondences, candidate node-to-node mappings are initialized and scheduled in decreasing order of expected similarity. For increased efficiency (in principle tractability, in fact), `mtool` will return the best available solution when it exhausts its preset search space limits. This anytime behavior of the scores provides a distinction between *exact* vs. *approximate* solutions (which contrasts with

the greedy hill-climbing search of e.g. `Smatch`; Cai and Knight, 2013). MRP scoring is robust with respect to equivalent variations of values, e.g. case and string vs. number type distinctions for all literals. Comparison of anchor values ignores whitespace character positions, internal segmentation of adjacent anchors, and basic punctuation marks in the left or right periphery of a normalized anchor. Assuming the string *Oh no!* as a hypothetical parser input, the following anchorings will all be considered equivalent: $\{\langle 0{:}6\rangle\}$, $\{\langle 0{:}2\rangle, \langle 3{:}6\rangle\}$, $\{\langle 0{:}1\rangle, \langle 1{:}6\rangle\}$, and $\{\langle 0{:}5\rangle\}$.

6 Submissions and Results

Six teams submitted parser outputs to the shared task within the official evaluation period. In addition, we received two submissions after the submission deadline, which we mark as 'unofficial'. We further include results from an additional 'reference' system by one of the task co-organizers, namely EDS outputs from the grammar-based ERG parser (Oepen and Flickinger, 2019).

Table 5 presents an overview of the participating systems and the tracks and frameworks they submitted results for. All official systems submitted results for the cross-framework track (across all frameworks), and additionally five of them submitted results to the cross-lingual track as well (where TJU-BLCU did not submit UCCA parser outputs in the cross-lingual track). We note that the shared task explicitly allowed partial submissions, in order to lower the bar for participation (which is no doubt substantial). Two of the teams—ISCAS and TJU-BLCU—declined the invitation to submit a system description paper to the shared task proceedings.

[11] https://github.com/cfmrp/mtool

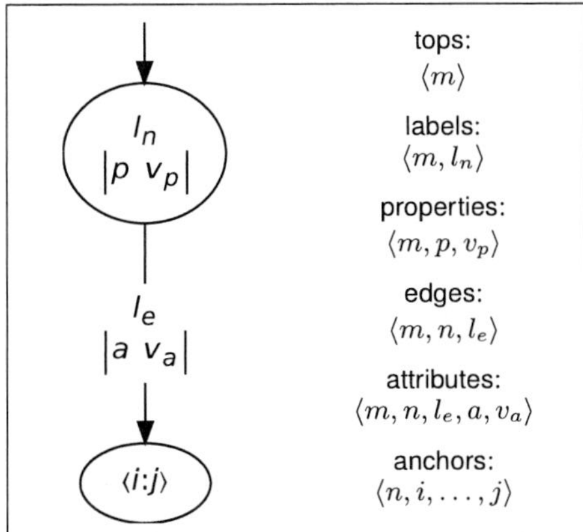

Figure 6: Representing an abstractMRP graph as a set of typed tuples, with m and n as node identifiers for the top and bottom node, respectively.

Team	Cross-Framework						Cross-Lingual				
	All	EDS	PTG	UCCA	AMR	DRG	All	PTG	UCCA	AMR	DRG
Hitachi	1	1	2	1	1	–	–	–	–	–	–
	1	1	1	2	1	2	1	2	3	1	1
ÚFAL	1	2	1	1	2	–	–	–	–	–	–
	1	2	2	1	1	1	1	1	1	2	2
HIT-SCIR	3	3	3	3	3	–	–	–	–	–	–
	3	3	3	2	3	3	3	3	2	3	3
HUJI-KU	4	5	4	4	5	–	–	–	–	–	–
	4	5	4	4	5	5	4	4	4	4	4
ISCAS	5	4	6	6	4	–	–	–	–	–	–
	5	4	6	6	4	4	–	–	–	–	–
TJU-BLCU	6	6	5	5	6	–	–	–	–	–	–
	6	6	5	5	6	6	5	5	–	5	5

Team	Tops			Labels			Properties			Anchors			Edges			Attributes			All		
	P	R	F	P	R	F	P	R	F	P	R	F	P	R	F	P	R	F	P	R	F
Hitachi	.93	.93	.93	.65	.68	.66	.63	.62	.62	.71	.70	.70	.82	.80	.81	.39	.32	.34	.85	.85	.85
	.95	.95	.95	.72	.72	.72	.54	.54	.54	.57	.55	.56	.83	.80	.82	.24	.23	.24	.88	.85	.86
ÚFAL	.93	.93	.93	.68	.68	.68	.61	.60	.60	.69	.71	.70	.80	.79	.80	.42	.33	.36	.85	.85	.85
	.94	.94	.94	.74	.73	.74	.55	.54	.54	.56	.57	.56	.80	.80	.80	.23	.24	.24	.87	.86	.86
HIT-SCIR	.94	.94	.94	.63	.64	.64	.45	.41	.43	.71	.71	.71	.77	.76	.77	.37	.30	.33	.80	.80	.80
	.94	.94	.94	.70	.69	.69	.44	.37	.40	.57	.56	.57	.77	.75	.76	.22	.22	.22	.82	.80	.81
HUJI-KU	.87	.84	.85	.36	.36	.36	.29	.18	.20	.66	.67	.67	.67	.62	.64	.15	.07	.10	.73	.63	.67
	.88	.83	.85	.29	.29	.29	.40	.24	.28	.51	.51	.51	.65	.62	.64	.07	.08	.07	.73	.58	.64
ISCAS	.70	.70	.70	.50	.49	.48	.22	.26	.24	.35	.41	.37	.52	.35	.39	–	–	–	.53	.43	.43
	.75	.74	.74	.56	.55	.55	.22	.22	.21	.29	.31	.29	.57	.40	.44	–	–	–	.58	.46	.48
TJU-BLCU	.83	.82	.83	.41	.29	.34	–	–	–	.45	.30	.35	.53	.30	.37	–	–	–	.57	.30	.39
	.75	.74	.75	.54	.29	.38	–	–	–	.33	.14	.19	.44	.18	.24	–	–	–	.55	.22	.30
ÚFAL	.93	.93	.93	.68	.68	.68	.61	.60	.60	.71	.71	.71	.80	.80	.80	.43	.34	.37	.85	.85	.85
	.94	.94	.94	.74	.73	.74	.55	.54	.54	.57	.57	.57	.80	.80	.80	.23	.24	.24	.87	.86	.87

Team	Tops			Labels			Properties			Anchors			Edges			Attributes			All		
	P	R	F	P	R	F	P	R	F	P	R	F	P	R	F	P	R	F	P	R	F
Hitachi	.96	.96	.96	.65	.65	.65	.44	.42	.43	.7	.68	.69	.8	.77	.78	.27	.27	.26	.86	.84	.85
ÚFAL	.95	.95	.95	.66	.66	.66	.43	.43	.43	.65	.72	.68	.78	.79	.79	.3	.33	.31	.84	.86	.85
HIT-SCIR	.95	.95	.95	.53	.52	.53	.21	.18	.20	.47	.47	.47	.66	.65	.66	.23	.24	.23	.72	.67	.69
HUJI-KU	.9	.84	.87	.15	.15	.15	.31	.32	.32	.42	.42	.42	.59	.58	.59	.08	.08	.08	.69	.54	.60
TJU-BLCU	.56	.55	.56	.41	.21	.27	–	–	–	.23	.12	.15	.28	.13	.18	–	–	–	.35	.15	.20
ÚFAL	.95	.95	.95	.66	.66	.66	.43	.43	.43	.71	.72	.72	.79	.79	.79	.3	.33	.31	.86	.86	.86

Table 6: Official rankings (top) for both tracks, and MRP scores for the cross-framework (middle) and cross-lingual (bottom) tracks. Each cross-framework submission is evaluated in two settings, where the top scores present results for the LPPS sub-corpus, and the bottom ones for the full English evaluation set. The rankings are presented both for the overall average scores (All), and separately per framework. Evaluation results are broken down by 'atomic' component pieces. For each component we report precision (P), recall (R), and F_1 score (F). Entries in the two MRP tables are split into the same blocks as in Table 5: official (top) vs. unofficial (bottom) submissions, omitting the two highly partial unofficial submissions by JBNU and ERG.

	EDS			PTG			UCCA			AMR			DRG		
	P	R	F	P	R	F	P	R	F	P	R	F	P	R	F
Hitachi	0.97	0.97	0.97	0.80	0.84	0.82	0.86	0.80	0.83	0.78	0.79	0.79	–	–	–
	0.94	0.93	0.94	0.89	0.89	0.89	0.78	0.72	0.75	0.83	0.80	0.82	0.94	0.92	0.93
ÚFAL	0.96	0.95	0.95	0.81	0.84	0.83	0.84	0.82	0.83	0.77	0.79	0.78	–	–	–
	0.93	0.92	0.93	0.88	0.89	0.88	0.75	0.78	0.76	0.81	0.79	0.80	0.95	0.93	0.94
HIT-SCIR	0.90	0.89	0.89	0.78	0.78	0.78	0.84	0.80	0.82	0.68	0.71	0.70	–	–	–
	0.87	0.88	0.87	0.85	0.84	0.84	0.75	0.74	0.75	0.74	0.66	0.70	0.90	0.89	0.89
HUJI-KU	0.83	0.76	0.79	0.71	0.49	0.58	0.80	0.76	0.78	0.56	0.5	0.53	–	–	–
	0.83	0.76	0.80	0.69	0.44	0.54	0.73	0.73	0.73	0.57	0.49	0.52	0.84	0.5	0.63
ISCAS	0.86	0.90	0.88	0.12	0.25	0.16	0.45	0.08	0.13	0.68	0.47	0.56	–	–	–
	0.85	0.87	0.86	0.14	0.26	0.18	0.42	0.03	0.06	0.74	0.53	0.61	0.78	0.63	0.69
TJU-BLCU	0.83	0.51	0.64	0.41	0.24	0.30	0.52	0.13	0.21	0.50	0.34	0.4	–	–	–
	0.84	0.35	0.49	0.38	0.15	0.21	0.50	0.06	0.10	0.54	0.21	0.30	0.49	0.34	0.40
JBNU	–	–	–	–	–	–	–	–	–	0.74	0.73	0.74	–	–	–
	–	–	–	–	–	–	–	–	–	0.71	0.62	0.66	–	–	–
ÚFAL	0.96	0.95	0.95	0.83	0.84	0.84	0.84	0.81	0.83	0.77	0.79	0.78	–	–	–
	0.93	0.92	0.93	0.89	0.89	0.89	0.75	0.78	0.76	0.81	0.79	0.80	0.95	0.93	0.94
ERG	0.95	0.96	0.96	–	–	–	–	–	–	–	–	–	–	–	–
	0.94	0.91	0.93	–	–	–	–	–	–	–	–	–	–	–	–

Table 7: Per-framework results for the cross-framework track, using the same groupings as in Table 6.

Table 6 presents the official rankings for the official submissions (top), including an overall score for each track and per-framework rankings. Rankings are given over the LPPS dataset, a sample from the Little Prince annotated by all frameworks save for DRG, and over the entire test set. Results are consequently more readily comparable for the LPPS sub-corpus, but should be more robust on the entire test corpus, due to its larger size (see § 4). That said, LPPS and overall test results are very similar, both in terms of ranking and in terms of bottom line scores.

The main task results are summarized in Table 6 for both the cross-framwork (middle) and cross-lingual (bottom) tracks. Results are broken down into component pieces. Edge attributes are only present in PTG and UCCA. While they are still predicted with fairly low results, this constitutes a notable improvement over the findings of MRP 2019 (the best score on the official track on UCCA edge attributes was 0.12 F_1 then, as opposed to 0.36 now). Anchors are predicted with substantially lower scores compared to MRP 2019, probably since we did not include in MRP 2020 the bi-lexical Flavor (0) frameworks. Edges and tops are slightly more accurate, while labels and properties slightly less, but these are not directly comparable since the frameworks and data are different. See § 8 for an overall discussion of the state of the art, considering MRP 2019 and MRP 2020.

Results show that the Hitachi and ÚFAL sub-missions share the first place for both tracks, and together rank first or second for almost all the individual frameworks (save for UCCA parsing in the cross-lingual track, where Hitachi ranks third). HIT-SCIR further ranks second for UCCA parsing in both tracks. Interestingly, rankings in the per-framework track are similar across frameworks, which may indicate some similarity in the parsing problem exhibited by different linguistic schemes, despite differences in structure and content.

Per-framework scores using the official MRP metric are given in Table 7 for the cross-framework track and Table 8 for the cross-lingual track. Examining these results, we note that cross-framework and cross-lingual scores are quite similar, an encouraging sign of cross-linguistic applicability. Another trend to note is that precision and recall are surprisingly close to each other for many systems, often identical.

7 Overview of Approaches

Compared with systems from MRP 2019, there has been a fairly clear shift in approaches for participating systems this year, resulting in significant improvements in performance. The improvements for some of the frameworks are fairly substantial. For example, the Hitachi system, one of the two winning systems, achieves a score of 0.82 F_1 in AMR parsing, in comparison to 0.73 F_1 achieved by the top AMR parser in MRP 2019. This reflects an improvement of over eight points, reflecting a

	PTG			UCCA			AMR			DRG		
	P	R	F	P	R	F	P	R	F	P	R	F
Hitachi	.89	.86	.87	.79	.79	.79	.82	.79	.8	.93	.94	.93
ÚFAL	.91	.91	.91	.79	.83	.81	.75	.81	.78	.90	.89	.90
HIT-SCIR	.82	.75	.78	.78	.82	.80	.60	.42	.49	.68	.69	.68
HUJI-KU	.65	.53	.58	.74	.76	.75	.55	.38	.45	.82	.50	.62
TJU-BLCU	.51	.14	.22	–	–	–	.46	.17	.25	.42	.28	.34
ÚFAL	.93	.92	.92	.79	.83	.81	.81	.8	.81	.9	.89	.9

Table 8: Per-framework results for the cross-lingual track.

number of innovations from the participants this year, as well as contemporaneous developments outside the shared task (see §8).

Broadly speaking, top performers at MRP 2020 have all adopted a system architecture that is based on an encoder–decoder framework in which the input sentence is encoded into contextualized token embeddings that are used as input to the decoder. The system vary in the decoding strategies.

The Hitachi system adopts a transformer-based encoder–decoder architecture. The system uses the standard transformer encoder in which self-attention and position embeddings are used to compute the contextualized token embeddings. In its decoder, this system has a number of innovations, however. First of all, the system rewrites the meaning representation graphs into a reversible Plain Graph Notation (PGN), and enhances PGN with a number of pseudo-nodes that indicate the end of node prediction, the end of label prediction, etc. These correspond well with parsing actions commonly found in transition-based systems. In this sense, the systems combines the strengths of graph-based parsing on the encoder side resulting from self attention with efficiency of transition-based parsing on the decoder side. Another innovation is the use of a 'hierarchical' decoding process in which the model first predicts a *mode*, and then predicts the next action conditioned on the mode. For example, if the mode is G(raph), the decoder predicts a meta node, and if the mode is S(urface), the decoder predicts the node label of a specific concept. This allows a fair competition among actions that are similar in nature.

The PERIN system computes contextualized token embeddings with XLM-R (Conneau et al., 2019) on the encoder side, and then on the decoder side, uses separate attention heads to predict the node labels, identify anchors for nodes, and predict edges between nodes, as well as edge labels. Because the label set for nodes is typically very large, rather than predicting the node labels directly, the PERIN system reduces the search space by predicting 'relative rules' that can be used to map surface token strings to node labels in meaning representation graphs, an idea that is similar to the use of Factored Concept Labels in Wang and Xue (2017). Another innovation of the PERIN system is that it is trained with a permutation-invariant loss function that returns the same value independently of how the nodes in the graph are ordered. This captures the unordered nature of nodes in (most of the MRP 2020) meaning representation graphs and prevents situations in which the model is penalized for generating the correct nodes in an order that is different from that in the training data.

The HIT-SCIR and JBNU systems adopt the iterative inference framework first proposed by Cai and Lam (2020) for Flavor (2) meaning representation graphs that do not enforce strict correspondences between tokens in the input sentence and the concepts in meaning representation graphs. The iterative inference framework is also based on an encoder–decoder architecture. The encoder takes the sentence as input and computes contextualized token embeddings that are used as text memory by a decoder that iteratively predicts the next node given the text memory and a predicted parent node in the partially constructed graph memory at the previous time step, and then identifies the parent node for the newly predicted node from the partially constructed graph. While the HIT-SCIR system essentially uses the Cai and Lam (2020) architecture with little modification, the JBNU system attempts to extend the work of Cai and Lam (2020) by using a shared state to make both predictions but did not observe substantial improvements.

Transition-based systems, which had achieved strong performance in the 2019 shared task, are also represented in the competition this year. The HIT-SCIR team uses a transition-based system to parse Flavor (1) meaning representations where there is a stricter correspondence between tokens in the input sentence and concepts in the meaning representation graph. The HIT-SCIR transition-based system is essentially the overall top performing system they developed for MRP 2019. It uses Stack LSTM to compute transition states in the parsing process, and the parsing actions are tailored to specific meaning representation frameworks. In the training process, the system fine-tunes BERT contextualized encodings.

The HUJI-KU system also extends an entry in the 2019 MRP shared task (originally called TUPA) to parse additional frameworks and handle meaning representation parsing in a multilingual setting. TUPA is a transition-based system that supports general DAG parsing. TUPA applies separate constraints tailored to each meaning representation framework. When parsing cross-framework meaning representations for English, the system is trained with a *BERT-large-cased* pretrained encoder, and when parsing cross-lingual meaning representations, it is trained with multilingual BERT.

8   On the State of the Art

MRP 2019 (Oepen et al., 2019) yielded parsers for five frameworks in a uniform format, of which EDS, UCCA, and AMR are represented in MRP 2020 again. Submissions included transition-, factorization-, and composition-based systems, and gold-standard target structures in 2019 were solely for English. Comparability is limited by the fact that two of the 2020 frameworks (PTG and DRG) are new, training and (in particular) evaluation sets for the others have been updated since MRP 2019, and additional validation sets was introduced. However, the LPPS evaluation sub-corpus (*Le Petite Prince*) is identical between the two years for EDS, UCCA, and AMR. This allows a comparison on nearly equal grounds: as Table 9 shows, in terms of LPPS F_1, the state-of-the-art has substantially improved for EDS and AMR parsing, but stayed the same for UCCA. However, as mentioned in §6, remote edge detection for UCCA improved substantially, though it carries only a small weight in terms of overall scores due to the scarcity of remote edges.

For EDS, the strongest results were obtained in the MRP 2019 official competition by SUDA–Alibaba (Zhang et al., 2019c). However, in the post-evaluation stage, they were outperformed by the Peking system (Chen et al., 2019). Both used factorization-based parsing with pre-trained contextualized language model embeddings (which has consistently proved to be very effective for other frameworks too). These parsers even approached the performance of the carefully designed grammar-based ERG parser (Oepen and Flickinger, 2019).

English PTG has not been comprehensively addressed by parsers prior to MRP 2020, but a bi-lexical framework called PSD is a subset of PTG. It was included in the SDP shared tasks (Oepen et al., 2014, 2015) as well as in MRP 2019, and has been addressed by numerous parsers since (Kurita and Søgaard, 2019; Kurtz et al., 2019; Jia et al., 2020, among others). Wang et al. (2019) established the state of the art in supervised PSD using a second-order factorization-based parser, and Fernández-González and Gómez-Rodríguez (2020) matched it using a stack-pointer parser.

Czech PTG, in its original form as published in the Prague Dependency Treebank (Hajič et al., 2018), has been used in several version of the TectoMT machine translation system (Rosa et al., 2016); however, parsing results have not been published separately. A (lossy) conversion has been included in the CoNLL 2009 Shared Task on Semantic Role Labeling (Hajič et al., 2009), but the differences in task design are and conversion make empirical comparison impossible.

UCCA parsing has been dominated by transition-based methods (Hershcovich et al., 2017, 2018; Che et al., 2019). However, both English and German UCCA parsing featured in a SemEval shared task (Hershcovich et al., 2019b), where the best system, a composition-based parser (Jiang et al., 2019), treated the task as constituency tree parsing with the recovery of remote edges as a postprocess-

	EDS			UCCA			AMR		
	P	R	F	P	R	F	P	R	F
2019	.92	.93	.93	.84	.82	.83	.74	.72	.73
2020	.97	.97	.97	.86	.80	.83	.78	.79	.79

Table 9: Per-framework cross-task comparison of top MRP metric scores on LPPS between the 2019 and 2020 editions of the MRP task, on the three frameworks represented in both year, for English. The top systems in MRP 2019 for EDS, UCCA, and AMR were Peking (Chen et al., 2019), HIT-SCIR (Che et al., 2019), and Saarland (Donatelli et al., 2019), respectively; in MRP 2020 the Hitachi system (Ozaki et al., 2020) was at the top for all three frameworks, sharing the UCCA first rank with ÚFAL (Samuel and Straka, 2020).

ing task.

Prior to MRP 2019, Lyu and Titov (2018) parsed AMR using a joint probabilistic model with latent alignments, avoiding cascading errors due to alignment inaccuracies and outperforming previous approaches. Lyu et al. (2020) recently improved the latent alignment parser using stochastic softmax. Lindemann et al. (2019) trained a composition-based parser on five frameworks including AMR and EDS, using the Apply–Modify algebra, on which the third-ranked Saarland submission to MRP 2019 was based (Donatelli et al., 2019). They employed multi-task training with all tackled semantic frameworks and UD, establishing the state of the art on all graph banks but AMR 2017. Since then, a new state-of-the-art has been established for English AMR, using sequence-to-sequence transduction (Zhang et al., 2019a,b) and iterative inference with graph encoding (Cai and Lam, 2019, 2020). Xu et al. (2020a) improved sequence-to-sequence parsing for AMR by using pre-trained encoders, reaching similar performance to Cai and Lam (2020). Astudillo et al. (2020) introduced a stack-transformer to enhance transition-based AMR parsing (Ballesteros and Al-Onaizan, 2017), and Lee et al. (2020) improved it further, using a trained parser for mining oracle actions and combining it with AMR-to-text generation to outperform the state of the-art.

Wang et al. (2018) parsed Chinese AMR with a transition-based system. For cross-lingual AMR parsing, Blloshmi et al. (2020) trained an AMR parser similar to the approach of Zhang et al. (2019b), using cross-lingual transfer learning, outperforming the transition-based cross-lingual AMR parser of Damonte and Cohen (2018) on German, Spanish, Italian, and Chinese.

DRG is a novel graph representation format for DRS that was specially designed for MRP 2020 to make it structurally as close as possible to other frameworks (Abzianidze et al., 2020). However, several semantic parsers exist for DRS, which employ different encodings. Liu et al. (2018) used a DRG format that dominantly labels edges compared to nodes. van Noord et al. (2018) process DRSs in a clausal form, sets of triples and quadruples. The latter format is more common among DRS parsers, as it was officially used by the shared task on DRS parsing (Abzianidze et al., 2019). The shared task gave rise to several DRS parsers: Evang (2019); Liu et al. (2019); van Noord (2019);

Fancellu et al. (2019), among which the best results ($F_1 = 0.85$) were achieved by the word-level sequence-to-sequence model with Tranformer (Liu et al., 2019). Note that the DRS shared task used F_1 calculated based on the DRS clausal forms, which is not comparable to MRP F_1 over DRGs.

Similarly to English DRG, German DRG has not been used for semantic parsing prior to the shared task due to the new DRG format. Moreover, semantic parsing with German DRG is novel in the sense that its DRS counterpart is also new. In German DRG, concepts are grounded in English WordNet 3.0 (Fellbaum, 2012) senses assuming that synsets are language-neutral. The mismatch between German tokens and English lemmas of senses must be expected to add additional complexity to German DRG parsing.

Direct comparison to non-MRP results is impossible: we are using a new version of AMRbank. Gold-standard tokenization is not provided for any of the frameworks. We use the MRP scorer. However, general trends appear consistent with recent developments. Pretrained embeddings and cross-lingual transfer help; but multi-task learning less so. There is yet progress to be made in sharing information between parsers for different frameworks and making better use of their overlap.

9 Reflections and Outlook

The MRP series of shared tasks has contributed to general availability of accurate data-driven parsers for a broad range of different frameworks, with performance levels ranging between 0.76 MRP F_1 (English UCCA) and 0.94 F_1 (English EDS). Parsing accuracies in the cross-lingual track present comparable levels of performance, despite limited training data in the case of UCCA and DRG. Furthermore, the evaluation sets for most of the frameworks comprise different text types and subject matters—offering some hope of robustness to domain variation. We expect that these parsers will enable follow-up experimentation on the utility of explicit meaning representation in downstream tasks like, for example, relation extraction, argumentation mining, summarization, or text generation.

Maybe equally importantly, the MRP task design capitalizes on uniformity of representations and evaluation, enabling resource creators and parser developers to more closely (inter)relate representations and parsing approaches across a diverse range of semantic graph frameworks. This facilitates both quantitative contrastive studies (e.g. the 'post-mortem' analysis by Buljan et al. (2020), which observes that top-performing MRP 2019 parsers have complementary strengths and weaknesses) but also more linguistic, qualitative comparison. General availability of parallel gold-standard annotations over the same text samples—drawing from the WSJ and LPPS corpora—enables side-by-side comparison of linguistic design choices in the different frameworks. This is an area of investigation that we hope will see increased interest in the aftermath of the MRP task series, to go well beyond the impressionistic observations from § 3 and ideally lead to contrastive refinement across linguistic schools and traditions.

Despite uniformity in packaging and evaluation, cumulative overall complexity and inherent diversity of the frameworks deemed participation in the shared task a formidable challenge. Of the sixteen teams who participated in MRP 2019, only four teams (predominantly strong performers from before) decided to submit parser outputs in 2020. The two 'newcomer' teams, by comparison, only made partial submissions in the cross-lingual track and ended up not competing for top ranks overall. Similar trends of 'competitive self-selection' and declining participant groups for consecutive instances have been observed with earlier CoNLL shared task and similar benchmarking series. On the upside, with the possible exception of English AMR (where there has been much contemporaneous progress recently), the MRP 2020 empirical results present a strong state-of-the-art benchmark for meaning representation parsing.

On the more foundational question of the relevance of explicit, discrete representations of sentence meaning, the past several years of breakthrough neural advances have been comparatively insensitive to syntactico-semantic structure. In our view, these developments have at least in part been reflective of the stark lack of general techniques for the encoding of hierarchical structure in end-to-end neural architectures. Increased adoption of Graph Convolutional Networks (Kipf and Welling, 2017) and other hierarchical modeling techniques suggest new opportunities for the exploration of both structurally informed end-to-end architectures or e.g. multi-task learning setups. Beyond such ultimately performance-driven research, explicit encoding of syntactico-semantic structure in our view further bears promise in terms of model interpretability and

safe-guarding against 'neural meltdown' (e.g. discarding something as foundational as negation or inadvertently altering a date expression in summarization or translation). In a similar vain, meaning representations are being successfully applied in evaluation, e.g. to quantify system output vs. gold standard similarity beyond surface n-grams (Sulem et al., 2018b; Xu et al., 2020b, inter alios).

All technical information regarding the MRP 2019 shared task, including system submissions, detailed official results, and links to supporting resources and software are available from the task web site at:

`http://mrp.nlpl.eu`

Acknowledgments

Several colleagues have assisted in designing the task and preparing its data and software resources. We thank Dotan Dvir (Hebrew University of Jerusalem) for leading the annotation efforts on UCCA. Dan Flickinger (Stanford University) created fresh gold-standard annotations of some 1,000 WSJ strings, which form part of the EDS evaluation graphs in 2020. Sebastian Schuster (Stanford University) advised on how to convert the gold-standard syntactic annotations from the venerable PTB and OntoNotes treebanks to Universal Dependencies, version 2.x, using 'modern' tokenization. Anna Nedoluzhko and Jiří Mírovský (Charles University in Prague) enhanced the PTG annotation of LPPS data with previously missing items, most notably coreference. Milan Straka (Charles University in Prague) made available an enhanced version of his UDPipe parser and assisted in training Czech, English, and German morpho-syntacic parsing models (for the MRP companion trees). Jayeol Chun (Brandeis University) provided invaluable assistance in conversion of the Chinese AMR annotations, preparation of the Chinese morpho-syntactic companion trees, and provisioning of companion alignments for the English AMR graphs.

We are grateful to the Nordic Language Processing Laboratory (NLPL) and Uninett Sigma2, which provided technical infrastructure for the MRP 2020 task. Also, we warmly acknowledge the assistance of the Linguistic Data Consortium (LDC) in distributing the training data for the task to participants at no cost to anyone.

The work on UCCA and the HUJI-KU submission was partially supported by the Israel Science Foundation (grant No. 929/17). The work on PTG has been partially supported by the Ministry of Education, Youth and Sports of the Czech Republic (project LINDAT/CLARIAH-CZ, grant No. LM2018101) and partially by the Grant Agency of the Czech Republic (project LUSyD, grant No. GX20-16819X). The work on DRG was supported by the NWO-VICI grant (288-89-003) and the European Union Horizon 2020 research and innovation programme (under grant agreement No. 742204). The work on Chinese AMR data is partially supported by project 18BYY127 under the National Social Science Foundation of China and project 61772278 under the National Science Foundation of China.

References

Omri Abend and Ari Rappoport. 2013. UCCA. A semantics-based grammatical annotation scheme. In *Proceedings of the 10th International Conference on Computational Semantics*, pages 1 – 12, Potsdam, Germany.

Lasha Abzianidze, Johannes Bjerva, Kilian Evang, Hessel Haagsma, Rik van Noord, Pierre Ludmann, Duc-Duy Nguyen, and Johan Bos. 2017. The Parallel Meaning Bank: Towards a multilingual corpus of translations annotated with compositional meaning representations. In *Proceedings of the 15th Conference of the European Chapter of the Association for Computational Linguistics: Volume 2, Short Papers*, pages 242–247, Valencia, Spain. Association for Computational Linguistics.

Lasha Abzianidze, Johan Bos, and Stephan Oepen. 2020. DRS at MRP 2020: Dressing up Discourse Representation Structures as graphs. In *Proceedings of the CoNLL 2020 Shared Task: Cross-Framework Meaning Representation Parsing*, pages 23 – 32, Online.

Lasha Abzianidze, Rik van Noord, Hessel Haagsma, and Johan Bos. 2019. The first shared task on discourse representation structure parsing. In *Proceedings of the IWCS Shared Task on Semantic Parsing*, Gothenburg, Sweden. Association for Computational Linguistics.

Ofir Arviv, Ruixiang Cui, and Daniel Hershcovich. 2020. HUJI-KU at MRP 2020: Two transition-based neural parsers. In *Proceedings of the CoNLL 2020 Shared Task: Cross-Framework Meaning Representation Parsing*, pages 73 – 82, Online.

Nicholas Asher. 1993. *Reference to Abstract Objects in Discourse*. Kluwer Academic Publishers.

Ramon Fernandez Astudillo, Miguel Ballesteros, Tahira Naseem, Austin Blodgett, and Radu Florian. 2020. Transition-based parsing with stack-transformers. In *Findings of EMNLP*.

Miguel Ballesteros and Yaser Al-Onaizan. 2017. AMR parsing using stack-LSTMs. In *Proceedings of the 2017 Conference on Empirical Methods in Natural Language Processing*, pages 1269–1275, Copenhagen, Denmark. Association for Computational Linguistics.

Laura Banarescu, Claire Bonial, Shu Cai, Madalina Georgescu, Kira Griffitt, Ulf Hermjakob, Kevin Knight, Philipp Koehn, Martha Palmer, and Nathan Schneider. 2013. Abstract Meaning Representation for sembanking. In *Proceedings of the 7th Linguistic Annotation Workshop and Interoperability with Discourse*, pages 178 – 186, Sofia, Bulgaria.

Emily M. Bender, Dan Flickinger, Stephan Oepen, Woodley Packard, and Ann Copestake. 2015. Layers of interpretation. On grammar and compositionality. In *Proceedings of the 11th International Conference on Computational Semantics*, pages 239 – 249, London, UK.

Alexandra Birch, Omri Abend, Ondřej Bojar, and Barry Haddow. 2016. HUME. Human UCCA-based evaluation of machine translation. In *Proceedings of the 2016 Conference on Empirical Methods in Natural Language Processing*, pages 1264 – 1274, Austin, TX, USA.

Rexhina Blloshmi, Rocco Tripodi, and Roberto Navigli. 2020. XL-AMR: Enabling cross-lingual AMR parsing with transfer learning techniques. In *Proceedings of the 2020 Conference on Empirical Methods in Natural Language Processing*.

Alena Böhmová, Jan Hajič, Eva Hajičová, and Barbora Hladká. 2003. The Prague Dependency Treebank: A three-level annotation scenario. In Anne Abeillé, editor, *Treebanks. Building and Using Parsed Corpora*, pages 103 – 127. Kluwer Academic Publishers, Dordrecht, The Netherlands.

Johan Bos, Valerio Basile, Kilian Evang, Noortje Venhuizen, and Johannes Bjerva. 2017. The Groningen Meaning Bank. In Nancy Ide and James Pustejovsky, editors, *Handbook of Linguistic Annotation*. Springer Netherlands.

Maja Buljan, Joakim Nivre, Stephan Oepen, and Lilja Øvrelid. 2020. A tale of three parsers: Towards diagnostic evaluation for meaning representation parsing. In *Proceedings of the 12th Language Resources and Evaluation Conference*, pages 1902–1909, Marseille, France. European Language Resources Association.

Deng Cai and Wai Lam. 2019. Core semantic first: A top-down approach for AMR parsing. In *Proceedings of the 2019 Conference on Empirical Methods in Natural Language Processing and the 9th International Joint Conference on Natural Language Processing (EMNLP-IJCNLP)*, pages 3799–3809, Hong Kong, China. Association for Computational Linguistics.

Deng Cai and Wai Lam. 2020. AMR parsing via graph-sequence iterative inference. In *Proceedings of the*

58th Annual Meeting of the Association for Computational Linguistics, pages 1290–1301, Online. Association for Computational Linguistics.

Shu Cai and Kevin Knight. 2013. Smatch. An evaluation metric for semantic feature structures. In *Proceedings of the 51th Meeting of the Association for Computational Linguistics*, pages 748–752, Sofia, Bulgaria.

Wanxiang Che, Longxu Dou, Yang Xu, Yuxuan Wang, Yijia Liu, and Ting Liu. 2019. HIT-SCIR at MRP 2019: A unified pipeline for meaning representation parsing via efficient training and effective encoding. In *Proceedings of the Shared Task on Cross-Framework Meaning Representation Parsing at the 2019 Conference on Computational Natural Language Learning*, pages 76–85, Hong Kong, China.

Yufei Chen, Yajie Ye, and Weiwei Sun. 2019. Peking at MRP 2019: Factorization- and composition-based parsing for Elementary Dependency Structures. In *Proceedings of the Shared Task on Cross-Framework Meaning Representation Parsing at the 2019 Conference on Computational Natural Language Learning*, pages 166–176, Hong Kong, China.

Leshem Choshen and Omri Abend. 2018. Reference-less measure of faithfulness for grammatical error correction. In *Proceedings of the 2015 Conference of the North American Chapter of the Association for Computational Linguistics*, New Orleans, LA, USA.

Alexis Conneau, Kartikay Khandelwal, Naman Goyal, Vishrav Chaudhary, Guillaume Wenzek, Francisco Guzmán, Edouard Grave, Myle Ott, Luke Zettlemoyer, and Veselin Stoyanov. 2019. Unsupervised cross-lingual representation learning at scale. *arXiv preprint arXiv:1911.02116*.

Ann Copestake, Dan Flickinger, Carl Pollard, and Ivan A. Sag. 2005. Minimal Recursion Semantics. An introduction. *Research on Language and Computation*, 3(4):281–332.

Marco Damonte and Shay B. Cohen. 2018. Cross-lingual Abstract Meaning Representation parsing. In *Proceedings of the 2018 Conference of the North American Chapter of the Association for Computational Linguistics: Human Language Technologies, Volume 1 (Long Papers)*, pages 1146–1155, New Orleans, Louisiana. Association for Computational Linguistics.

Robert M. W. Dixon. 2010/2012. *Basic Linguistic Theory*. Oxford University Press.

Lucia Donatelli, Meaghan Fowlie, Jonas Groschwitz, Alexander Koller, Matthias Lindemann, Mario Mina, and Pia Weißenhorn. 2019. Saarland at MRP 2019: Compositional parsing across all graphbanks. In *Proceedings of the Shared Task on Cross-Framework Meaning Representation Parsing at the 2019 Conference on Computational Natural Language Learning*, pages 66–75, Hong Kong, China.

Longxu Dou, Yunlong Feng, Yuqiu Ji, Wanxiang Che, and Ting Liu. 2020. HIT-SCIR at MRP 2020: Transition-based parser and iterative inference parser. In *Proceedings of the CoNLL 2020 Shared Task: Cross-Framework Meaning Representation Parsing*, pages 65–72, Online.

Rebecca Dridan and Stephan Oepen. 2011. Parser evaluation using elementary dependency matching. In *Proceedings of the 12th International Conference on Parsing Technologies*, pages 225–230, Dublin, Ireland.

Jason Eisner. 1997. Bilexical grammars and a cubic-time probabilistic parser. In *Proceedings of the Fifth International Workshop on Parsing Technologies*, pages 54–65, Boston/Cambridge, Massachusetts, USA. Association for Computational Linguistics.

Kilian Evang. 2019. Transition-based DRS parsing using stack-LSTMs. In *Proceedings of the IWCS Shared Task on Semantic Parsing*, Gothenburg, Sweden. Association for Computational Linguistics.

Federico Fancellu, Sorcha Gilroy, Adam Lopez, and Mirella Lapata. 2019. Semantic graph parsing with recurrent neural network DAG grammars. In *Proceedings of the 2019 Conference on Empirical Methods in Natural Language Processing and the 9th International Joint Conference on Natural Language Processing (EMNLP-IJCNLP)*, pages 2769–2778, Hong Kong, China. Association for Computational Linguistics.

Christiane Fellbaum. 2012. Wordnet. *The Encyclopedia of Applied Linguistics*.

Daniel Fernández-González and Carlos Gómez-Rodríguez. 2020. Transition-based semantic dependency parsing with pointer networks. In *Proceedings of the 58th Annual Meeting of the Association for Computational Linguistics*, pages 7035–7046, Online. Association for Computational Linguistics.

Dan Flickinger, Stephan Oepen, and Emily M. Bender. 2017. Sustainable development and refinement of complex linguistic annotations at scale. In Nacy Ide and James Pustejovsky, editors, *Handbook of Linguistic Annotation*, pages 353–377. Springer, Dordrecht, The Netherlands.

Jan Hajič, Eduard Bejček, Alevtina Bémová, Eva Buráňová, Eva Hajičová, Jiří Havelka, Petr Homola, Jiří Kárník, Václava Kettnerová, Natalia Klyueva, Veronika Kolářová, Lucie Kučová, Markéta Lopatková, Marie Mikulová, Jiří Mírovský, Anna Nedoluzhko, Petr Pajas, Jarmila Panevová, Lucie Poláková, Magdaléna Rysová, Petr Sgall, Johanka Spoustová, Pavel Straňák, Pavlína Synková, Magda Ševčíková, Jan Štěpánek, Zdeňka Urešová, Barbora Vidová Hladká, Daniel Zeman, Šárka Zikánová, and Zdeněk Žabokrtský. 2018. Prague dependency treebank 3.5. LINDAT/CLARIAH-CZ digital library at the Institute of Formal and Applied Linguistics (ÚFAL), Faculty of Mathematics and Physics, Charles University.

Jan Hajič, Massimiliano Ciaramita, Richard Johansson, Daisuke Kawahara, Maria Antònia Martí, Lluís Màrquez, Adam Meyers, Joakim Nivre, Sebastian Padó, Jan Štěpánek, Pavel Straňák, Mihai Surdeanu, Nianwen Xue, and Yi Zhang. 2009. The CoNLL-2009 shared task: Syntactic and semantic dependencies in multiple languages. In *Proceedings of the Thirteenth Conference on Computational Natural Language Learning (CoNLL 2009): Shared Task*, pages 1–18, Boulder, Colorado. Association for Computational Linguistics.

Jan Hajič, Eva Hajičová, Jarmila Panevová, Petr Sgall, Ondřej Bojar, Silvie Cinková, Eva Fučíková, Marie Mikulová, Petr Pajas, Jan Popelka, Jiří Semecký, Jana Šindlerová, Jan Štěpánek, Josef Toman, Zdeňka Urešová, and Zdeněk Žabokrtský. 2012. Announcing Prague Czech-English Dependency Treebank 2.0. In *Proceedings of the 8th International Conference on Language Resources and Evaluation*, pages 3153–3160, Istanbul, Turkey.

Eva Hajičová, Barbara Partee, and Petr Sgall. 1998. *Topic–Focus Articulation, Tripartite Structures, and Semantic Content*. Kluwer, Dordrecht, The Netherlands.

Daniel Hershcovich, Omri Abend, and Ari Rappoport. 2017. A transition-based directed acyclic graph parser for UCCA. In *Proceedings of the 55th Annual Meeting of the Association for Computational Linguistics (Volume 1: Long Papers)*, pages 1127–1138, Vancouver, Canada. Association for Computational Linguistics.

Daniel Hershcovich, Omri Abend, and Ari Rappoport. 2018. Multitask parsing across semantic representations. In *Proceedings of the 56th Meeting of the Association for Computational Linguistics*, pages 373–385, Melbourne, Australia.

Daniel Hershcovich, Zohar Aizenbud, Leshem Choshen, Elior Sulem, Ari Rappoport, and Omri Abend. 2019a. SemEval-2019 task 1. Cross-lingual semantic parsing with UCCA. In *Proceedings of the 13th International Workshop on Semantic Evaluation*, pages 1–10, Minneapolis, MN, USA.

Daniel Hershcovich, Zohar Aizenbud, Leshem Choshen, Elior Sulem, Ari Rappoport, and Omri Abend. 2019b. SemEval-2019 task 1: Cross-lingual semantic parsing with UCCA. In *Proceedings of the 13th International Workshop on Semantic Evaluation*, pages 1–10, Minneapolis, Minnesota, USA. Association for Computational Linguistics.

Eduard Hovy, Mitchell Marcus, Martha Palmer, Lance Ramshaw, and Ralph Weischedel. 2006. OntoNotes. The 90% solution. In *Proceedings of Human Language Technologies: The 2006 Annual Conference of the North American Chapter of the Association for Computational Linguistics, Companion Volume: Short Papers*, pages 57–60, New York City, USA.

Zixia Jia, Youmi Ma, Jiong Cai, and Kewei Tu. 2020. Semi-supervised semantic dependency parsing using CRF autoencoders. In *Proceedings of the 58th Annual Meeting of the Association for Computational Linguistics*, pages 6795–6805, Online. Association for Computational Linguistics.

Wei Jiang, Zhenghua Li, Yu Zhang, and Min Zhang. 2019. HLT@SUDA at SemEval-2019 task 1: UCCA graph parsing as constituent tree parsing. In *Proceedings of the 13th International Workshop on Semantic Evaluation*, pages 11–15, Minneapolis, Minnesota, USA. Association for Computational Linguistics.

Hans Kamp and Uwe Reyle. 1993. *From Discourse to Logic; An Introduction to Modeltheoretic Semantics of Natural Language, Formal Logic and DRT*. Kluwer, Dordrecht.

Paul Kingsbury and Martha Palmer. 2002. From Tree-Bank to PropBank. In *Proceedings of the 3rd International Conference on Language Resources and Evaluation*, pages 1989–1993, Las Palmas, Spain.

Thomas N. Kipf and Max Welling. 2017. Semi-supervised classification with graph convolutional networks. In *5th International Conference on Learning Representations*, Toulon, France.

Marco Kuhlmann and Stephan Oepen. 2016. Towards a catalogue of linguistic graph banks. *Computational Linguistics*, 42(4):819–827.

Shuhei Kurita and Anders Søgaard. 2019. Multi-task semantic dependency parsing with policy gradient for learning easy-first strategies. In *Proceedings of the 57th Annual Meeting of the Association for Computational Linguistics*, pages 2420–2430, Florence, Italy. Association for Computational Linguistics.

Robin Kurtz, Daniel Roxbo, and Marco Kuhlmann. 2019. Improving semantic dependency parsing with syntactic features. In *Proceedings of the First NLPL Workshop on Deep Learning for Natural Language Processing*, pages 12–21, Turku, Finland. Linköping University Electronic Press.

Young-Suk Lee, Ramon Fernandez Astudillo, Tahira Naseem, Revanth Gangi Reddy, Radu Florian, and Salim Roukos. 2020. Pushing the limits of AMR parsing with self-learning. In *Findings of EMNLP*.

Matthias Lindemann, Jonas Groschwitz, and Alexander Koller. 2019. Compositional semantic parsing across graphbanks. In *Proceedings of the 57th Annual Meeting of the Association for Computational Linguistics*, pages 4576–4585, Florence, Italy. Association for Computational Linguistics.

Jiangming Liu, Shay B. Cohen, and Mirella Lapata. 2018. Discourse representation structure parsing. In *Proceedings of the 56th Annual Meeting of the Association for Computational Linguistics (Volume 1: Long Papers)*, pages 429–439, Melbourne, Australia. Association for Computational Linguistics.

Jiangming Liu, Shay B. Cohen, and Mirella Lapata. 2019. Discourse representation structure parsing with recurrent neural networks and the transformer model. In *Proceedings of the IWCS Shared Task on Semantic Parsing*, Gothenburg, Sweden. Association for Computational Linguistics.

Chunchuan Lyu, Shay B. Cohen, and Ivan Titov. 2020. A differentiable relaxation of graph segmentation and alignment for AMR parsing.

Chunchuan Lyu and Ivan Titov. 2018. AMR parsing as graph prediction with latent alignment. In *Proceedings of the 56th Annual Meeting of the Association for Computational Linguistics (Volume 1: Long Papers)*, pages 397–407, Melbourne, Australia. Association for Computational Linguistics.

Christopher Manning, Mihai Surdeanu, John Bauer, Jenny Finkel, Steven Bethard, and David McClosky. 2014. The Stanford CoreNLP natural language processing toolkit. In *Proceedings of 52nd Annual Meeting of the Association for Computational Linguistics: System Demonstrations*, pages 55–60, Baltimore, Maryland. Association for Computational Linguistics.

Mitchell Marcus, Beatrice Santorini, and Mary Ann Marcinkiewicz. 1993. Building a large annotated corpus of English. The Penn Treebank. *Computational Linguistics*, 19:313 – 330.

Jonathan May. 2016. SemEval-2016 Task 8. Meaning representation parsing. In *Proceedings of the 10th International Workshop on Semantic Evaluation*, pages 1063 – 1073, San Diego, CA, USA.

Jonathan May and Jay Priyadarshi. 2017. SemEval-2017 Task 9. Abstract Meaning Representation parsing and generation. In *Proceedings of the 11th International Workshop on Semantic Evaluation*, pages 536 – 545.

James J. McGregor. 1982. Backtrack search algorithms and the maximal common subgraph problem. *Software: Practice and Experience*, 12(1):23 – 34.

Seung-Hoon Na and Jinwoo Min. 2020. JBNU at MRP 2020: AMR parsing using a joint state model for graph-sequence iterative inference. In *Proceedings of the CoNLL 2020 Shared Task: Cross-Framework Meaning Representation Parsing*, pages 83 – 87, Online.

Joakim Nivre, Marie-Catherine de Marneffe, Filip Ginter, Jan Hajič, Christopher D. Manning, Sampo Pyysalo, Sebastian Schuster, Francis Tyers, and Daniel Zeman. 2020. Universal Dependencies v2: An evergrowing multilingual treebank collection. In *Proceedings of the 12th Language Resources and Evaluation Conference*, pages 4034–4043, Marseille, France. European Language Resources Association.

Rik van Noord. 2019. Neural Boxer at the IWCS shared task on DRS parsing. In *Proceedings of the IWCS Shared Task on Semantic Parsing*, Gothenburg, Sweden. Association for Computational Linguistics.

Rik van Noord, Lasha Abzianidze, Antonio Toral, and Johan Bos. 2018. Exploring neural methods for parsing discourse representation structures. *Transactions of the Association for Computational Linguistics*, 6:619–633.

Stephan Oepen, Omri Abend, Jan Hajič, Daniel Hershcovich, Marco Kuhlmann, Tim O'Gorman, Nianwen Xue, Jayeol Chun, Milan Straka, and Zdeňka Urešová. 2019. MRP 2019: Cross-framework Meaning Representation Parsing. In *Proceedings of the Shared Task on Cross-Framework Meaning Representation Parsing at the 2019 Conference on Computational Natural Language Learning*, pages 1 – 27, Hong Kong, China.

Stephan Oepen and Dan Flickinger. 2019. The ERG at MRP 2019: Radically compositional semantic dependencies. In *Proceedings of the Shared Task on Cross-Framework Meaning Representation Parsing at the 2019 Conference on Computational Natural Language Learning*, pages 40 – 44, Hong Kong, China.

Stephan Oepen, Marco Kuhlmann, Yusuke Miyao, Daniel Zeman, Silvie Cinková, Dan Flickinger, Jan Hajič, and Zdeňka Urešová. 2015. SemEval 2015 Task 18. Broad-coverage semantic dependency parsing. In *Proceedings of the 9th International Workshop on Semantic Evaluation*, pages 915 – 926, Denver, CO, USA.

Stephan Oepen, Marco Kuhlmann, Yusuke Miyao, Daniel Zeman, Dan Flickinger, Jan Hajič, Angelina Ivanova, and Yi Zhang. 2014. SemEval 2014 Task 8. Broad-coverage semantic dependency parsing. In *Proceedings of the 8th International Workshop on Semantic Evaluation*, pages 63 – 72, Dublin, Ireland.

Stephan Oepen and Jan Tore Lønning. 2006. Discriminant-based MRS banking. In *Proceedings of the 5th International Conference on Language Resources and Evaluation*, pages 1250 – 1255, Genoa, Italy.

Hiroaki Ozaki, Gaku Morio, Yuta Koreeda, Terufumi Morishita, and Toshinori Miyoshi. 2020. Hitachi at MRP 2020: Text-to-graph-notation transducer. In *Proceedings of the CoNLL 2020 Shared Task: Cross-Framework Meaning Representation Parsing*, pages 40 – 52, Online.

Hao Peng, Sam Thomson, and Noah A. Smith. 2017. Deep multitask learning for semantic dependency parsing. In *Proceedings of the 55th Meeting of the Association for Computational Linguistics*, pages 2037 – 2048, Vancouver, Canada.

Carl Pollard and Ivan A. Sag. 1994. *Head-Driven Phrase Structure Grammar*. Studies in Contemporary Linguistics. The University of Chicago Press, Chicago, USA.

Rudolf Rosa, Martin Popel, Ondřej Bojar, David Mareček, and Ondřej Dušek. 2016. Moses & treex hybrid MT systems bestiary. In *Proceedings of the 2nd Deep Machine Translation Workshop*, pages 1 – 10, Lisbon, Portugal. ÚFAL MFF UK.

David Samuel and Milan Straka. 2020. ÚFAL at MRP 2020: Permutation-invariant semantic parsing in PERIN. In *Proceedings of the CoNLL 2020 Shared Task: Cross-Framework Meaning Representation Parsing*, pages 53 – 64, Online.

Rob A. Van der Sandt. 1992. Presupposition projection as anaphora resolution. *Journal of Semantics*, 9(4):333–377.

Sebastian Schuster and Christopher D. Manning. 2016. Enhanced English Universal Dependencies: An improved representation for natural language understanding tasks. In *Proceedings of the Tenth International Conference on Language Resources and Evaluation (LREC'16)*, pages 2371–2378, Portorož, Slovenia. European Language Resources Association (ELRA).

Petr Sgall, Eva Hajičová, and Jarmila Panevová. 1986. *The Meaning of the Sentence and Its Semantic and Pragmatic Aspects*. D. Reidel Publishing Company, Dordrecht, The Netherlands.

Gabriel Stanovsky and Ido Dagan. 2018. Semantics as a foreign language. In *Proceedings of the 2018 Conference on Empirical Methods in Natural Language Processing*, pages 2412–2421, Brussels, Belgium.

Mark Steedman. 2011. *Taking Scope*. MIT Press, Cambridge, MA, USA.

Milan Straka. 2018. UDPipe 2.0 prototype at CoNLL 2018 UD shared task. In *Proceedings of the CoNLL 2018 Shared Task: Multilingual Parsing from Raw Text to Universal Dependencies*, pages 197–207.

Milan Straka and Jana Straková. 2020. UDPipe at EvaLatin 2020: Contextualized embeddings and treebank embeddings. In *Proceedings of LT4HALA 2020 - 1st Workshop on Language Technologies for Historical and Ancient Languages*, pages 124–129, Marseille, France. European Language Resources Association (ELRA).

Elior Sulem, Omri Abend, and Ari Rappoport. 2015. Conceptual annotations preserve structure across translations. A French–English case study. In *Proceedings of the 1st Workshop on Semantics-Driven Statistical Machine Translation*, pages 11–22.

Elior Sulem, Omri Abend, and Ari Rappoport. 2018a. Semantic structural annotation for text simplification. In *Proceedings of the 2015 Conference of the North American Chapter of the Association for Computational Linguistics*, New Orleans, LA, USA.

Elior Sulem, Omri Abend, and Ari Rappoport. 2018b. Semantic structural evaluation for text simplification. In *Proceedings of the 2018 Conference of the North American Chapter of the Association for Computational Linguistics: Human Language Technologies, Volume 1 (Long Papers)*, pages 685–696, New Orleans, Louisiana. Association for Computational Linguistics.

Elior Sulem, Omri Abend, and Ari Rappoport. 2018c. Simple and effective text simplification using semantic and neural methods. In *Proceedings of the 56th Meeting of the Association for Computational Linguistics*, Melbourne, Australia.

Zdeňka Urešová, Eva Fučíková, and Jana Šindlerová. 2016. CzEngVallex. A bilingual Czech–English valency lexicon. *The Prague Bulletin of Mathematical Linguistics*, 105:17–50.

Chuan Wang, Bin Li, and Nianwen Xue. 2018. Transition-based Chinese AMR parsing. In *Proceedings of the 2018 Conference of the North American Chapter of the Association for Computational Linguistics: Human Language Technologies, Volume 2 (Short Papers)*, pages 247–252, New Orleans, Louisiana. Association for Computational Linguistics.

Chuan Wang and Nianwen Xue. 2017. Getting the most out of AMR parsing. In *Proceedings of the 2017 Conference on Empirical Methods in Natural Language Processing*, pages 1257–1268, Copenhagen, Denmark.

Xinyu Wang, Jingxian Huang, and Kewei Tu. 2019. Second-order semantic dependency parsing with end-to-end neural networks. In *Proceedings of the 57th Annual Meeting of the Association for Computational Linguistics*, pages 4609–4618, Florence, Italy. Association for Computational Linguistics.

Dongqin Xu, Junhui Li, Muhua Zhu, Min Zhang, and Guodong Zhou. 2020a. Improving AMR parsing with sequence-to-sequence pre-training. In *Proceedings of the 2020 Conference on Empirical Methods in Natural Language Processing*.

Jin Xu, Yinuo Guo, and Junfeng Hu. 2020b. Incorporate semantic structures into machine translation evaluation via UCCA. In *Proceedings of the International Conference on Machine Translation*, Online.

Daniel Zeman and Jan Hajič. 2020. FGD at MRP 2020: Prague Tectogrammatical Graphs. In *Proceedings of the CoNLL 2020 Shared Task: Cross-Framework Meaning Representation Parsing*, pages 33–39, Online.

Sheng Zhang, Xutai Ma, Kevin Duh, and Benjamin Van Durme. 2019a. AMR parsing as sequence-to-graph transduction. In *Proceedings of the 57th Annual Meeting of the Association for Computational Linguistics*, pages 80–94, Florence, Italy. Association for Computational Linguistics.

Sheng Zhang, Xutai Ma, Kevin Duh, and Benjamin Van Durme. 2019b. Broad-coverage semantic parsing as transduction. In *Proceedings of the 2019 Conference on Empirical Methods in Natural Language Processing and the 9th International Joint Conference on Natural Language Processing (EMNLP-IJCNLP)*, pages 3786–3798, Hong Kong, China. Association for Computational Linguistics.

Yue Zhang, Wei Jiang, Qingrong Xia, Junjie Cao, Rui Wang, Zhenghua Li, and Min Zhang. 2019c. SUDA–Alibaba at MRP 2019: Graph-based models with BERT. In *Proceedings of the Shared Task on Cross-Framework Meaning Representation Parsing at the 2019 Conference on Computational Natural Language Learning*, pages 149–157, Hong Kong, China.

DRS at MRP 2020:
Dressing up Discourse Representation Structures as Graphs

Lasha Abzianidze[*]
UiL OTS
Utrecht University
l.abzianidze@uu.nl

Johan Bos
CLCG
University of Groningen
johan.bos@rug.nl

Stephan Oepen
Department of Informatics
University of Oslo
oe@ifi.uio.no

Abstract

Discourse Representation Theory (DRT) is a formal account for representing the meaning of natural language discourse. Meaning in DRT is modeled via a Discourse Representation Structure (DRS), a meaning representation with a model-theoretic interpretation, which is usually depicted as nested boxes. In contrast, a directed labeled graph is a common data structure used to encode semantics of natural language texts. The paper describes the procedure of dressing up DRSs as directed labeled graphs to include DRT as a new framework in the 2020 shared task on Cross-Framework and Cross-Lingual Meaning Representation Parsing. Since one of the goals of the shared task is to encourage unified models for several semantic graph frameworks, the conversion procedure was biased towards making the DRT graph framework somewhat similar to other graph-based meaning representation frameworks.

1 Introduction

Graphs are a common data structure for representing meaning of natural language sentences or texts. Several shared tasks on semantic parsing have been organized, and the target meaning representations of the shared tasks were predominantly encoded as directed labeled graphs:[1] Semantic Dependency Graphs (Oepen et al., 2014, 2015), Abstract Meaning Representation (May, 2016; May and Priyadarshi, 2017), and Universal Conceptual Cognitive Annotation (Hershcovich et al., 2019). Some of these graphs are presented in Figure 1. Recently, Oepen et al. (2019) packaged several meaning representation graphs in a uniform graph abstraction and serialization for cross-framework meaning representation parsing.

Parallel to these developments our point of departure is Discourse Representation Theory (DRT, Kamp and Reyle, 1993), a well-studied framework for studying formal semantics beyond sentences. Its meaning representation structures, Discourse Representation Structure (DRS), are directly translatable into formal logic. A sample DRS, in its traditional box format, is illustrated in Figure 2. We will discuss the DRS in more details in Section 2.

Obviously, DRSs are meaning representation structures, but they are different from the already mentioned graph-based meaning representations in two aspects. First, **DRSs are not inherently graphs**. A DRS is more like a formula of predicate logic which is further organized in sub-formulas and governed with additional operations that account for co-reference and presupposition. That's why DRSs are usually not considered as graph-based meaning representations. For example, DRT was not among the frameworks of the shared task on cross-framework meaning representation parsing (MRP 2019, Oepen et al., 2019) since the meaning representations at the shared task were all uniformly formatted as graphs. Žabokrtský et al. (2020) excluded DRSs when surveying sentence meaning representations as they "limit [themselves] to meaning representations whose backbone structure can be described as a graph over words (possibly with added non-lexical nodes) [...]". The second main contrast between DRSs and several of the graph-based meaning representations is that **DRSs are very different from syntactic structures**. DRSs have roots in formal semantics, and they are geared to account for negation, quantification, and semantic scope rather than for syntactic

---

[*]Part of the work was done while the author was at the University of Groningen.

[1]Throughout the paper, we mean a directed labeled graph when simply talking about graphs, unless stated otherwise.

Proceedings of the CoNLL 2020 Shared Task: Cross-Framework Meaning Representation Parsing, pages 23–32
Online, Nov. 19-20, 2020. ©2020 Association for Computational Linguistics

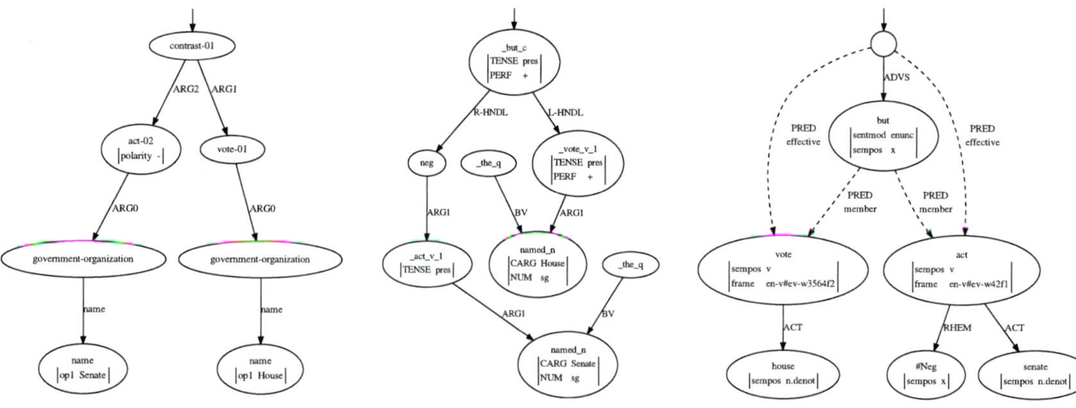

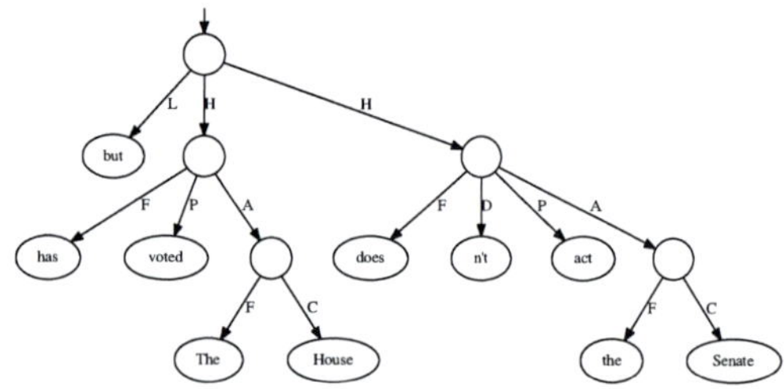

(a) AMR: Abstract Meaning Representation (Banarescu et al., 2013)

(b) EDS: Elementary Dependency Structures (Oepen and Lønning, 2006)

(c) PTG: Prague Tectogrammatical Graphs (Sgall et al., 1986; Hajič et al., 2012; Zeman and Hajič, 2020)

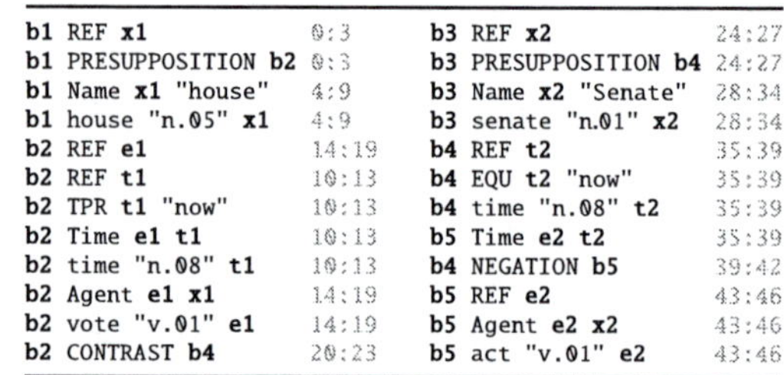

(d) UCCA: Universal Conceptual Cognitive Annotation (Abend and Rappoport, 2013)

(e) DRS: Discourse Representation Structure in a clausal form (Kamp and Reyle, 1993; Bos et al., 2017; Abzianidze et al., 2017)

Figure 1: The meaning representation graphs (a-d) of the MRP 2020 frameworks for the sentence *The House has voted but the Senate doesn't act.* (e) is the DRS of Figure 2 in the clausal form, a suitable format for semantic parsing. The goal is to convert (e) into a graph somewhat similar to (a-d).

structures.[2]

Given that graphs are mainstream when it comes to representing meaning and semantically parsing wide-coverage natural language texts, it is important that DRSs are also convertible into graphs, and we refer to these structures as Discourse Representation Graphs (DRGs). This will make DRSs accessible for researchers that primarily focus on graph-based meaning representations and parsing: (a) already existing graph-based semantic parsing models can be re-used or tested on DRGs; and (b) the specific structure of DRGs, reflecting formal semantics of the meaning, will pose new challenges for graph representation learning.

In a nutshell, to embrace DRSs in the second edition of the shared task on cross-framework (and cross-lingual) meaning representation pars-

ing (MRP 2020; Oepen et al., 2020), we investigate the conversion of DRSs from clausal form (the form adapted to semantic parsing, see Figure 1e) into graphs. While doing so, our goal is to (i) make DRGs structurally as close as possible to the graphs of other frameworks in MRP 2020 (see Figure 1), and (ii) keeping redundant information in DRGs to a minimum to prevent graphs of extensive size and to avoid inflation of the evaluation score. Our efforts contribute to unified parsing models and evaluation tools across the frameworks. Hopefully, it will also save the time of participants by preventing them from developing a completely new parsing model for DRGs.

The rest of the paper is organized as follows. First, Section 2 briefly describes the building blocks of DRSs, and then Section 3 outlines already existing approaches of converting DRSs into graphs. In addition to the existing ones, Section 4 introduces several candidate graph-based encodings of DRSs. In Section 5, we compare several

____

[2]For instance, this fact is another reason for excluding DRSs from the survey by Žabokrtský et al. (2020): "we do not include primarily logical representations which are too distant from sentence structures; this leaves out some prominent frameworks such as the Groningen Meaning Bank [...]".

Class		Type symbol	SDRS signature	Examples
Entity	t	C	constant	`now`, `house`, `senate`
		r	discourse referent	$x_1, x_2, e_1, e_2, t_1, t_2$
		B	box label	`b1`, `b2`, `b3`, `b4`, `b5`
Predicate	B	S	semantic role	`Agent`, `Name`, `Time`
		M	comparison relation	`<`, `=`
		C	concept	`house.n.05`, `act.v.01`
Discourse connective		R	discourse relation	`CONTRAST`
		O	DRS operator	`NEGATION`, `PRESUPPOSITION`

Table 1: Classification of the DRS signature. Each element of the signature has a type symbol (in a bold font). t is for terms, which might be a constant or a discourse referent, while B stands for binary relations, which are semantic roles and comparison relations.

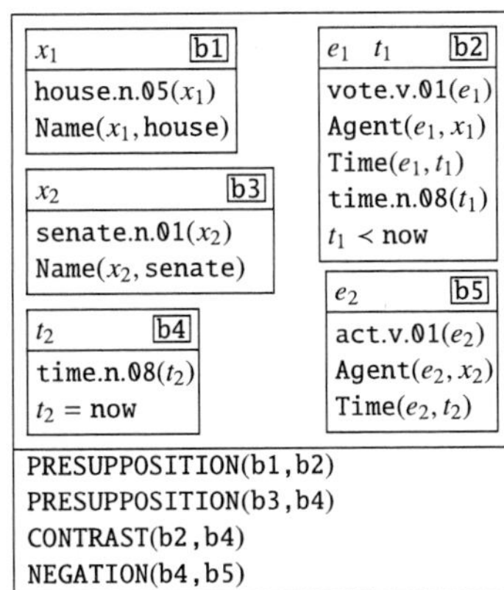

Figure 2: A flat visualization of a box-formatted DRS for the sentence *The House has voted but the Senate doesn't act.*

DRG formats on the computational feasibility of finding maximum common edge subgraph (MCES) because the computational feasibility is crucial for evaluating the meaning representation graphs against the gold standard. In the end, based on the findings of the MCES experiment and our desire for similarity with other graph-based frameworks, we select the specific DRG format that is included in MRP 2020.

2 Discourse Representation Structures

DRT is a framework that dates back to the early 1980s (Kamp, 1981; Heim, 1982). Since then, the framework has gone through several extensions and modifications to account for certain semantic or pragmatic phenomena. Throughout the paper we use DRSs that are derived from the Parallel Meaning Bank (PMB, Abzianidze et al., 2017). One such DRS is presented in Figure 2. The DRS signature is given in Table 1.

The PMB incorporates several extensions to DRSs. On a micro level, the extensions aim to make DRSs language-neutral by disambiguating non-logical symbols with WordNet (Miller, 1995) synsets and VerbNet (Bonial et al., 2011) roles, where the VerbNet roles are used in combination with neo-Davidsonian event semantics (Parsons, 1990). On a macro level, presuppositions are modeled and explicitly represented following Van der Sandt (1992) and Projective DRT (Venhuizen et al., 2013) while discourse is analyzed following Segmented DRT (Asher and Lascarides, 2003) and flattened by treating discourse relations and DRS operators in a unified way. Due to these extensions,

all boxes are labeled with identifiers.

Let's decipher what the DRS in Figure 2 is expressing. It consists of two parts: a set of boxes and a set of *discourse connectives* applied to box labels (i.e., identifiers). Boxes can be seen as sub-formulas whose separation is relevant for fine-grained semantics. Each box includes a (possibly empty) set of *discourse referents* stacked on a (possibly empty) set of *conditions*. The example sentence contains two clauses, corresponding to boxes b2 and b4, that are related with each other via the `CONTRAST` discourse relation. Both b2 and b4 presuppose the existence of entities x_1 (for *the House*) and x_2 (for *the Senate*), which are further characterized with concepts (using WordNet synsets) and the naming semantic role. The presuppositions are put in separate boxes labeled with b1 and b3. The presupposition relations are explicitly stated with the binary `PRESUPPOSITION` DRS operator. Since we use a flat visualization of DRSs, b5, which is negated and nested in b4 (expressed by `NEGATION(b4,b5)`), is depicted outside b4. In addition to modeling verb argument structure via neo-Davidsonian event semantics and semantic roles, the DRS also contains information about tense.[3]

3 Related Work

There have been several approaches to represent DRSs as graphs. These representations are put side-by-side in Figure 3.

---

[3]Note that t_2 is in b4 because it has to be out of the scope of negation: there is a time t_2, and it is not the case that at t_2 *the Senate acts.*

25

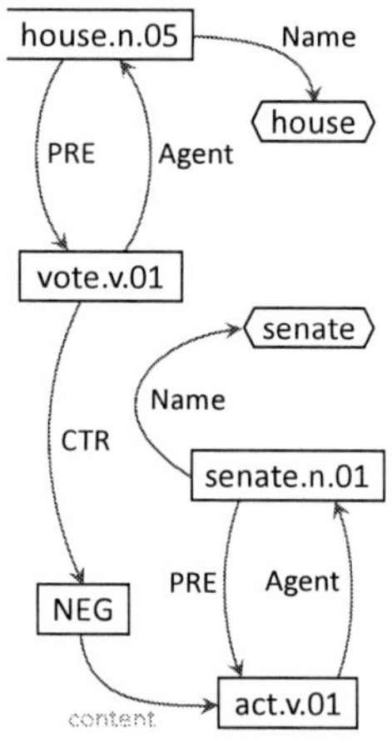 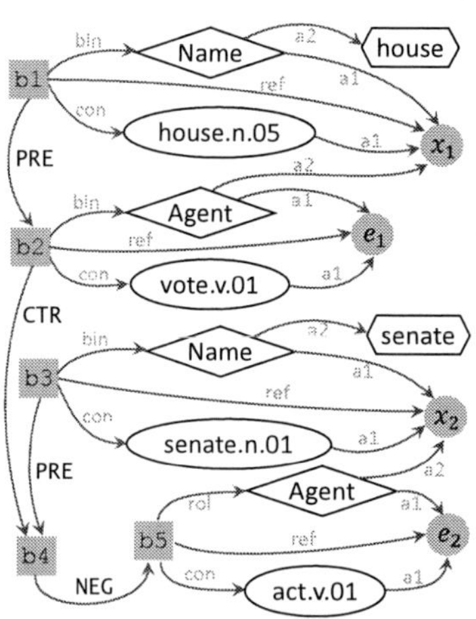 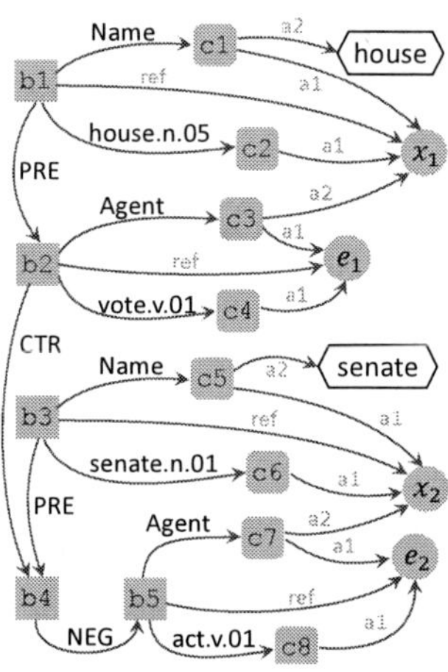

(a) The augmented graph of Power (1999) corresponding to the simplified sample DRS. The graph is a felicitous extension of Power's original proposal over DRSs with presuppositions and discourse relations.

(b) The BB* encoding largely follows Basile and Bos (2013) and incorporates several additional simplifications. The encoding is node-centric. B and C are encoded as labeled nodes while R, O and argument positions (A) as labeled edges. Only B and r are unlabeled nodes.

(c) L18 is the edge-centric encoding by Liu et al. (2018). B and C are represented as unlabeled nodes with B- and C-labeled incoming edges. R, O and argument positions (A) are encoded as labeled edges. Unlabeled nodes are introduced not only by B and r but also by B and C.

Figure 3: Contrasting the existing graph representations of DRSs. The graphs encode the sample DRS from Figure 2. For brevity, the tense information is omitted from the DRS. Unlabeled nodes have a gray background. The shapes of nodes are not part of the graphs but simply help with reading to distinguish the types of symbols.

The work by Power (1999) doesn't aim to convert DRSs into graphs as such, but it proposes to augment object-oriented knowledge representation (OOKR) graphs with additional scope information to establish correspondence with DRSs. Although the correspondence is incomplete, e.g., some OOKR graphs might have no corresponding DRS. The augmentation of Power (1999) doesn't cover DRSs with discourse relations, presuppositions (e.g., b1 to b2 in Figure 2) or with an embedded box that contains base and complex conditions (like b4 in Figure 2). Nevertheless, for demonstration purposes, we still present Power (1999)'s augmented graph for a felicitous, simplified DRS of Figure 2.

Basile and Bos (2013) proposed converting DRSs into graphs, calling them Discourse Representation Graphs (DRGs). Their goal was to facilitate word-level alignment between surface forms and the corresponding DRSs to generate texts from DRSs. The graph encoding, with several simplifications, is exemplified in Figure 3b.[4] The simplifications decrease the number of nodes and out-of-signature labels in the graph. The encoding can be seen as node-centric since the most frequent signature symbols, namely the symbols of type B and C, are modeled as labeled nodes. Argument positions (A) of binary predicates are distinguished via edge labels. We call this DRG format BB*.

To evaluate the output of their DRS parser, Liu et al. (2018) converted DRSs into graphs, demonstrated in Figure 3c. This graph encoding, in contrast to BB*, is edge-centric as the symbols of type B and C are used as edge labels. Moreover, compared to BB*, the encoding contains more unlabeled nodes since B and C are also modeled with reified nodes. We call Liu et al. (2018)'s encoding L18.

Interestingly, in contrast to the proposed graph encodings of DRS, van Noord et al. (2018a) refused to convert DRSs into graphs and instead used so-called *clausal form* of DRSs (see Figure 1e). The clauses in clausal form are triples, e.g., ⟨b4, NEGATION, b5⟩, or quadruples, e.g., ⟨b2, Agent, e1, x1⟩, where the quadruples are hyper-edges and fall out of the scope of standard graph encodings. The official evaluation of the shared task on DRS parsing (Abzianidze et al.,

---

[4]Originally Basile and Bos (2013) use more labels for edges that expresses type-specific information of nodes. For example, they use different edge labels to distinguish the first argument position of B from the only argument position of C while in the paper we use the same label for both. Basile and Bos (2013) also encodes O as a reified node that introduces two edges b4 $\xrightarrow{\text{unary}}$ NEG $\xrightarrow{\text{scope}}$ b5. Instead, we simply model O with a single edge b4 $\xrightarrow{\text{NEG}}$ b5.

2019) was also based on clausal form of DRSs.

4 More Graph-based Encodings of DRS

As illustrated in the previous section, there is no agreement on how DRSs should be converted into graphs (or whether they should be converted at all). The range of graph encodings in Figure 3 presents anything but an exhaustive list. Some encoding can even be further refined and compressed without affecting the readability or expressivness. For instance, as explained in footnote 4, BB* represents a refined version of DRGs proposed by Basile and Bos (2013). L18 can also be further compressed by discarding reified concept nodes and their outgoing a1 edges, e.g., replacing $b5 \xrightarrow{\text{act.v.01}} c8 \xrightarrow{\text{a1}} e_2$ with $b5 \xrightarrow{\text{act.v.01}} e_2$. We will use L18* to refer to the DRGs refined in such a way.

In general, the choices in which DRG formats might differ are several. Here we will discuss some of them, namely (see also Table 2):

(A) Expressing *Argument* positions of B via forking and labeled edges ($\textcircled{B}\!\leftarrow^1_2$, like BB*) or solely via graph configuration ($1\!\to\!\textcircled{B}\!\to\!2$, without labeled edges), e.g., encoding $\text{Agent}(e_1, x_1)$ as $e_1 \to \text{Agent} \to x_1$;

(B) Representing *Binary* predicates as labeled nodes ($\textcircled{B}$, like BB*) or unlabeled nodes with B-labeled edges ($\xrightarrow{B}\bigcirc$, like L18);

(C) Encoding *Concepts* as labeled nodes ($\textcircled{C}$, like BB*), unlabeled nodes with incoming C-labeled edges ($\xrightarrow{C}\bigcirc$, like L18), labeled edges ($\xrightarrow{C}\bullet$, like L18*), or as a label on an r node ($c\,\textcircled{\bullet}$, which will be discussed further);

(I) Expressing box membership explicitly (Exp) or implicitly (Imp). Whether a node (corresponding to B, C, or r) is *In* a particular B, can be depicted via an explicit connecting edge or implicitly via graph configuration.

Here we would like to elaborate more on (I). The box membership in DRT directly accounts for a semantic scope. Like discourse referents, conditions are also members of boxes. So, we also need to express the box membership of condition predicates in the graphs. All the encodings in Figure 3 explicitly express box membership. For instance, $\text{Agent}(e_1, x_1)$ belonging to b2 is expressed via connecting b2 to the Agent node (see Figure 3b) or via the outgoing Agent edge from b2 to c3. Explicating all box memberships via labeled edges

DRG encoding	Args	B	C	In-box
BB*+typed edges	$\textcircled{B}\!\leftarrow^1_2$	$\textcircled{B}$	$\textcircled{C}$	Exp
$A_a^< B^\circ C^\circ$	$\textcircled{B}\!\leftarrow^1_2$	$\textcircled{B}$	$\textcircled{C}$	Exp
$A_a^< C^\flat B^\flat$ (L18)	$\textcircled{B}\!\leftarrow^1_2$	$\xrightarrow{B}\bigcirc$	$\xrightarrow{C}\bigcirc$	Exp
$A_a^< B^\flat C^\downarrow$ (L18*)	$\textcircled{B}\!\leftarrow^1_2$	$\xrightarrow{B}\bigcirc$	$\xrightarrow{C}\bullet$	Exp
$A_a^< B^\circ C^\downarrow$	$\textcircled{B}\!\leftarrow^1_2$	$\textcircled{B}$	$\xrightarrow{C}\bullet$	Exp
$A^\uparrow B^\circ C^\downarrow$	$1\!\to\!\textcircled{B}\!\to\!2$	$\textcircled{B}$	$\xrightarrow{C}\bullet$	Exp
$A_a^< B^\flat C$	$\textcircled{B}\!\leftarrow^1_2$	$\xrightarrow{B}\bigcirc$	$c\,\textcircled{\bullet}$	Exp
$A_a^< B^\circ C$	$\textcircled{B}\!\leftarrow^1_2$	$\textcircled{B}$	$c\,\textcircled{\bullet}$	Exp
$A^\uparrow B^\circ C$	$1\!\to\!\textcircled{B}\!\to\!2$	$\textcircled{B}$	$c\,\textcircled{\bullet}$	Exp
$A^\uparrow B^\circ C I$	$1\!\to\!\textcircled{B}\!\to\!2$	$\textcircled{B}$	$c\,\textcircled{\bullet}$	Im-a1
$A^\uparrow_a B^\circ C I$	$1\!\to\!\textcircled{B}\!\to\!2$	$\textcircled{B}$	$c\,\textcircled{\bullet}$	Im-a1

Table 2: Several combinations of the choices in DRG design. The choices concern representation of argument positions, B symbols, C symbols, and in-box relations. The names of encodings visually follow the combinations of the choices.

increases the graphs in size. To prevent this, one can make box membership of certain predicates or their arguments implicit but at the same time easily and unambiguously recoverable from the graphs. For example, if we assume that directionality of arrows carries the in-box inheritance and consider the case when argument positions are configurationally encoded ($1\!\to\!\textcircled{B}\!\to\!2$), then there is no need to explicate the in-box relation for Name in $x_1 \to \text{Name} \to \text{house}$ whenever the Name condition and x_1 are in the same box.[5] We dub such an implication of box membership of B from the first argument as 'Im-a1'.

Table 2 lists several DRG formats based on combinations of how argument positions, binary predicates, concepts, and in-box relations are represented in a graph. While modeling the argument position, $1\!\to\!\textcircled{B}\!\to\!2$ is preferred over $\textcircled{B}\!\leftarrow^1_2$ from a theoretical point of view because a1 and a2 labels are not part of the DRS signature; They are ad-hoc ingredients only helping with distinguishing argument positions. When it comes to modeling concepts, as we already discussed, $\xrightarrow{C}\bullet$ leads to more economic graphs than $\xrightarrow{C}\bigcirc$.

In the PMB annotation, for almost any discourse referent, there exists the most specific concept among the concepts applied to it. For example, a discourse referent might have only two con-

---

[5]Remember that a discourse *r*eferent is considered to be *in a box* if it is introduced in the top row of the box.

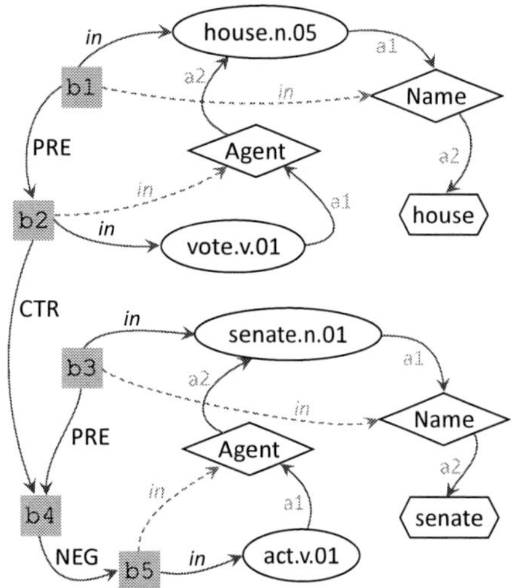

Figure 4: $A\!\!\uparrow_a B°C$ and $A\!\!\uparrow B°C\!I$ encodings. The r nodes are labeled with Concepts and connected to the boxes via *in*-edges. Dashed *in*-edges for Binary predicates and the aN edge labels are recoverable. $A\!\!\uparrow B°C\!I$ is obtained by ignoring dashed edges and gray edge labels. Unlabeled nodes are colored in grey where their labels merely serve to match graph components across the different visualizations.

cepts, `male.n.02` and `person.n.01`, applied to it, but among these concepts there exists the most specific concept, namely `male.n.02`, as `male.n.02` is a hyponym of `person.n.01` according to WordNet. The $c\odot$ choice exploits this annotation property of concepts in the PMB and labels the node of a discourse referent with the corresponding most specific concept. This type of encoding of C is shown in Figure 4.

Figure 4 also depicts $A\!\!\uparrow B°C\!I$ DRG encoding with implicit box membership of B. Though all the box membership edges of B are made implicit in the encoding example, this is not the case in general. For example, attributive and predicative adjectives usually introduce $\langle$`b1`, `Attribute`, `x1`, `s1`$\rangle$ clause, where `x1` is the attributed entity which is not necessarily introduced in the same `b1` box as the attributing state `s1`. Another example is a construction with a locative preposition and a definite noun phrase, e.g., *hid a parcel under the bed*, whose DRS contains the following fragment:

```
b2 REF e1              b2 Location e1 x3
b2 hide "v.01" e1      b2 SZP x2 x3
b2 REF x1              b3 REF x2
b2 parcel "n.01" x1    b3 bed "n.01" x2
b2 Patient e1 x1
```

where the binary relation SZP (spatial above) is in

a different box than its first argument.

As we have shown, there are at least a dozen ways to dress up DRSs as graphs. Some of the DRG formats are verbose, some can employ default rules to ignore certain redundancies, some require out-of-signature symbols, and some prefer labeled edges over labeled nodes. There isn't enough space to illustrate the graphs listed in Table 2, but each of the mentioned encoding choices is demonstrated by at least one of the graphs from Figure 3 and Figure 4.

5 Matching & Evaluating DRGs

In graph-based semantic parsing, system outputs are conventionally evaluated against the gold standard graphs by finding the maximum common edge subgraph (MCES) for each pair of produced and gold graphs, and then calculating macro-average F-score (Oepen et al., 2019). In general, the MCES problem is NP-complete, and finding the maximum subgraph *shared* between two relatively large graphs is sometimes computationally infeasible. In this section, we experiment on how computationally expensive is the MCES problem for each DRG design.

5.1 Data & Tools

We run the experiments on the output of existing DRS parsers. Four distinct parsing models are selected to achieve diversity in the system output graphs. Two of the parsers are end-to-end character-based LSTM models from van Noord et al. (2018b): one is their best model (chLSTM$^\uparrow$) while another one is trained on fewer data on purpose to have mediocre performance (chLSTM$^\downarrow$). Another two parsers are based on the semantic

DRS parsers	DRS	BB^*	$A^{<_a}_a B^i_\delta C^i_\delta$	$A^{<_a}_a B° C^i_\bullet$	$A^{<_a}_a B° \mathcal{C}$	$A\!\!\uparrow B° \mathcal{C}I$
			DRGs			
chLSTM$^\downarrow$	64.6	79.6	74.3	77.7	77.9	78.2
Boxer$^\downarrow$	78.2	89.5	86.8	87.5	87.6	87.7
chLSTM$^\uparrow$	84.3	92.3	88.4	90.9	90.9	91.1
Boxer$^\uparrow$	87.2	94.2	92.3	92.9	92.9	93.0

Table 3: Macro F-scores of the models when their output is treated as DRS or DRG. F-score for DRS is computed with `Counter` while for DRG with `mtool`.

DRS parser	✗	$\mathcal{C}^{✂}$	BB^*	$A_a^{\vee}B^{\circ}C^{\circ}$	$A_a^{\vee}C_{\flat}B_{\flat}$	$A_a^{\vee}B_{\flat}C^{\bullet}$	$A_a^{\vee}B^{\circ}C^{\bullet}$	$A^{\bullet}B^{\circ}C^{\bullet}$	$A_a^{\bullet}B^{\circ}C^{\bullet}$	$A_a^{\vee}B_{\flat}\mathcal{C}$	$A_a^{\vee}B^{\circ}\mathcal{C}$	$A^{\bullet}B^{\circ}\mathcal{C}$	$A_a^{\bullet}B^{\circ}\mathcal{C}$	$A^{\bullet}B^{\circ}\mathcal{C}I$	$A_a^{\bullet}B^{\circ}\mathcal{C}I$
chLSTM$^{\downarrow}$	13	11	27.2	30.4	28.0	12.5	15.0	18.1	15.0	9.3	10.3	12.8	10.3	8.1	7.0
Boxer$^{\downarrow}$	7	9	9.2	10.3	9.7	3.6	4.8	6.7	4.8	2.0	2.2	3.5	2.2	1.0	0.1
chLSTM$^{\uparrow}$	4	3	8.3	9.8	13.1	4.3	5.2	6.6	5.2	3.0	3.2	4.4	3.2	2.2	1.6
Boxer$^{\uparrow}$	7	3	4.4	5.1	4.8	1.3	2.7	3.3	2.7	1.0	1.0	1.8	1.0	0.9	0.3

Table 4: The percentage of approximate (i.e., non-exact) matches w.r.t. the total non-null DRGs. Lower numbers are better as more graph matches corresponding to MCES are found. The total number of DRSs is 885. While converting DRSs into DRGs, ✗-number of DRGs become null due to ill-formed DRSs and are excluded during calculating the percentages. Encoding with $\mathcal{C}$ additionally renders $\mathcal{C}^{✂}$-number of DRSs untranslatable.

parser Boxer (Bos, 2008), which is used in the PMB to *pack* all annotations layers into DRS boxes. Boxer$^{\downarrow}$ is Boxer based on the NLP tools of the PMB pipeline[6], on the other hand, Boxer$^{\uparrow}$ is Boxer employing annotation layers output by MaChAmp (van der Goot et al., 2020). As the names suggest, Boxer$^{\uparrow}$ is a better model than Boxer$^{\downarrow}$. The output DRSs are obtained by parsing the development set (885 documents) of the PMB v3.0.0.[7] Evaluation of the models based on the DRSs of the dev set is given in Table 3. DRSs are scored with `Counter` (van Noord et al., 2018a), the clause matching tool for DRSs in clausal form.[8]

For MCES-based matching of DRGs, we use `mtool`[9], the Swiss Army Knife for Graph-Based Meaning Representation. Based on the graph configurations, `mtool` schedules potential node-to-node mappings between two graphs. This information is used to initialize *promising* node-to-node mappings that might lead to finding the MCES early. `mtool` is the official scorer in both the MRP 2019 and MRP 2020 shared tasks.

All types of graph encodings employed in the experiments are obtained with the `DRS2Graph` tool.[10] This new converter from clause-based DRSs to labeled directed graphs is one of the contributions of the paper.

5.2 Results & Analysis

The results of finding MCES between the system generated and converted DRGs and reference DRGs are provided in Table 4. The reference DRGs were obtained by converting the gold standard DRS of the PMB 3.0.0 development set. We run experiments with 13 DRG formats. All 885 DRSs were converted in each DRG format without problems. In principle, the encodings with the $\mathcal{C}$ choice are lossy, however, they were successfully applied to the gold DRSs. Several parser-produced DRSs were not converted according to the $\mathcal{C}$ choice since the parsers assert the inconsistent concepts for discourse referents. For example, Boxer$^{\uparrow}$ produced a DRS with `measure.n.02` and `book.n.01` applied to the same discourse referent. Since these senses are not in hyponymy/hypernymy relation, the DRS didn't meet the requirement from $\mathcal{C}$ and was one of the three DRSs of Boxer$^{\uparrow}$ that couldn't be dressed up as $\mathcal{C}$-based graphs.[11]

Table 4 shows the computational (in)feasibility of the MCES problem across the combinations of parsing models and graph encodings (using the `mtool` implementation with default limits on its search space). Given that models are sorted according to their performance in ascending order from top to bottom, the table shows that for relatively distinct graphs it can be difficult to guarantee the MCES solution.[12] But things are not so straightforward as chLSTM$^{\uparrow}$ outperforms Boxer$^{\downarrow}$ but finding MCES for Boxer$^{\downarrow}$ is easier for 10 encodings out of 13. This can be explained by the fact that gold DRSs are obtained from Boxer$^{\downarrow}$ while taking into account added human annotations. Given this, it is

---

[6]https://pmb.let.rug.nl/software.php
[7]https://pmb.let.rug.nl/data.php
[8]https://github.com/RikVN/DRS_parsing
[9]https://github.com/cfmrp/mtool
[10]https://github.com/kovvalsky/DRS2Graph

[11]From 6620 gold DRSs of the PMB 3.0.0 training part, only 16 (0.24%) DRSs didn't satisfy the constraint of $\mathcal{C}$.

[12]When exhausting its search space limits, `mtool` falls back to an anytime strategy, returning the best overall match found up to that point. This match will often correspond to the MCES, but there is no correctness guarantee in this mode.

expected that gold and Boxer$^{\downarrow}$'s DRSs have in common substantial chunks of boxes, and this sharing is transferred on the DRGs too.

Interestingly, the encodings BB* (Basile and Bos, 2013) and $A_a^{<a}B^{\flat}C^{\flat}$ (Liu et al., 2018) are one of the most inefficient encodings across all the models. For instance, non-exact (i.e., approximate) MCES was found for 237 DRG pairs out of 872 for chLSTM$^{\downarrow}$ and BB* encoding. For other encodings the ratio of approximate matches halves.

Among the encodings with the $C^{\downarrow}$ choice, $A_a^{<a}B^{\flat}C^{\downarrow}$ appears to provide most computationally *friendly* graphs. Every encoding with $C^{\downarrow}$ becomes even better when $C^{\downarrow}$ is replaced with C. This is because C brings at least a 16% reduction in the number of edges and increases the number of labeled nodes. The latter apparently helps `mtool` to get better initializations for node mappings.

$A_a^{<a}B^{\flat}C$ is the best among C-featured encodings with explicit box membership. It doesn't improve further when changing its encoding choices, including switching to $A^{\downarrow}$. The results show that $A_a^{<a}$ is consistently better than $A^{\downarrow}$. Even when they are combined, $A^{\downarrow}$ adds no value to $A_a^{<a}$. However, the advantage of $A^{\downarrow}$ over $A_a^{<a}$ is that it configurationally distinguishes argument positions and there is no need for out-of-signature labels. Moreover, $A^{\downarrow}$ invites the intuitive inheritance property about in-box relation (see (I) discussed in Section 4). When incorporating the implicit in-box relation with $A^{\downarrow}$, the combination $A^{\downarrow}B^{\circ}CI$ yields a substantial decrease in the number of approximate matches. This is explained by the fact that the number of edges decreases by at least 23%. Adding the out-of-signature edge labels for marking argument positions further improves the encoding.

Differences between F-scores calculated over DRS (with `Counter`) and DRGs (with `mtool`) are significant (see Table 3). The gap between low- and high-performing model is greater than 10% and 5%, respectively. The DRS-based score is more strict than the DRG-based one because DRSs are evaluated in the clausal form, where some DRSs conditions (e.g., built with B) are modeled via quadruples, i.e., hyper-edges. In DRGs, the hyper-edges are represented by multiple triples ($\langle$nodeID, edgeLabel, nodeID$\rangle$ or $\langle$nodeID, label, labelValue$\rangle$), and this additionally rewards the models when they get parts of hyper-edges correctly.

6 Conclusion

There have been several approaches that encoded DRSs as graphs (surveyed in Section 3), but their objectives were to transform DRSs in a suitable format for particular applications rather than exploring and comparing different types of DRG encodings. This paper fills this gap. We have systematically characterized a dozen of DRG encodings and contrasted them with each other, and compared them to the DRS clausal form from an evaluation perspective.

We opt for the $A^{\downarrow}B^{\circ}CI$ DRG encoding (see Figure 4) to represent DRSs at the MRP 2020 shared task. Despite the encoding being lossy, it represents an excellent trade-off due to the advantages it brings: (a) the encoding has at least 23% fewer edges than other encodings, which makes the DRGs more compact and easier to read; (b) given that scope information inflates DRSs, learning relatively compact DRGs seems a good starting point for the shared task; (c) only less than 0.25% DRSs are lost when applying the encoding; (d) it doesn't employ the out-of-signature labels a1 and a2; (e) for the DRGs obtained from the average-performing DRS parsers, the evaluation tool can find exact maximal matches for at least 98.4% of DRG pairs.

When abstracting from the reification of the roles as nodes, the chosen DRG encoding and the graphs of other frameworks in MRP 2020 have abstractly parallel graph topologies for linguistically parallel predicate-argument structures.

Acknowledgments

We thank Rik van Noord for providing us with outputs of the DRS parsers. We acknowledge access to the Peregrine HPC cluster provided by the CIT of the University of Groningen, and to the NLPL infrastructure provided by Sigma2 in Norway. The first two authors were supported by the NWO-VICI grant (288-89-003). The first author was additionally supported by the European Research Council (ERC) under the European Unions Horizon 2020 research and innovation programme (grant agreement No. 742204).

References

Omri Abend and Ari Rappoport. 2013. UCCA: A semantics-based grammatical annotation scheme. In *Proceedings of the 10th International Conference on Computational Semantics (IWCS 2013) – Long Papers*, pages 1–12, Potsdam, Germany. Association for Computational Linguistics.

Lasha Abzianidze, Johannes Bjerva, Kilian Evang, Hessel Haagsma, Rik van Noord, Pierre Ludmann, Duc-Duy Nguyen, and Johan Bos. 2017. The Parallel Meaning Bank: Towards a multilingual corpus of translations annotated with compositional meaning representations. In *Proceedings of the 15th Conference of the European Chapter of the Association for Computational Linguistics: Volume 2, Short Papers*, pages 242–247, Valencia, Spain. Association for Computational Linguistics.

Lasha Abzianidze, Rik van Noord, Hessel Haagsma, and Johan Bos. 2019. The first shared task on discourse representation structure parsing. In *Proceedings of the IWCS Shared Task on Semantic Parsing*, Gothenburg, Sweden. Association for Computational Linguistics.

N. Asher and A. Lascarides. 2003. *Logics of conversation*. Studies in natural language processing. Cambridge University Press.

Laura Banarescu, Claire Bonial, Shu Cai, Madalina Georgescu, Kira Griffitt, Ulf Hermjakob, Kevin Knight, Philipp Koehn, Martha Palmer, and Nathan Schneider. 2013. Abstract Meaning Representation for sembanking. In *Proceedings of the 7th Linguistic Annotation Workshop and Interoperability with Discourse*, pages 178–186, Sofia, Bulgaria. Association for Computational Linguistics.

Valerio Basile and Johan Bos. 2013. Aligning formal meaning representations with surface strings for wide-coverage text generation. In *Proceedings of the 14th European Workshop on Natural Language Generation*, pages 1–9, Sofia, Bulgaria. Association for Computational Linguistics.

Claire Bonial, William J. Corvey, Martha Palmer, Volha Petukhova, and Harry Bunt. 2011. A hierarchical unification of LIRICS and VerbNet semantic roles. In *Proceedings of the 5th IEEE International Conference on Semantic Computing (ICSC 2011)*, pages 483–489.

Johan Bos. 2008. Wide-Coverage Semantic Analysis with Boxer. In Johan Bos and Rodolfo Delmonte, editors, *Semantics in Text Processing. STEP 2008 Conference Proceedings*, volume 1 of *Research in Computational Semantics*, pages 277–286. College Publications.

Johan Bos, Valerio Basile, Kilian Evang, Noortje Venhuizen, and Johannes Bjerva. 2017. The Groningen Meaning Bank. In Nancy Ide and James Pustejovsky, editors, *Handbook of Linguistic Annotation*. Springer Netherlands.

Rob van der Goot, Ahmet Üstün, Alan Ramponi, and Barbara Plank. 2020. Massive choice, ample tasks (machamp): A toolkit for multi-task learning in nlp.

Jan Hajič, Eva Hajičová, Jarmila Panevová, Petr Sgall, Ondřej Bojar, Silvie Cinková, Eva Fučíková, Marie Mikulová, Petr Pajas, Jan Popelka, Jiří Semecký, Jana Šindlerová, Jan Štěpánek, Josef Toman, Zdeňka Urešová, and Zdeněk Žabokrtský. 2012. Announcing Prague Czech-English Dependency Treebank 2.0. In *Proceedings of the Eighth International Conference on Language Resources and Evaluation (LREC'12)*, pages 3153–3160, Istanbul, Turkey. European Language Resources Association (ELRA).

Irene Heim. 1982. *The Semantics of Definite and Indefinite Noun Phrases*. Ph.D. thesis, University of Massachusetts, Amherst.

Daniel Hershcovich, Zohar Aizenbud, Leshem Choshen, Elior Sulem, Ari Rappoport, and Omri Abend. 2019. SemEval-2019 task 1: Cross-lingual semantic parsing with UCCA. In *Proceedings of the 13th International Workshop on Semantic Evaluation*, pages 1–10, Minneapolis, Minnesota, USA. Association for Computational Linguistics.

Hans Kamp. 1981. A theory of truth and semantic representation. In J. A. G. Groenendijk, T. M. V. Janssen, and M. B. J. Stokhof, editors, *Formal Methods in the Study of Language*, volume 1, pages 277–322. Mathematisch Centrum, Amsterdam.

Hans Kamp and Uwe Reyle. 1993. *From Discourse to Logic; An Introduction to Modeltheoretic Semantics of Natural Language, Formal Logic and DRT*. Kluwer, Dordrecht.

Jiangming Liu, Shay B. Cohen, and Mirella Lapata. 2018. Discourse representation structure parsing. In *Proceedings of the 56th Annual Meeting of the Association for Computational Linguistics (Volume 1: Long Papers)*, pages 429–439, Melbourne, Australia. Association for Computational Linguistics.

Jonathan May. 2016. SemEval-2016 task 8: Meaning representation parsing. In *Proceedings of the 10th International Workshop on Semantic Evaluation (SemEval-2016)*, pages 1063–1073, San Diego, California. Association for Computational Linguistics.

Jonathan May and Jay Priyadarshi. 2017. SemEval-2017 task 9: Abstract Meaning Representation parsing and generation. In *Proceedings of the 11th International Workshop on Semantic Evaluation (SemEval-2017)*, pages 536–545, Vancouver, Canada. Association for Computational Linguistics.

George A Miller. 1995. Wordnet: a lexical database for english. *Communications of the ACM*, 38(11):39–41.

Rik van Noord, Lasha Abzianidze, Hessel Haagsma, and Johan Bos. 2018a. Evaluating scoped meaning representations. In *Proceedings of the Eleventh*

International Conference on Language Resources and Evaluation (LREC-2018), Miyazaki, Japan. European Languages Resources Association (ELRA).

Rik van Noord, Lasha Abzianidze, Antonio Toral, and Johan Bos. 2018b. Exploring neural methods for parsing discourse representation structures. *Transactions of the Association for Computational Linguistics*, 6:619–633.

Stephan Oepen, Omri Abend, Lasha Abzianidze, Johan Bos, Jan Hajič, Daniel Hershcovich, Bin Li, Tim O'Gorman, Nianwen Xue, and Daniel Zeman. 2020. MRP 2020: The Second Shared Task on Cross-framework and Cross-Lingual Meaning Representation Parsing. In *Proceedings of the CoNLL 2020 Shared Task: Cross-Framework Meaning Representation Parsing*, pages 1–22, Online.

Stephan Oepen, Omri Abend, Jan Hajič, Daniel Hershcovich, Marco Kuhlmann, Tim O'Gorman, Nianwen Xue, Jayeol Chun, Milan Straka, and Zdeňka Urešová. 2019. MRP 2019: Cross-framework Meaning Representation Parsing. In *Proceedings of the Shared Task on Cross-Framework Meaning Representation Parsing at the 2019 Conference on Computational Natural Language Learning*, pages 1–27, Hong Kong, China.

Stephan Oepen, Marco Kuhlmann, Yusuke Miyao, Daniel Zeman, Silvie Cinková, Dan Flickinger, Jan Hajič, and Zdeňka Urešová. 2015. SemEval 2015 task 18: Broad-coverage semantic dependency parsing. In *Proceedings of the 9th International Workshop on Semantic Evaluation (SemEval 2015)*, pages 915–926, Denver, Colorado. Association for Computational Linguistics.

Stephan Oepen, Marco Kuhlmann, Yusuke Miyao, Daniel Zeman, Dan Flickinger, Jan Hajič, Angelina Ivanova, and Yi Zhang. 2014. SemEval 2014 task 8: Broad-coverage semantic dependency parsing. In *Proceedings of the 8th International Workshop on Semantic Evaluation (SemEval 2014)*, pages 63–72, Dublin, Ireland. Association for Computational Linguistics.

Stephan Oepen and Jan Tore Lønning. 2006. Discriminant-based MRS banking. In *Proceedings of the Fifth International Conference on Language Resources and Evaluation (LREC'06)*, Genoa, Italy. European Language Resources Association (ELRA).

Terence Parsons. 1990. *Events in the Semantics of English: A Study in Subatomic Semantics*. MIT Press.

Richard Power. 1999. Controlling logical scope in text generation. In *Proceedings of the 7th. European Workshop on Natural Language Generation (EWNLG'99)*, pages 1–9, Toulouse.

Rob A. Van der Sandt. 1992. Presupposition projection as anaphora resolution. *Journal of Semantics*, 9(4):333–377.

Petr Sgall, Eva Hajičová, and Jarmila Panevová. 1986. *The Meaning of the Sentence and Its Semantic and Pragmatic Aspects*. Academia/Reidel Publishing Company, Prague, Czech Republic/Dordrecht, Netherlands.

Noortje J. Venhuizen, Johan Bos, and Harm Brouwer. 2013. Parsimonious semantic representations with projection pointers. In *Proceedings of the 10th International Conference on Computational Semantics (IWCS 2013) – Long Papers*, pages 252–263, Potsdam, Germany. Association for Computational Linguistics.

Daniel Zeman and Jan Hajič. 2020. FGD at MRP 2020: Prague Tectogrammatical Graphs. In *Proceedings of the CoNLL 2020 Shared Task: Cross-Framework Meaning Representation Parsing*, pages 33–39, Online.

Zdeněk Žabokrtský, Daniel Zeman, and Magda Ševčíková. 2020. Sentence meaning representations across languages: What can we learn from existing frameworks? *Computational Linguistics*, 0(0):605–665.

FGD at MRP 2020: Prague Tectogrammatical Graphs

Daniel Zeman and Jan Hajič

Charles University in Prague
Faculty of Mathematics and Physics
Institute of Formal and Applied Linguistics (ÚFAL)
`{zeman|hajic}@ufal.mff.cuni.cz`

Abstract

Prague Tectogrammatical Graphs (PTG) is a meaning representation framework that originates in the tectogrammatical layer of the Prague Dependency Treebank (PDT) and is theoretically founded in Functional Generative Description of language (FGD). PTG in its present form has been prepared for the CoNLL 2020 shared task on Cross-Framework Meaning Representation Parsing (MRP). It is generated automatically from the Prague treebanks and stored in the JSON-based MRP graph interchange format. The conversion is partially lossy; in this paper we describe what part of annotation was included and how it is represented in PTG.

1 Introduction

The Functional Generative Description (FGD) (Sgall, 1967; Sgall et al., 1986), as instantiated in the Prague family of dependency treebanks, defines four layers of description: 1. the word layer; 2. the morphological layer; 3. the analytical (surface-syntactic) layer; 4. the tectogrammatical (deep-syntactic) layer. The meaning representation used in the CoNLL 2020 shared task (Oepen et al., 2020) is based mostly on the tectogrammatical layer; however, references have to be followed all the way down to the word layer in order to provide anchoring of graph nodes in the underlying text.

The shared task featured PTG data in two languages: English and Czech. The English data was taken from the same sources as in the previous shared task (CoNLL MRP 2019, Oepen et al. 2019); however, a different conversion procedure had been used in the previous task, leading to different (and simpler) target graphs, known as Prague Semantic Dependencies (PSD, Miyao et al. 2014). The source text originates in the Wall Street Journal portion of the Penn TreeBank and the source

annotation stems from the Prague Czech-English Dependency Treebank 2.0 (PCEDT, Hajič et al. 2012). As there are other frameworks in which the same data is annotated in the shared task, the training-development-test split was synchronized across frameworks,[1] and a handful of sentences were omitted because they did not align with the original WSJ text. In addition, the test set includes 100 out-of-domain sentences from The Little Prince short novel by Antoine de Saint-Exupéry. The Czech data was taken from the Prague Dependency Treebank 3.5 (PDT, Hajič et al. 2017) and its standard training-development-evaluation split was used.

The meaning representation in P(CE)DT is called *tectogrammatical tree* or *t-tree*. The structure meets the tree constraints only because

- paratactic structures such as coordination are encoded using technical dependencies, special edge labels and attributes;

- coreference links are encoded as node attributes instead of being treated as edges.

As the representations in the shared task are not restricted to trees, additional edges were added to more directly encode paratactic structures and coreference. The resulting structures are called **Prague Tectogrammatical Graphs (PTG).**

2 Graph Properties and Anchoring

The typical node in a tectogrammatical graph corresponds to a content word, which is its anchoring in the surface sentence. Pronouns are treated as content words in this respect. Function words normally

---

[1] Sections 00–20 of WSJ served as training data; section 21 was used for development/validation and section 23 for evaluation.

Proceedings of the CoNLL 2020 Shared Task: Cross-Framework Meaning Representation Parsing, pages 33–39
Online, Nov. 19-20, 2020. ©2020 Association for Computational Linguistics

DENOM	independent nominal
PAR	parenthetic clause
PARTL	independent interjection
PRED	independent verbal clause
VOCAT	independent vocative

Table 1: Five PTG functors for "independent" nodes. Except for PAR, these functors typically occur at edges going out of the artificial root node.

ACT	argument: actor
ADDR	argument: addressee
EFF	argument: effect
ORIG	argument: origo
PAT	argument: patient

Table 2: Five argument functors in PTG.

do not have nodes of their own.[2] They are treated as attributes of the content word they "belong to". This association is projected to anchoring and one node can thus be anchored to multiple surface sub-strings, even discontinuous. Punctuation symbols are even less prominent than function words and are not included in node anchoring.

On the other hand, there are *generated (empty) nodes* that represent reconstructed material, deleted on the surface. These nodes are usually unanchored. Unanchored is also the artificial root node. Despite not being trees, the graphs are rooted and every node is reachable from the single root node[3] via at least one directed path. Some nodes are reachable via multiple paths and the graph may also contain cycles.

In the classification of the MRP shared task, Prague Tectogrammatical Graphs represent a Flavor 1 framework.

3 Edge Types

Most edges in PTG are understood as dependencies. In each clause, the backbone of the representation is formed by edges going from a verbal predicate

---

[2]Coordinating conjunctions (or even coordinating punctuation) are an exception. Despite being function words, they may be used as technical means to capture coordination, in which case they will have their own node.

[3]One could argue that the root node could be removed in the MRP environment and its children marked as *top nodes* instead. However, we stick to this representation because 1. the root is considered a node in the Prague tectogrammatical trees; 2. there may be multiple outgoing edges from the root, and 3. the labels and attributes of the edges are not necessarily identical. Root nodes are not labeled in the data, but in the diagrams in this paper, we use '#Root' to represent them.

ACMP	adjunct: accompaniment
AIM	adjunct: purpose
BEN	adjunct: benefactor
CAUS	adjunct: cause
CNCS	adjunct: concession
COMPL	adjunct: predicative complement
COND	adjunct: condition
CONTRD	adjunct: confrontation
CPR	adjunct: comparison
CRIT	adjunct: criterion
DIFF	adjunct: difference
DIR1	adjunct: where from
DIR2	adjunct: which way
DIR3	adjunct: where to
EXT	adjunct: extent
HER	adjunct: inheritance
INTT	adjunct: intention
LOC	adjunct: where
MANN	adjunct: manner
MEANS	adjunct: means
REG	adjunct: with regard to
RESL	adjunct: result
RESTR	adjunct: exception, restriction
SUBS	adjunct: substitution
TFHL	adjunct: for how long
TFRWH	adjunct: from when
THL	adjunct: (after) how long
THO	adjunct: how often
TOWH	adjunct: to when
TPAR	adjunct: in parallel with what
TSIN	adjunct: since when
TTILL	adjunct: until when
TWHEN	adjunct: when

Table 3: Thirty-three adjunct functors in PTG.

APP	adnominal adjunct: appurtenance
AUTH	adnominal adjunct: author
DESCR	adnominal description (only PCEDT)
ID	adnominal specification of identity
MAT	adnominal argument: content
RSTR	adnominal adjunct: modification

Table 4: Six adnominal functors in PTG.

to its arguments and adjuncts (both of which can be clauses themselves, represented by their predicates). Copular clauses are headed by the copula (meaning that the copula is not treated as a function word) and the non-verbal component of the predicate is analyzed as an argument of the cop-

ATT	speaker's attitude
CM	conjunction modifier
CPHR	nominal part of complex predicate
DPHR	dependent part of idiom
FPHR	part of foreign expression
INTF	expletive subject
MOD	some modal expressions
NE	part of named entity (only PCEDT)
PREC	preceding context
RHEM	rhematizer

Table 5: Ten PTG functors for miscellaneous dependents.

ADVS	parataxis: adversative
APPS	parataxis: apposition
CONFR	parataxis: confrontation
CONJ	parataxis: conjunction
CONTRA	parataxis: conflict
CSQ	parataxis: consequence
DISJ	parataxis: disjunction
GRAD	parataxis: gradation
OPER	parataxis: math operation
REAS	parataxis: cause

Table 6: PTG functors for 10 types of paratactic relations.

ula. There is no direct edge between the non-verbal or secondary predicate and the subject argument (Figure 1).

Unlike in some other meaning representation frameworks, attributes of nominals (and adjuncts of clauses) are not treated as predicates and the edge goes from the nominal to its attribute, not the other way around.

Overall the tectogrammatical layer defines[4] 67 relation types, called *functors*; a few extra functors are defined in PCEDT. Relations between the artificial root node and the most independent word of the sentence are listed in Table 1. Tables 2, 3 and 4 list the functors for arguments, adjuncts and adnominal modifiers, respectively. Miscellaneous other dependencies are covered by Table 5.

Optionally, some functors may be further subclassified using *subfunctors*. In the PTG data for the shared task, we merge the functor with its subfunctor into a single label, using the period

---

[4]See `https://ufal.mff.cuni.cz/pdt2.0/doc/manuals/en/t-layer/html/ch07.html` for detailed documentation.

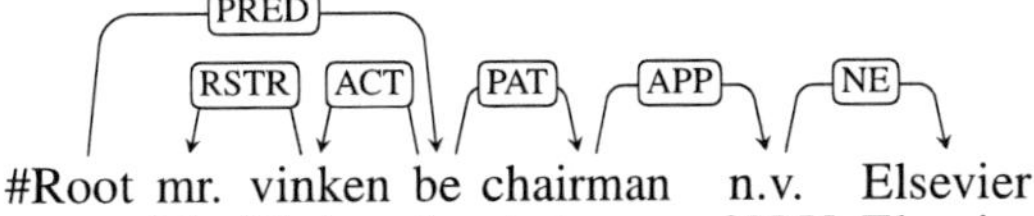

Figure 1: PTG of a simple clause with a copula. The sentence is *Mr. Vinken is chairman of Elsevier N.V.* The preposition *of* does not have a node of its own but it is considered an attribute of the head node of the named entity. The text anchoring of that node (shown in the second line) is thus *of N. V.* The linear ordering of nodes in our diagrams is not significant.

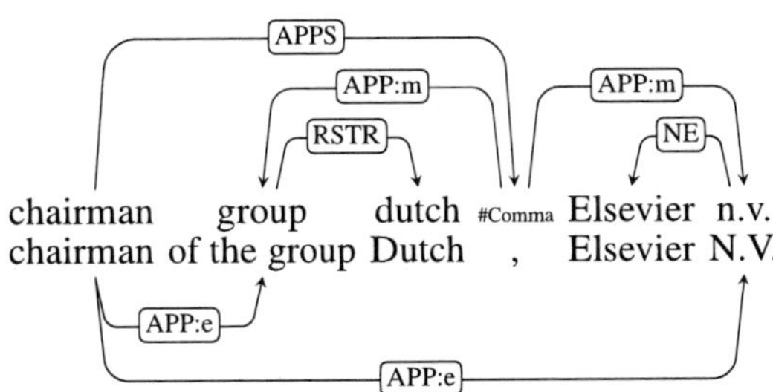

Figure 2: PTG of a paratactic structure (apposition). The phrase is *chairman of Elsevier N.V., the Dutch group*. Note that APPS means 'apposition' while APP stands for 'appurtenance'. The suffix :m in the edge labels is not a subfunctor. It is a shortcut for the *member* attribute, indicating that this node is a member of the paratactic structure, rather than its shared dependent. The edges below the nodes were added during the conversion from t-trees to PTG and connect the members of the apposition with their effective parent. The suffix :e is a shortcut for the *effective* attribute of the edge.

as a delimiter. For example, the locative adjunct LOC may be further specified as LOC.above, LOC.around etc.

Paratactic structures such as coordination and apposition call for special treatment within this prevailingly dependency-based framework. They are always headed by a technical node which is typically anchored in a coordinating conjunction or punctuation. The functor of the incoming edge only classifies the type of the paratactic relation (see Table 6 for available functors). Edges outgoing from the technical node lead to members of the paratactic relation and their functors reflect the actual relation between the parent of the structure and the member.

The technical node and the edges described so far are present also in the source t-trees in the Prague treebanks. During conversion to PTG, we

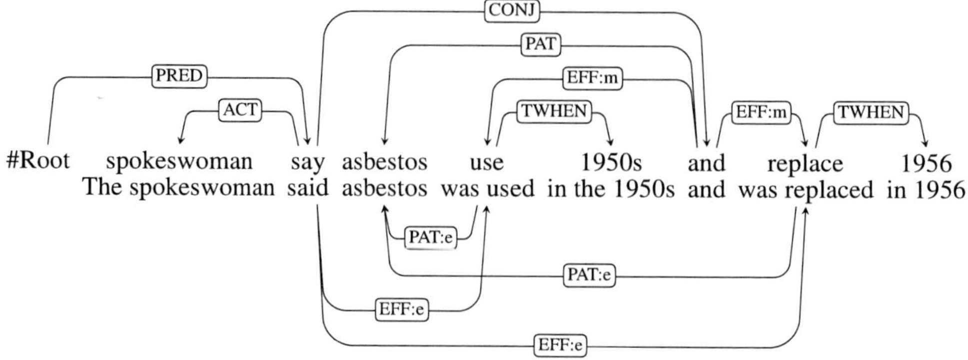

Figure 3: Propagation of effective dependencies to a shared argument of coordinate verbs. The sentence is *The spokeswoman said asbestos was used in the 1950s and replaced in 1956.* Note that the auxiliary *was* occurs only once but is included in anchoring of two nodes.

deterministically add extra edges that propagate dependencies across the paratactic structure and connect children with their *effective* parents. An example is given in Figure 2. A larger example in Figure 3 shows dependency propagation to a dependent shared by the conjuncts.

The last category of edges, also added during conversion to PTG, is related to coreference and will be described in §5.

4 Generated Nodes

Material may be missing (elided, deleted) from the surface sentence if it is unimportant or understandable from context. The tectogrammatical representation uses *generated nodes* to account for the missing material. If there is no surface word representing an obligatory valency-licensed argument of a verb, a generated node will be added and attached to the predicate with an appropriate functor. In fact, the graph in Figure 3 should include two generated nodes which we omitted for simplicity: the ADDR argument of *say* and the ACT argument of *use* and *replace*.

The labels of the generated nodes further distinguish their type and purpose. #PersPron is used for personal pronouns, regardless whether they are overt or generated. #Cor is a grammatically controlled coreferential argument (see §5), and #Gen is a general actor, not identifiable with a concrete entity (as in Czech *Tohle se tak prostě dělá.* "One simply does it this way."[5]

While most generated nodes are unanchored,

sometimes a generated node is a copy of a regular node and inherits its anchoring (and label). Such copied nodes may be observed in coordination, as in Figure 4.

5 Coreference

Coreference is a relation between two nodes that have the same referent in the scene described by the text. While most participants in coreference are nouns or pronouns, sometimes a referent may also be described by a clause. T-trees capture coreference as a node attribute which refers to another node by its unique identifier. In PTG these links are converted to edges, as in Figure 4, where a generated node is coreferential with an overt pronoun.

While coreference is naturally a symmetric relation, only one-way direction is explicitly captured by the edge in PTG. The rules that govern the direction (inherited from the t-trees) are complex. For example, if the edge connects an overt pronoun with an overt noun, it always points from the pronoun to the noun. There may be chains of coreference edges that connect more than two coreferential nodes, and coreference edges may also cause the graph to contain cycles (Figure 5). Coreference in the Prague treebanks may even cross sentence boundaries; however, only intra-sentence relations are preserved in PTG.

There are two types of coreference edges. Grammatical coreference (coref.gram) follows deterministically from grammatical rules (e.g., the subject of an infinitive must be coreferential with one of the arguments of the matrix verb). The instances that do not fall under grammatical coreference are called textual coreference (coref.text); the

---

[5]The Czech sentence does not contain a word directly corresponding to the English pronoun *one*, so a #Gen node must be generated instead.

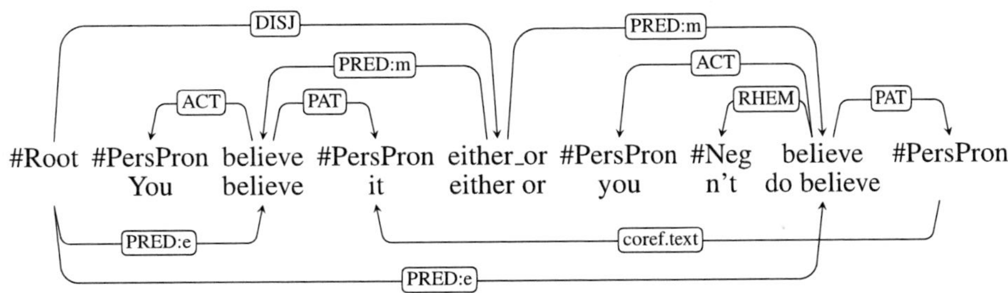

Figure 4: Ellipsis and generated nodes. The sentence is *You either believe it or you don't.* There are two nodes anchored to the surface word *believe*: the first one is a regular node, the second one is generated (in addition, the anchoring of the second node includes the auxiliary *do*). Another generated node represents the hypothetical patient of the second *believe*. The `coref.text` edge indicates that the patients of the two verbs are coreferential.

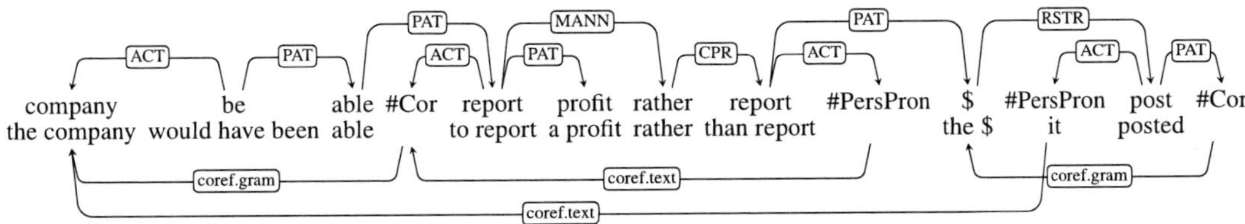

Figure 5: Coreference. The full sentence is *Without the Cray-3 research and development expenses, the company would have been able to report a profit of $19.3 million for the first half of 1989 rather than the $5.9 million it posted.* We have omitted some nodes for simplicity.

prototypical case is a pronoun linked to a noun.

Finally, the graphs may also contain edges that represent *bridging* relations. Bridging is similar to coreference but different in that the participants are not fully identical. Instead, one may be a subset of the other (then the edge label is `bridging.SUB_SET`). Bridging relations are currently available in the Czech data but not in English.

6 Node Properties

The main label that represents a node is its tectogrammatical lemma or *t_lemma*.[6] Besides it, a t-tree node has a number of attributes and 'grammatemes', both of which translate as node *properties* in the file format used in the shared task. Not all properties are available in both Czech and English, and not all properties are preserved during the conversion to PTG. The Prague treebanks, especially the Czech PDT, contain a number of grammatemes that were assigned semi-automatically without much human intervention. Such properties were omitted and only the manually assigned (or checked) ones were carried over to PTG.

The following node properties appear in the data:[7]

- **sempos** – semantic part-of-speech category. Older data, such as the English part of PCEDT, do not have sempos but they have a 'formeme', first part of which corresponds to sempos (while the second part corresponds to what newer data captures in subfunctors). The first part of a formeme is thus converted to sempos in PTG.

- **sentmod** – sentence modality, 5 values: `enunc` (declarative), `excl` (exclamative), `desid` (desiderative), `imper` (imperative), `inter` (interrogative). Occurs at the main predicate node, both in Czech and English.

- **factmod** – factual modality: is the event presented as given, or hypothetical? Four values: `asserted`, `potential`, `irreal`, `appeal`. Occurs at predicate nodes, in Czech data only.

- **diatgram** – diathesis, 7 values: `act` (active), `pas` (passive), `res1` and `res2` (resul-

---

[6]In the diagrams throughout this paper, the first line of each node shows its t_lemma and the second line shows the surface strings it is anchored to, if any.

[7]See `https://ufal.mff.cuni.cz/pdt3.0/documentation` for detailed documentation.

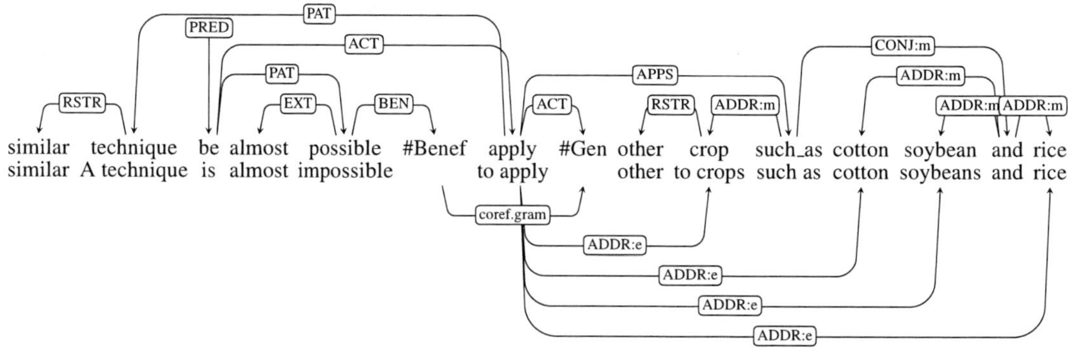

Figure 6: PTG representation of the sentence *A similar technique is almost impossible to apply to other crops, such as cotton, soybeans and rice.* (Sentence 13 of file 0209 from the Wall Street Journal / Prague Czech-English Dependency Treebank.) We have omitted the artificial #Root node in order to fit the graph on the page.

tative), `recip` (reciprocal), `disp` (dispositional), and `deagent` (deagentive). Occurs with finite verbs, in Czech data only.

- **typgroup** – does the noun in plural signify a pair/tuple? Seven possible values, e.g., `sg.group` or `pl.single`. Occurs with nouns, in Czech data only.

- **frame** – frame identifier (can be used as an index to the valency dictionary Vallex). In English, frames are available only for verbs. In Czech they are available also for some adjectives and nouns.

- **tfa** – topic-focus articulation, 3 values: `t` (topic), `f` (focus), `c` (contrast). Only in Czech data, available for most nodes (also generated ones), except the artificial root and the technical heads of paratactic structures.

Related to topic-focus articulation, the tectogrammatical layer also defines a *deep ordering* of nodes. It is reflected in the numerical node ids in Czech PTG, hence it could be considered as another node property. Note however that the diagrams in this paper do *not* reflect the deep order.

7 Other Crops

Instead of a summary, we provide in Figure 6 the PTG representation of sentence 13 of file 0209 from the Wall Street Journal, which has become a standard running example throughout many papers on semantic representations and parsing. See also Oepen et al. (2020) for an alternative but equivalent visualization of the graph.

Acknowledgments

This work was supported by the the Grant No. GX20-16819X of the Czech Science Foundation (LUSyD) and by the LINDAT/CLARIAH-CZ project of the Ministry of Education, Youth and Sports of the Czech Republic (project LM2018101).

References

Jan Hajič, Eva Hajičová, Jarmila Panevová, Petr Sgall, Ondřej Bojar, Silvie Cinková, Eva Fučíková, Marie Mikulová, Petr Pajas, Jan Popelka, Jiří Semecký, Jana Šindlerová, Jan Štěpánek, Josef Toman, Zdeňka Urešová, and Zdeněk Žabokrtský. 2012. Announcing Prague Czech-English Dependency Treebank 2.0. In *Proceedings of the 8th International Conference on Language Resources and Evaluation (LREC 2012)*, pages 3153–3160, İstanbul, Turkey. ELRA, European Language Resources Association.

Jan Hajič, Eva Hajičová, Marie Mikulová, and Jiří Mírovský. 2017. Prague Dependency Treebank. In *Handbook of Linguistic Annotation*, pages 555–594. Springer.

Yusuke Miyao, Stephan Oepen, and Daniel Zeman. 2014. In-house: An ensemble of pre-existing off-the-shelf parsers. In *Proceedings of the Eighth International Workshop on Semantic Evaluation (SemEval 2014)*, pages 335–340, Dublin, Ireland. Dublin City University.

Stephan Oepen, Omri Abend, Lasha Abzianidze, Johan Bos, Jan Hajič, Daniel Hershcovich, Bin Li, Tim O'Gorman, Nianwen Xue, and Daniel Zeman. 2020. MRP 2020: The Second Shared Task on Cross-framework and Cross-Lingual Meaning Representation Parsing. In *Proceedings of the CoNLL 2020 Shared Task: Cross-Framework Meaning Representation Parsing*, pages 1–22, Online.

Stephan Oepen, Omri Abend, Jan Hajič, Daniel Hershcovich, Marco Kuhlmann, Tim O'Gorman, Nianwen Xue, Jayeol Chun, Milan Straka, and Zdeňka Urešová. 2019. MRP 2019: Cross-framework Meaning Representation Parsing. In *Proceedings of the Shared Task on Cross-Framework Meaning Representation Parsing at the 2019 Conference on Computational Natural Language Learning*, pages 1 – 27, Hong Kong, China.

Petr Sgall. 1967. Functional sentence perspective in a generative description. *Prague Studies in Mathematical Linguistics*, 2:203–225.

Petr Sgall, Eva Hajičová, and Jarmila Panevová. 1986. *The Meaning of the Sentence in its Semantic and Pragmatic Aspects*. Springer Science & Business Media.

Hitachi at MRP 2020: Text-to-Graph-Notation Transducer

Hiroaki Ozaki,* **Gaku Morio***, [†]**Yuta Koreeda, Terufumi Morishita** and **Toshinori Miyoshi**
Research and Development Group, Hitachi, Ltd., Japan
[†]Research and Development Group, Hitachi America, Ltd., USA
{hiroaki.ozaki.yu, gaku.morio.vn, terufumi.morishita.wp,
toshinori.miyoshi.pd}@hitachi.com, [†]yuta.koreeda@hal.hitachi.com

Abstract

This paper presents our proposed parser for the shared task on Meaning Representation Parsing (MRP 2020) at CoNLL, where participant systems were required to parse five types of graphs in different languages. We propose to unify these tasks as a text-to-graph-notation transduction in which we convert an input text into a graph notation. To this end, we designed a novel Plain Graph Notation (PGN) that handles various graphs universally. Then, our parser predicts a PGN-based sequence by leveraging Transformers and biaffine attentions. Notably, our parser can handle any PGN-formatted graphs with fewer framework-specific modifications. As a result, ensemble versions of the parser tied for **1st** place in both cross-framework and cross-lingual tracks.

1 Introduction

This paper introduces the proposed parser of the Hitachi team for the CoNLL 2020 Cross-Framework Meaning Representation Parsing (MRP 2020) shared task (Oepen et al., 2020). Different from the previous MRP 2019 shared task (Oepen et al., 2019), there are two tracks. The first is a *cross-framework* track that aims at parsing English sentences to five different meaning representation graphs, i.e., EDS (Oepen and Lønning, 2006), PTG (Hajič et al., 2012), UCCA (Abend and Rappoport, 2013; Hershcovich et al., 2017), AMR (Banarescu et al., 2013), and DRG (Van Der Sandt, 1992; Bos et al., 2017). The other is a *cross-lingual* track that targets four different frameworks and three languages, i.e., German UCCA and DRG, Chinese AMR (Li et al., 2016), and Czech PTG. In both tracks, the goal was to design a unified parser for all graphs.

---

* Contributed equally. Ozaki mainly developed PGN parser. Morio mainly developed neural models.

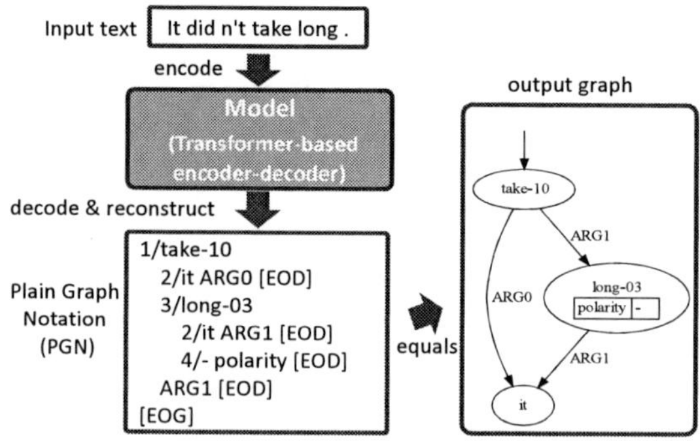

Figure 1: Given an input text, we tokenize and encode the text by pre-trained Transformer encoder (e.g., BERT). Then, Transformer decoder is applied to produce a Plain Graph Notation (PGN) that is convertible into a general graph.

In this paper, we propose a novel parser to unify graph predictions across all frameworks and languages. To this end, we introduce a *text-to-graph-notation* transduction. The overview of our parser is shown in Figure 1. Our parser utilizes sequence-to-sequence Transformer architectures (Vaswani et al., 2017) to generate a plain graph notation (PGN), which we newly designed as a context-free language. PGN is a simplified notation based on the PENMAN notation (Matthiessen and Bateman, 1991) that is generally used for AMR graphs. However, PGN is tailored for direct generation by sequence-to-sequence architecture.

Our parser is expected to combine both strengths of the neural graph-based and transition-based parsers (McDonald et al., 2005; Yamada and Matsumoto, 2003; Kulmizev et al., 2019; Ma et al., 2018). This is because the Transformer decoder directly draws attentions like a graph-based parser does, as well as handles higher-level effects of graph structures by sequence prediction like a transition-based parser does. Moreover, our parser is practically able to parse most of the graph vari-

Proceedings of the CoNLL 2020 Shared Task: Cross-Framework Meaning Representation Parsing, pages 40–52
Online, Nov. 19-20, 2020. ©2020 Association for Computational Linguistics

ants in a unified manner. For example, our parser is able to predict directed acyclic graphs, disconnected graphs, directed multigraphs, reentrancy edges (Vilares and Gómez-Rodríguez, 2018), and source-side anchors without complicated language-dependent architectures.

Consequently, ensemble versions of our parser officially tied for 1st place in both the cross-framework track and cross-lingual track, achieving the top performances for English EDS, PTG, and AMR graphs. We also summarize other contributions as follows:

Alignment Free: PGN generation allows us to achieve completely alignment-free parsing.

Action Design Free: Compared to a transition-based parser, there is no need to design a complex transition strategy.

Fast Training: Since we leverage attentions, train speed is faster than a transition-based parser.

2 Related Work

2.1 Previous Systems for Cross-Framework Meaning Representation Parsing

MRP 2019 (Oepen et al., 2019) brought various parsing techniques together. According to Oepen et al. (2019), MRP systems can be characterized into three broad families of approaches: transition-, factorization-, or composition-based architectures. For example, the winning technique of HIT-SCIR (Che et al., 2019) at MRP 2019 used a transition-based parser based on a BERT encoder (Devlin et al., 2019). SUDA-Alibaba (Zhang et al., 2019c) proposed a graph-based approach with BERT. They used biaffine attention (Dozat and Manning, 2018) for the edge prediction. Donatelli et al. (2019) employed a compositional approach that represents each graph with its compositional tree structure (Lindemann et al., 2019).

2.2 Comparison with Other Systems

Like Zhang et al. (2019a), we model a context-free language instead of a sequence of transition actions, and parser states can be regarded as being implicitly materialized inside BERT's memory. However, our parser jointly generates nodes and edges based on PGN, making the system consider higher-level effects of graph structures.

The work most closely related to our study is (Zhang et al., 2019b), where the authors provided an encoder-decoder architecture to predict a sequence of semantic relations, employing a target

```
graph       = {target "[EOG]"};
edge        = node_id {dep "[EOD]"};
dep         = target edge_label;
target      = node_id | edge;
node_id     = {digit};
edge_label  = {letter};
```

Figure 2: PGN grammar described in EBNF. Essentially, a graph can be represented by a set of edges. However, to support floating nodes, we defined a graph as a set of edges and floating nodes.

Name	Function
`attr2name`	Append -{attr name} suffix to edge label name instead of having attributes.
`prop2node`	Make node properties independent nodes linked with edges named with properties' names.
`embed_label`	Replace node_id in PGN with {node_id}/{node_label}.

Table 1: List of PGN processors.

node-, relation type-, and source node-module in the decoder. Similar to our study, Zhang et al. (2019b) encoded node and edge representation with the modules. While they jointly predicted node and edge labels, our parser outputs node and edge labels separately. In addition, they provided LSTMs whereas we provide Transformers that can draw attentions from both past node and edge representations in the decoder. Also, while Zhang et al. (2019b) solved reentrancies by producing the same node ID, we solve them with a biaffine classifier, making our parser solve reentrancies with attentions.

The biggest difference between the transition-based architectures for MRP (Che et al., 2019) and our work is that we have designed PGN such that it unifies all graph generation processes and eliminates the need to design framework-specific actions. In addition, Che et al. (2019) relied on explicit alignment between input tokens and nodes, whereas our model utilizes biaffine attention for anchoring only when it is necessary, allowing our model to be alignment-free.

3 Plain Graph Notation

3.1 Format Design

To represent a graph as a text sequence, we newly designed a notation, called Plain Graph Notation (PGN), with the key principles shown below.

Simpler Format: Similar to PENMAN notation (Matthiessen and Bateman, 1991; Goodman, 2020), which is used to represent AMR graphs with text sequence, PGN is based on a context-free grammar.

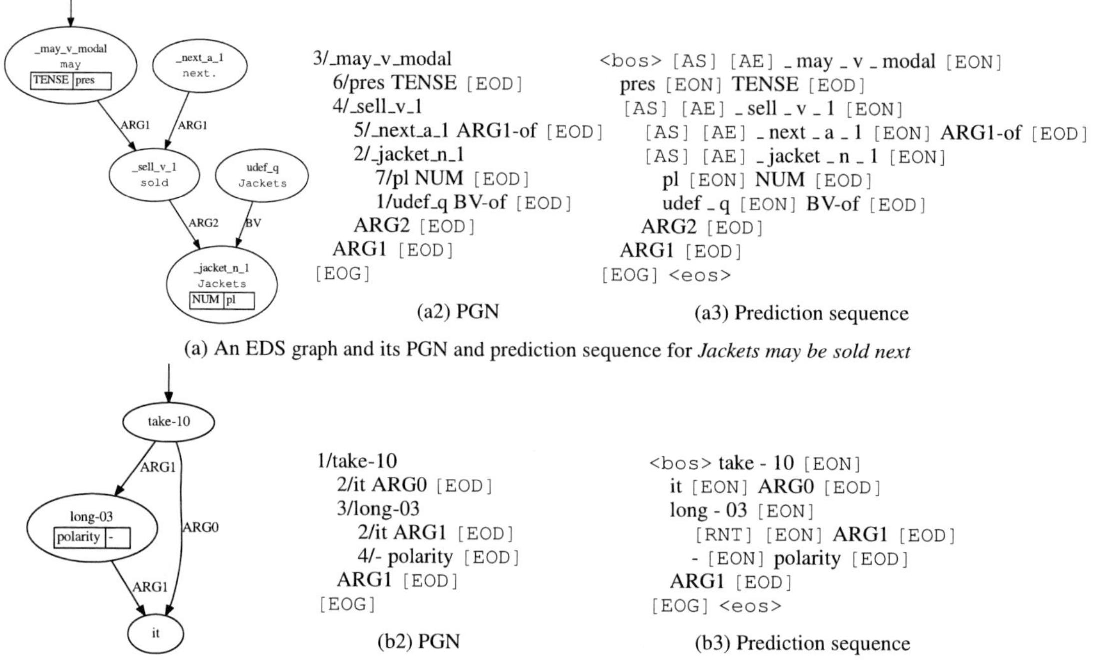

(a2) PGN   (a3) Prediction sequence

(a) An EDS graph and its PGN and prediction sequence for *Jackets may be sold next*

(b2) PGN   (b3) Prediction sequence

(b) An AMR graph and its PGN and prediction sequence for *it didn't take long.*

Figure 3: MRP graph examples and their PGN and prediction formatted expressions. We applied `prop2node` and `embed_label` processors to generate the PGN expressions.

However, PGN only represents a graph structure (namely, all edges in the graph) for simplicity. All node properties are omitted from PGN while we preserve the properties separately. In addition, we reduce redundant meta-tokens appearing in the notation as much as possible. Figure 2 shows the Extended Backus–Naur Form (EBNF)[1] of PGN grammar.

Tree-Like Structure: We employed an essentially tree-like structure[2] because all spanning graphs with a root can be converted into tree-like structures by flipping the directions of appropriate edges. This structure is useful when we convert graphs to PGN.

Left-to-Right Decodable: To make our parser robust, we allow it to convert a notation into a graph in a left-to-right manner. This operation makes us decode an ill-formatted sequence with a *best-effort* strategy. We briefly explain this algorithm in a later sub-section.

3.2 Graph to PGN Conversion

MRP graph to PGN conversion starts with the top nodes. We recursively apply the grammar shown in Figure 2 from parents to children by depth first search. In addition to the depth first search, at finding a next path, we select a child node in increasing order of the numbers of outgoing edges in all descendant nodes (i.e., we select *shallow* branch first) to convert. Since we assume the input graph consists of a tree-like structure, finding children is just extracting out-going edges. However, several frameworks such as EDS, DRG, and AMR may not form a tree-like structure. Thus, we provide an option using all edges instead of out-going edges with flipping edge directions of in-coming edges (we append "-of" suffix to labels of flipped edges). To deal with the reentrancy problem, our recursive search is applied when the node first appears. Here we describe various framework-specific modifications.

Floating Nodes: We found that some EDS and AMR graphs have floating nodes in which no incoming or outgoing edges are annotated. Thus, the PGN grammar supports floating nodes.

Floating Sub-Graphs: We found that some EDS graphs have floating sub-graphs that have no con-

---

[1] https://www.iso.org/obp/ui/#iso:std: iso-iec:14977:ed-1:v1:en

[2] Here we define "tree-like" graph as a graph whose root node is always an ancestor of all nodes in the graph.

nection to the top. Therefore, we add temporal top nodes for floating sub-graphs to convert all sub-graphs on the basis of the following criteria.

1. First predicate node that has *frame* property, with the first priority.
2. First node that has smallest ID in a sub-graph, with the second priority.

3.3 Left-to-Right Decoding

This left-to-right decoding system consists of a stack and an input stream. Every time a token is fed from the input stream, we take an action of ADD (put the token to the stack), ARC (create an edge between the top two tokens on the stack), POP (pop out the top token from the stack), or CLEAR (pop out all tokens in the stack, and add them to the node list). These actions correspond to `node_id`, `edge_label`, `[EOD]`, and `[EOG]` in Figure 2, respectively.

Since neural networks may produce ill-formatted PGN, the left-to-right decoding finds as many edges as possible.[3] If there is an ill-formatted action such that a PGN sequence terminates with a non-empty stack, we generate additional edges according to the stack state.

3.4 PGN Processors

We define PGN processors, which are a set of invertible functions to apply small modification PGN formatted sequences. Table 1 shows all PGN processors and their description. To better understand these processors, Figure 3 (a2 and b2) shows example PGN formatted graphs of EDS and AMR. Actual PGN expressions are a list of serialized tokens, but here we add indentations for ease of reading. According to the PGN grammar, a `node_id` should be digits representing a node ID, but we insert node labels by the `embed_label` processor. In Figure 3 (a2), there are two flipped edges in the graph to form a tree-like structure, i.e., (_next_a_1, _sell_v_1, ARG1) and (udef_q, _jacket_n_1, BV). Also, Figure 3 (a2 and b2) depicts a larger number of nodes than that in original MRP graphs because node properties are converted into additional nodes by `prop2node` processor, e.g., 6/pres and 7/pl in the EDS graph.

3.5 PGN to Prediction Sequence

Though existing text generation techniques are applicable to generate PGN as is, we provide further modification for PGN expressions to obtain more suitable prediction sequences for a neural decoder. Figure 3 (a3 and b3) shows example prediction sequences derived from PGN. As can be seen, we split a node label into multiple tokens (e.g., subword tokens) and add some special tokens. We add an end-of-node token (`[EON]`) just after the end of subword elements because we should know where the node label token generation terminates. Since `[EON]` is inserted as the end of node token, we can consider `[EON]` as the node's representative token, which will be used for reentrancy classifiers and property classifiers (described later). To handle anchors, we add a place-holder token for anchor starting and ending (`[AS]` and `[AE]`) before node label tokens. When our parser predicts `[AS]` and `[AE]` tokens, we resolve anchors by a biaffine classifier described later. We also add a place-holder token (`[RNT]`) to generate a reentrancy edge after all decoding steps have been completed.

4 Model

4.1 Problem Formalization

We describe the conceptual formalization similarly to the work of Zhang et al. (2019b). Given an input sequence X (i.e., tokens in the text), we optimize an output sequence $\hat{Y} = \langle y_1, y_2, \ldots y_n \rangle$, where y can be represented by a tuple $\langle y^{\text{mode}}, y^{\text{G}}, y^{\text{E}}, y^{\text{L}}, y^{\text{AS}}, y^{\text{AE}} \rangle$,[4] consisting of a model label (y^{mode}), mode-wise labels (y^{G}, y^{E} and y^{L}), and an index of a source-side token for anchoring (y^{AS} and y^{AE}), defined as follows:

$$\hat{Y} = \arg\max_Y \prod_i^n \mathrm{P}(y_i \mid y_{<i}, X).$$

4.2 Overview

To generate the prediction sequence, we provide a sequence-to-sequence model. Figure 4 illustrates an example of AMR parsing (i.e., the graph of Figure 3 (b3)). Our parser is based on a typical encoder-decoder architecture but has several proposed architectures on the decoder side. Given an input text, our parser encodes the tokens by a pre-trained language model (PLM) such as BERT (Devlin et al., 2019). At decoding, a Transformer decoder produces the prediction sequence. To effectively control the decoder, we propose a *mode switching* mechanism. At the i-th decode step, our

---

[3]In practice, ill-formatted outputs were very few in experiments.

[4]We omit reentrancy and property outputs for simplicity.

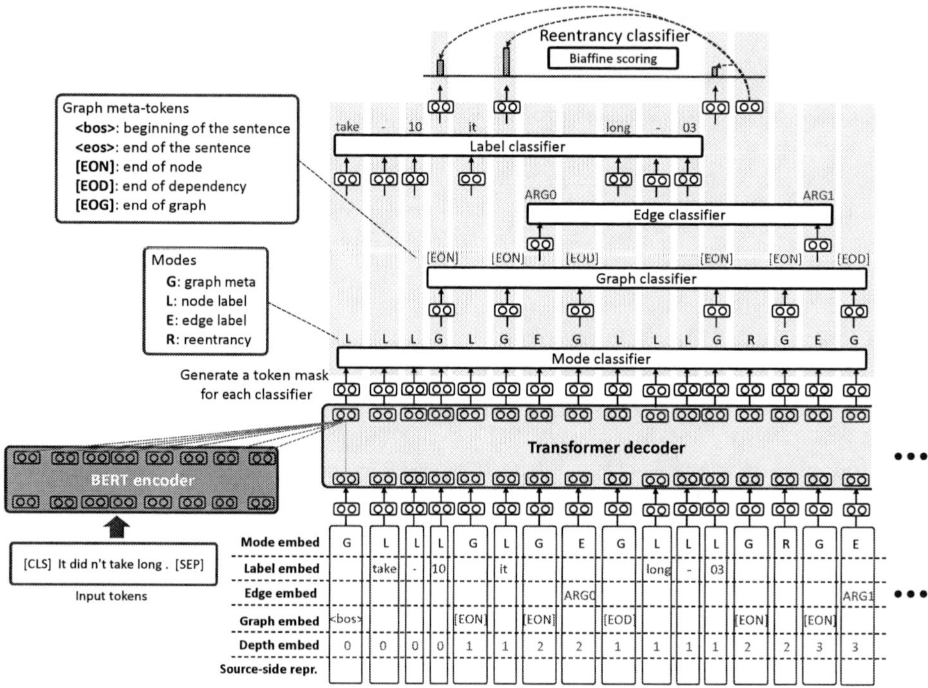

Figure 4: Overview of our proposed parser, showing an example of AMR parsing, assuming PLM = BERT. We encode input tokens that are fed into the decoder. In the decoder, each mode is embedded and the decoder produces an output label for each classifier.

parser decides which mode to execute amongst the following six modes:

G (graph) generates the meta tokens: `<bos>`, `<eos>`, `[EON]`, `[EOD]`, and `[EOG]`.

L (label) generates label tokens of a node, such as *take - 10*.

E (edge) generates an edge label such as *ARG0*.

AS (anchor start) produces an anchoring start representation corresponding to `[AS]`.

AE (anchor end) produces an anchoring end representation corresponding to `[AE]`.

R (reentrancy) generates a place-holder token `[RNT]` that is solved after all decoding steps have been completed.

Then, a classification layer of the selected mode is applied to predict the i-th output. For example, if mode E is selected, an edge classifier on the decoder is used to produce an edge label. If mode AS is selected, an anchoring classifier on the decoder is used to produce an anchor starting index in the encoder's subword tokens. If mode R is selected, we do nothing but generate a place-holder token. Instead, after all decoding steps, we apply biaffine attention, which solves the reentrancy edges for the place-holder tokens.

4.3 Encoder

Given an input text, a PLM-specific tokenizer tokenizes the text into the token sequence X. Note that we insert special tokens such as `[CLS]` and `[SEP]` according to the PLM type. To obtain PLM representations, a layer-wise attention is applied (Kondratyuk and Straka, 2019; Peters et al., 2018):

$$\mathbf{h}_{\text{PLM},i} = c \sum_j \text{PLM}_{ij} \cdot \text{softmax}\,(\mathbf{s})_j,$$

where $\mathbf{s}$ and c are parameters. Note that $\mathbf{h}_{\text{PLM},i} \in \mathbb{R}^{d(\text{PLM})}$, where $d(\text{PLM})$ represents the number of dimensions of the PLM layers. PLM_{ij} is an embedding of the i-th token in the j-th PLM layer. Note that $1 \leq i \leq N$, where N is the number of tokens.

4.4 Decoder

We employ a Transformer decoder to fully utilize a self-attention mechanism. The decoder includes a switching architecture of *modes* that makes the decoder explicitly learn structural representations.
Decoder Input Representation: For each decoding step i, we compute an input representation for the Transformer decoder:

$$\mathbf{e}_i = \left[\mathbf{e}_i^{\text{mode}}; \mathbf{e}_i^{\text{G}}; \mathbf{e}_i^{\text{L}}; \mathbf{e}_i^{\text{E}}; \mathbf{e}_i^{\text{AS}}; \mathbf{e}_i^{\text{AE}}; \mathbf{e}_i^{\text{depth}} \right],$$

where ; shows a concatenate operation, and each representation is obtained as follows:

$$e_i^{\text{mode}} = \text{EMB}^{(\text{mode})}\left(y_i^{\text{mode}}\right),$$
$$e_i^{\text{G}} = \text{EMB}^{(\text{G})}\left(y_i^{\text{G}}\right),$$
$$e_i^{\text{E}} = \text{EMB}^{(\text{E})}\left(y_i^{\text{E}}\right),$$
$$e_i^{\text{L}} = \text{EMB}^{(\text{L})}\left(y_i^{\text{L}}\right),$$
$$e_i^{\text{AS}} = W^{(\text{AS})}\mathbf{h}_{\text{PLM},k} + \mathbf{b}^{(\text{AS})},$$
$$e_i^{\text{AE}} = W^{(\text{AE})}\mathbf{h}_{\text{PLM},k} + \mathbf{b}^{(\text{AE})},$$
$$e_i^{\text{depth}} = \text{EMB}^{(\text{depth})}\left(y_i^{\text{depth}}\right),$$

where EMB is a layer that transfers the label into a fixed sized vector, and W and $\mathbf{b}$ are parameters. The following shows detailed descriptions.

- e_i^{mode}: This is a representation of the current mode label. $y_i^{\text{mode}} \in \{\text{G}, \text{E}, \text{L}, \text{AS}, \text{AE}, \text{R}\}$ denotes the mode label.
- $e_i^{\text{G}}, e_i^{\text{E}}, e_i^{\text{L}}$: These are representations of a graph meta-token, edge label, and node label, respectively. In turn, y_i^{G}, y_i^{E}, and y_i^{L} represent a mode-wise label. For example, $y_i^{\text{G}} \in \{\texttt{<bos>}, \texttt{<eos>}, \texttt{[EON]}, \texttt{[EOD]}, \texttt{[EOG]}\}$. $y_i^{\text{E}} \in \{\text{ARG0}, \text{ARG1}, \dots\}$ when the target framework is AMR. Note that G, E, and L are selected exclusively and thus zero embeddings are assigned for non-selected modes: for example, if y_i^{mode} is E, $e_i^{\text{G}} = e_i^{\text{L}} = \mathbf{0}$.
- $e_i^{\text{AS}}, e_i^{\text{AE}}$: These are input embedding of source-side anchors. $W^{(\text{AS})}, W^{(\text{AE})} \in \mathbb{R}^{d(\text{PLM}) \times d(\text{PLM})}$ and $\mathbf{b}^{(\text{AS})}, \mathbf{b}^{(\text{AE})} \in \mathbb{R}^{d(\text{PLM})}$ are trainable parameters. k is an index of the anchor starting token for AS, or an index of the anchor ending token for AE. Therefore, the Transformer decoder draws attentions from the encoder representation of source-side anchored tokens. Note that AS and AE are also exclusive.
- e_i^{depth}: This is a feature embedding to make the network consider the current depth from the top of the graph. The depth y_i^{depth} is obtained by starting from zero, adding one when $\texttt{[EON]}$ appears, and subtracting one when $\texttt{[EOD]}$ appears (see Figure 4).

Transformer Decoder: To leverage self-attentions throughout parsing, a multi-layered Transformer decoder (Vaswani et al., 2017) is applied to obtain an output sequence. Let $\mathbf{d}_i$ be a decoder representation at i-th step that is obtained by a multi-layered Transformer decoder where previous decoder inputs $(e_1 \dots e_i)$ and encoder repre-

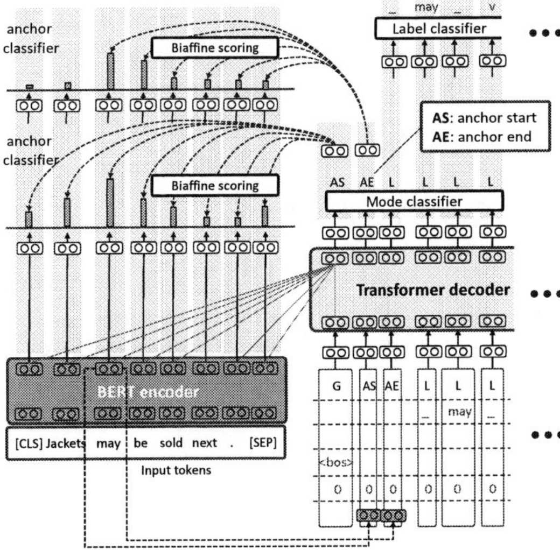

Figure 5: Overview of our proposed parser, showing an example EDS parsing with anchoring prediction.

sentations $(\mathbf{h}_{\text{PLM},1} \dots \mathbf{h}_{\text{PLM},N})$ are given. We also apply position-encoding (Sukhbaatar et al., 2015; Vaswani et al., 2017; Devlin et al., 2019) for the decoder input representation. By leveraging this decoder, we can consider the entire encoder representation and all decoder inputs throughout the decoding steps.

Mode Output Layers: Given the decoder representation $\mathbf{d}_i$, we produce a probability distribution of the next mode label with a softmax classifier and a feed forward network as follows:

$$\text{P}\left(y_{i+1}^{\text{mode}}\right) = \text{CLS}^{(\text{mode})}\left(\mathbf{d}_i\right),$$

where

$$\text{CLS}^{(t)}(\mathbf{x}) = \text{softmax}\left(W^{(t)}\text{FFN}^{(t)}\left(\mathbf{x}\right) + \mathbf{b}^{(t)}\right).$$

In the equation, y_{i+1}^{mode} denotes a mode label, i.e., G, E, L, AS, AE, or R. We chose the mode y_{i+1}^{mode} based on the maximum probability. Similarly, we obtain a probability distribution for each mode-wise label as follows:

$$\text{P}\left(y_{i+1}^{\text{G}}\right) = \text{CLS}^{(\text{G})}\left(\mathbf{d}_i\right),$$
$$\text{P}\left(y_{i+1}^{\text{E}}\right) = \text{CLS}^{(\text{E})}\left(\mathbf{d}_i\right),$$
$$\text{P}\left(y_{i+1}^{\text{L}}\right) = \text{CLS}^{(\text{L})}\left(\mathbf{d}_i\right),$$

After applying these layers above, we obtain output labels $y_{i+1}^{\text{mode}}, y_{i+1}^{\text{G}}, y_{i+1}^{\text{E}}, y_{i+1}^{\text{L}}$, and their corresponding embeddings $e_{i+1}^{\text{mode}}, e_{i+1}^{\text{G}}, e_{i+1}^{\text{E}}, e_{i+1}^{\text{L}}$, which are used for the next decoder input.

Anchoring Classifier: To compute source-side anchors (i.e., AS and AE), we employ biaffine attention (Dozat and Manning, 2017, 2018). The biaffine operation computes a relation for vector pairs as:

$$\text{BIAFFINE}^{(t)}(\mathbf{x}, \mathbf{y}) = \mathbf{x}^{\top}\mathbf{U}^{(t)}\mathbf{y} + W^{(t)}[\mathbf{x}; \mathbf{y}] + b^{(t)},$$

where $\mathbf{U}^{(t)}$, $W^{(t)}$, and $b^{(t)}$ are trainable parameters. We apply the biaffine operation between the decoder representation $\mathbf{d}_i$ and encoder representation $\mathbf{h}_{\text{PLM},j}$ to point a range of anchoring. If $y_{i+1}^{\text{mode}} = \text{AS}$, the anchor starting probability can be represented as

$$\mathbf{h}_i^{(A1)} = \text{FFN}^{(A1)}(\mathbf{d}_i),$$
$$\mathbf{h}_j^{(A2)} = \text{FFN}^{(A2)}(\mathbf{h}_{\text{PLM},j}),$$
$$P\left(y_{i \to j}^{\text{AS}}\right) = \sigma\left(\text{BIAFFINE}^{(A)}\left(\mathbf{h}_i^{(A1)}, \mathbf{h}_j^{(A2)}\right)\right),$$

where σ is a sigmoid function. $P\left(y_{i \to j}^{\text{AS}}\right)$ represents a probability that the j-th token in the encoder is an anchor starting token. After the output layer above, we draw encoder representations by selecting $\arg\max_{j \in 1,\dots,N} P\left(y_{i \to j}^{\text{AS}}\right)$ and its corresponding $\mathbf{h}_{\text{PLM},j}$, which is used as the next decoder input $\mathbf{e}_{i+1}^{\text{AS}}$. Also, $\mathbf{e}_{i+1}^{\text{AE}}$ can be calculated in the same manner.

Figure 5 shows an example of EDS parsing (the graph of Figure 3 (a3)). This example illustrates that AS is raised at the first decoding step, applying biaffine scoring and selecting the encoder's representation of *may* token. Similarly, the AE is raised at the second step.

Reentrancy Classifier: To solve reentrancy edges, we provide another biaffine layer. Given that this is a target-side (i.e., decoder-side) operation, we apply this classifier after all decoding steps have been finished to keep the training speed fast. If $y_{i+1}^{\text{mode}} = \text{R}$, the probability that a reentrancy edge exists between the i and j-th decoding steps can be represented as

$$\mathbf{h}_i^{(R1)} = \text{FFN}^{(R1)}(\mathbf{d}_i),$$
$$\mathbf{h}_j^{(R2)} = \text{FFN}^{(R2)}(\mathbf{d}_j),$$
$$P\left(y_{i \to j}^{\text{R}}\right) = \sigma\left(\text{BIAFFINE}^{(R)}\left(\mathbf{h}_i^{(R1)}, \mathbf{h}_j^{(R2)}\right)\right).$$

To restrict the search space, we only consider the end of node token (i.e., [EON]) for j (see Figure 4), since we assume [EON] is a representative token of the node.

Property Classifiers: Since we need to classify the properties of a node for PTG graphs, we provide property classifiers on the top of the decoder. Given that we consider [EON] as a representative token of a node, we use decoder representations of [EON] tokens to classify properties. Therefore, if $y_{i+1}^{\text{G}} = \text{[EON]}$, a probability distribution for the property is computed as

$$P\left(y_{i+1}^{\mathcal{P}}\right) = \text{CLS}^{(\mathcal{P})}(\mathbf{d}_i),$$

where $P\left(y_{i+1}^{\mathcal{P}}\right)$ represents a probability distribution of the label of property type $\mathcal{P}$ at the [EON] (i.e., a node representative token). Note that $\mathcal{P}$ contains a *no label* class where the node is considered to not have the property.

4.5 Loss and Decoding

Loss: We compute a mode output cross-entropy loss $\mathcal{L}_{\text{mode}}$ based on $P\left(y^{\text{mode}}\right)$. For each mode, we compute mode-specific cross-entropy loss $\mathcal{L}_{\text{G}}, \mathcal{L}_{\text{L}}$, and $\mathcal{L}_{\text{E}}$ based on $P\left(y^{\text{G}}\right), P\left(y^{\text{L}}\right)$, and $P\left(y^{\text{E}}\right)$. Note that loss is not computed if a different mode is selected for decode step i. For example, if $y_i^{\text{mode}} = \text{G}$, only $\mathcal{L}_{\text{G}}$ is computed, and others are ignored except the mode loss. Anchoring loss $\mathcal{L}_{\text{AS}}$ and $\mathcal{L}_{\text{AE}}$ are computed based on binary cross-entropy of the $P\left(y^{\text{AS}}\right)$ and $P\left(y^{\text{AE}}\right)$. Similarly, reentrancy loss is represented as $\mathcal{L}_{\text{R}}$. If the graph has property tasks (e.g., PTG graphs), we compute the cross-entropy of property label $\mathcal{L}_{\mathcal{P}}$ for property type $\mathcal{P}$. The following equation describes the combined loss to be optimized:

$$\mathcal{L} = \lambda_{\text{mode}}\mathcal{L}_{\text{mode}} + \lambda_{\text{G}}\mathcal{L}_{\text{G}} + \lambda_{\text{E}}\mathcal{L}_{\text{E}} + \lambda_{\text{L}}\mathcal{L}_{\text{L}}$$
$$+ \lambda_{\text{A}}\mathcal{L}_{\text{AS}} + \lambda_{\text{A}}\mathcal{L}_{\text{AE}} + \lambda_{\text{R}}\mathcal{L}_{\text{R}} + \lambda_{\text{P}}\sum_{\mathcal{P}}\mathcal{L}_{\mathcal{P}}.$$

where λ are hyperparameters to adjust loss scales. **Decoding:** For simplicity, we only consider greedy decoding. We also apply explicit restrictions. For example, the mode AE always comes after AS.

4.6 Ensemble

To further boost the performance of our parser, we provide an average ensemble. We apply mode-wise averaging over output probabilities. Therefore, we average probabilities for the mode layer, mode-specific layers, anchoring classifiers, reentrancy classifier, and property classifiers, respectively.

	Cross-framework					Cross-lingual			
	AMR	EDS	UCCA	PTG	DRG	PTG	UCCA	AMR	DRG
Data preparation									
No. of folds	36	24	12	52	16	52	12	16	8
Reverse edge		✓			✓				✓
`prop2node`	✓	✓						✓	
`embed_label`	✓	✓		✓	✓	✓		✓	✓
`attr2name`			✓	✓		✓	✓		
Hyperparameters									
Hugging Face PLM	roberta-large	roberta-large	roberta-large	roberta-large	roberta-large	bert-base-ml-cased	bert-base-ml-cased	chinese-roberta-wwm-ext-large	bert-base-ml-cased
Encoder dropout	.1	.1	.1	.1	.1	.1	.1	.1	.1
FFN dropout	.1	.1	.1	.1	.1	.1	.1	.1	.1
FFN activation	ReLU	ReLU	ReLU	ReLU	ReLU	ReLU	ReLU	ReLU	ReLU
BIAFFINE dim	400	400	400	400	400	400	400	400	400
Decoder layer, head	6, 4	6, 4	6, 4	6, 4	6, 4	6, 4	8, 4	6, 4	8 ,4
Decoder d_{ff}	256	256	256	256	256	256	256	256	256
Decoder dropout	.1	.1	.1	.1	.1	.1	.1	.1	.1
Depth embedding dim	100	100	100	100	100	100	100	100	100
λ_{mode}	1.0	1.0	1.0	1.0	1.0	1.0	1.0	1.0	1.0
λ_G	.137	1.0	.06	.459	.85	.45	.162	.15	.058
λ_E	.137	1.7	.09	.329	.25	.35	.058	.15	.613
λ_L	1.2	1.4	0	1.50	.4	1.5	0	1.5	.538
λ_A	0	2.0	1.73	2.0	0	2.0	2.96	3.0	0
λ_R	3.1	1.0	.50	1.5	2.0	1.5	.241	3.0	.885
λ_P	0	0	0	1.6	0	1.6	0	0	0
Encoder learning rate	1.4e-5	1e-5	1e-5	1e-5	5e-5	5e-5	1.6e-5	5e-6	5.4e-6
Decoder learning rate	5.4e-5	5e-5	5e-5	5e-5	1e-4	1e-4	1.2e-4	1e-4	8.0e-5
Adam beta1, 2	.9,.998	.9,.998	.9,.998	.9,.998	.9,.998	.9,.998	.9,.998	.9,.998	.9,.998
Warmup ratio	.01	.01	.01	.05	.05	.05	.05	.01	.05
Batch size	8	12	8	8	4	4	16	8	32
Maximum epochs	500	500	1000	500	500	500	1000	500	1000
CV ensemble	✓	✓	✓	✓	✓	✓	✓	✓	✓

Table 2: Experimental setup of submitted models: data preparation (**top**) and hyperparameter values (**bottom**).

4.7 Post-Processing

We incorporate framework-specific post-processing after reconstruction except for DRG.

For EDS, to support unknown words appearing as a named entity, we replace the `CARG` property with a node label expression extracted by anchors when the edit distance between node label expression and `CARG` is larger than 70% of the node label characters. Since the EDS frame dictionary is available[5], we correct frames by checking their arguments. When several candidates are available, we select the most frequent frame name.

For PTG, frame dictionaries for both English and Czech are also available[6], so we correct frames in the same manner.

For UCCA, we apply post-processing to follow UCCA restrictions. We remove non-anchored nodes appearing as terminal nodes. We also remove self-loop edges. We add `remote` attribute to all edges except primary edges.

For AMR, we replace `date-entity` and

---

[5] http://svn.delph-in.net/erg/tags/
1214/etc
[6] http://hdl.handle.net/11234/1-1512

`url-entity` with an extracted date and URL from the input by using regular expressions.

5 Experiments

Data Preparation: We first converted all MRP formatted training data into PGN format. Table 2 (top) summarizes the PGN conversion parameters. Since PTG and UCCA utilize tree-like structures, we did not use the reverse edge option, which flips edge directions to form a tree-like structure. AMR graphs form essentially non-tree-like structures; however, given MRP data have been converted to tree-like structures, we did not apply the reverse edge option to AMR graphs. We used `attr2name` on all graphs that have edge attributes (i.e., PTG and UCCA). We also applied `prop2node` to all graphs that have node properties, except PTG graphs.

We divided training data into folds to apply cross-validation (CV) (see No. of folds in Table 2 (top)). We decided a fold size should have about a half number of graphs in the official validation data.

Implementation: We utilize BERT (Devlin et al., 2019) and RoBERTa (Liu et al., 2019) models as

Team	Mean	EDS	PTG	UCCA	AMR	DRG
Hitachi (ours)	**.8642 /1**	**.9356 /1**	**.8873 /1**	.7507 /2	**.8154 /1**	.9319 /2
ÚFAL (Samuel and Straka, 2020)	**.8639 /1**	.9273 /2	.8844 /2	**.7640 /1**	.8023 /2	**.9416 /1**
HIT-SCIR (Dou et al., 2020)	.8106 /3	.8740 /3	.8426 /3	.7476 /3	.6980 /3	.8907 /3
HUJI-KU (Arviv et al., 2020)	.6429 /4	.7968 /5	.5376 /4	.7291 /4	.5236 /5	.6275 /5
ISCAS	.4813 /5	.8586 /4	.1799 /6	.0599 /6	.6148 /4	.6935 /4
TJU-BLCU	.3016 /6	.4904 /6	.2149 /5	.1041 /5	.2996 /6	.3991 /6
JBNU (Na and Min, 2020)	.1323 /-	-	-	-	.6613 /-	-

Table 3: Official MRP results for the cross-framework track (shown as score /rank).

Team	Mean	Czech PTG	German UCCA	Chinese AMR	German DRG
Hitachi (ours)	**.8505 /1**	.8735 /2	.7904 /3	**.8044 /1**	**.9336 /1**
ÚFAL (Samuel and Straka, 2020)	**.8507 /1**	**.9127 /1**	**.8101 /1**	.7817 /2	.8983 /2
HIT-SCIR (Dou et al., 2020)	.6891 /3	.7793 /3	.8002 /2	.4939 /3	.6831 /3
HUJI-KU (Arviv et al., 2020)	.6011 /4	.5849 /4	.7472 /4	.4492 /4	.6233 /4
ISCAS	-	-	-	-	-
TJU-BLCU	.2003 /5	.2171 /5	.0000 /5	.2464 /5	.3377 /5
JBNU (Na and Min, 2020)	-	-	-	-	-

Table 4: Official MRP results for the cross-lingual track (shown as score /rank).

PLMs from Hugging Face's Transformer library (Wolf et al., 2019), which is included on the official 'white-list' of legitimate resources in MRP 2020. RoBERTa large model is used for the cross-framework track because we found in our preliminary experiments that this model generally performs better. In the cross-lingual track, we utilize multi-lingual BERT (Devlin et al., 2019) except for Chinese AMR. Chinese RoBERTa (Cui et al., 2020) is used for the Chinese AMR graphs because the model is carefully tuned for Chinese.

At training, we split network parameters into two groups: one for the encoder and the other for all decoder parameters, applying discriminative fine-tuning (Kondratyuk and Straka, 2019). Each group-specific learning rate is provided and is tuned discriminatively. We select models by evaluating MRP scores on CV and official validation data.

Input texts are tokenized by the PLM-specific tokenizer. We utilized the tokenization scheme of the tokenizer for our decoder: we use the same vocabulary for the node labels y_i^L when decoding. The only exception is Czech PTG because node label tokens in Czech PTG graphs include accents that are removed from the vocabulary of multi-lingual BERT. Thus, we employ *character*-level decoding for Czech PTG, where the vocabulary was constructed to contain Czech characters.

Hyperparameters: Hyperparameters of the submitted models are shown in Table 2 (bottom). Adam (Kingma and Ba, 2015) was used as an optimizer, applying linear warmup scheduling. We preliminarily tuned hyperparameters for learning rates, the number of decoder layers, the number of decoder heads, and λ values.

Search ranges of hyperparameters were [1e-6, 1e-3] with log-uniform sampling for decoder learning rate, [1e-6, 1e-4] with log-uniform sampling for encoder learning rate, [4, 8] for Transformer layers and heads, and [0, 2] with uniform sampling for λ. We fixed $\lambda_{mode} = 1$. In terms of hidden dimensions, we did not aggressively tune them because we preliminarily found their impact on the final performance to be minuscule. In this work, we fixed the biaffine dimensions to 400 and the depth embedding dimensions to 100.

Validation: We used CV to validate our models to ensure robustness. We picked four folds from the training data in Table 2 for each framework/language.[7] For example, although we split the EDS training data into 24 folds, we only used four of these folds to validate the EDS model. We mixed official validation data with each fold to evaluate the model's performance. Then, validation performance was evaluated every 20 epochs, selecting the best model.

Through this validation, we obtained four (i.e., the number of CV folds) trained models for each framework/language with the same hyperparameters. The obtained models were then utilized for the average ensemble.

Setup for Cross-Lingual Pre-Training: Given the lower resource nature of the cross-lingual track, especially for the German UCCA and DRG graphs, we provided two-staged cross-lingual training. First, we concatenated the cross-framework (CF) (e.g., English DRG) and cross-lingual (CL)

---

[7] This was done to save the computation time.

	EDS	PTG	UCCA	AMR	DRG
roberta-large	**.9101**	**.8779**	**.7692**	**.7776**	**.9080**
bert-base-cased	.8964	.8589	.7473	.7634	.8675

Table 5: Comparison of MRP all-F scores between BERT base and RoBERTa large versions. Scores were evaluated with CV with no ensemble.

(e.g., German DRG) training data. Then, we applied pre-training on the concatenated data for each framework with multi-lingual BERT (Devlin et al., 2019). After that, we applied fine-tuning on only monolingual training data.

5.1 Results and Discussion

Overall Result: Table 3 shows the official cross-framework evaluation results in MRP metrics. As can be seen in the table, in terms of average MRP scores, our parser tied for 1st place: results were very close to the ÚFAL system (Samuel and Straka, 2020).[8] We achieved the top performances on EDS, PTG, and AMR, demonstrating the efficiency for these frameworks. Table 4, the official cross-lingual evaluation results, shows a similar tendency. In the cross-lingual track, we achieved a tie for 1st place, obtaining the best performance for Chinese AMR and German DRG. Notably, our parser performed well on flavor 2 graphs (Oepen et al., 2019) such as AMR and DRG, where no anchors exist in the graphs. This is because we generate node labels directly by the Transformer decoder, thus avoiding alignment errors. However, anchor-based graphs such as UCCA seem unsuitable for our parser when compared to the ÚFAL system. We presume that improving the biaffine scoring in anchoring classifiers would remedy this problem.

Comparing Pre-Trained Models: To better understand how we benefit from PLMs, we compare the `bert-base-cased` and `roberta-large` models. Table 5 shows MRP all-F scores of the cross-framework results. Note that the hyperparameters were slightly different for each model. RoBERTa large models were better than BERT small models, showing improvements ranging from one to four points.

Effectiveness of Depth Embeddings: We conduct an ablation study to examine the role of depth embedding. Table 6 shows a CV-averaged result on English DRG graphs. Note that the hyperparameters are different from Table 5. The result shows

	Label	Edge	All
w/ depth embedding	**.8661**	**.9200**	**.9011**
w/o depth embedding	.8611	.9138	.8952

Table 6: Ablation study of depth embedding for DRG's MRP metrics with CV results with no ensemble. We used BERT base in this run.

Language & Framework	Edge	All
German UCCA		
w/ cross-lingual pre-training	**.6942**	**.7791**
w/o cross-lingual pre-training	.6123	.6938
German DRG		
w/ cross-lingual pre-training	**.9479**	**.9044**
w/o cross-lingual pre-training	.9005	.8543

Table 7: Comparison of MRP scores between cross-lingual training and monolingual training. Scores were evaluated through CV by micro-averaging.

that our depth embedding is effective to boost performance. We presume this is because the decoder considers a kind of stack state in PGN, which helps the parser easily produce valid graphs.

Effectiveness of Cross-Lingual Pre-Training: Table 7 shows a comparison of F scores between CL and monolingual training. We used `bert-base-german` instead of `bert-base-ml-cased` for both monolingual trainings. CL training outperformed monolingual training. This indicates that both UCCA and DRG annotations are cross-lingually consistent, and our model can capture the consistency through the CL training. We estimate that our parser has a better transfer ability on cross-lingual graphs.

6 Conclusion

This paper described a novel parser for the shared task on Meaning Representation Parsing 2020. We proposed a text-to-graph-notation transduction that provides a novel graph notation. Our model effectively parsed the graph-notation. Experimental results showed that our parser achieved the top performances in many frameworks. Since our parser is not limited to the five frameworks, in future work we will extend our technique for other tasks.

Acknowledgments

Computational resource of AI Bridging Cloud Infrastructure (ABCI) provided by the National Institute of Advanced Industrial Science and Technology (AIST) was used. We would like to thank the anonymous reviewers for their helpful comments. We also thank Dr. Masaaki Shimizu for the convenience of the computational resources.

---

[8]Given randomness nature of the official evaluation tool and statistical significance concerns, system ranking was considered with rounded scores.

References

Omri Abend and Ari Rappoport. 2013. Universal conceptual cognitive annotation (UCCA). In *Proceedings of the 51st Annual Meeting of the Association for Computational Linguistics*.

Ofir Arviv, Ruixiang Cui, and Daniel Hershcovich. 2020. HUJI-KU at MRP 2020: Two transition-based neural parsers. In *Proceedings of the CoNLL 2020 Shared Task: Cross-Framework Meaning Representation Parsing*, pages 73–82, Online.

Laura Banarescu, Claire Bonial, Shu Cai, Madalina Georgescu, Kira Griffitt, Ulf Hermjakob, Kevin Knight, Philipp Koehn, Martha Palmer, and Nathan Schneider. 2013. Abstract meaning representation for sembanking. In *Proceedings of the 7th Linguistic Annotation Workshop and Interoperability with Discourse*.

Johan Bos, Valerio Basile, Kilian Evang, Noortje J. Venhuizen, and Johannes Bjerva. 2017. *The Groningen Meaning Bank*, pages 463–496. Springer.

Wanxiang Che, Longxu Dou, Yang Xu, Yuxuan Wang, Yijia Liu, and Ting Liu. 2019. HIT-SCIR at MRP 2019: A unified pipeline for meaning representation parsing via efficient training and effective encoding. In *Proceedings of the Shared Task on Cross-Framework Meaning Representation Parsing at the 2019 Conference on Natural Language Learning*, pages 76–85, Hong Kong. Association for Computational Linguistics.

Yiming Cui, Wanxiang Che, Ting Liu, Bing Qin, Shijin Wang, and Guoping Hu. 2020. Revisiting pre-trained models for chinese natural language processing. *arXiv preprint arXiv:2004.13922*.

Jacob Devlin, Ming-Wei Chang, Kenton Lee, and Kristina Toutanova. 2019. BERT: Pre-training of deep bidirectional transformers for language understanding. In *Proceedings of the 2019 Conference of the North American Chapter of the Association for Computational Linguistics: Human Language Technologies, Volume 1 (Long and Short Papers)*, pages 4171–4186, Minneapolis, Minnesota. Association for Computational Linguistics.

Lucia Donatelli, Meaghan Fowlie, Jonas Groschwitz, Alexander Koller, Matthias Lindemann, Mario Mina, and Pia Weißenhorn. 2019. Saarland at MRP 2019: Compositional parsing across all graphbanks. In *Proceedings of the Shared Task on Cross-Framework Meaning Representation Parsing at the 2019 Conference on Natural Language Learning*, pages 66–75, Hong Kong. Association for Computational Linguistics.

Longxu Dou, Yunlong Feng, Yuqiu Ji, Wanxiang Che, and Ting Liu. 2020. HIT-SCIR at MRP 2020: Transition-based parser and iterative inference parser. In *Proceedings of the CoNLL 2020 Shared Task: Cross-Framework Meaning Representation Parsing*, pages 65–72, Online.

Timothy Dozat and Christopher D. Manning. 2017. Deep biaffine attention for neural dependency parsing. In *the Fifth International Conference on Learning Representations*.

Timothy Dozat and Christopher D. Manning. 2018. Simpler but More Accurate Semantic Dependency Parsing. In *Proceedings of the 56th Annual Meeting of the Association for Computational Linguistics*.

Michael Wayne Goodman. 2020. Penman: An open-source library and tool for AMR graphs. In *Proceedings of the 58th Annual Meeting of the Association for Computational Linguistics: System Demonstrations*, pages 312–319, Online. Association for Computational Linguistics.

Jan Hajič, Eva Hajičová, Jarmila Panevová, Petr Sgall, Ondřej Bojar, Silvie Cinková, Eva Fučíková, Marie Mikulová, Petr Pajas, Jan Popelka, Jiří Semecký, Jana Šindlerová, Jan Štěpánek, Josef Toman, Zdeňka Urešová, and Zdeněk Žabokrtský. 2012. Announcing Prague Czech-English dependency treebank 2.0. In *Proceedings of the Eighth International Conference on Language Resources and Evaluation*.

Daniel Hershcovich, Omri Abend, and Ari Rappoport. 2017. A transition-based directed acyclic graph parser for UCCA. In *Proceedings of the 55th Annual Meeting of the Association for Computational Linguistics (Volume 1: Long Papers)*, pages 1127–1138, Vancouver, Canada. Association for Computational Linguistics.

Diederik P. Kingma and Jimmy Ba. 2015. Adam: A method for stochastic optimization. In *Proceedings of the 3rd International Conference on Learning Representations, ICLR 2015, San Diego, CA, USA, May 7-9, 2015*.

Dan Kondratyuk and Milan Straka. 2019. 75 languages, 1 model: Parsing universal dependencies universally. In *Proceedings of the 2019 Conference on Empirical Methods in Natural Language Processing and the 9th International Joint Conference on Natural Language Processing (EMNLP-IJCNLP)*, pages 2779–2795, Hong Kong, China. Association for Computational Linguistics.

Artur Kulmizev, Miryam de Lhoneux, Johannes Gontrum, Elena Fano, and Joakim Nivre. 2019. Deep contextualized word embeddings in transition-based and graph-based dependency parsing - a tale of two parsers revisited. In *Proceedings of the 2019 Conference on Empirical Methods in Natural Language Processing and the 9th International Joint Conference on Natural Language Processing (EMNLP-IJCNLP)*, pages 2755–2768, Hong Kong, China. Association for Computational Linguistics.

Bin Li, Yuan Wen, Weiguang Qu, Lijun Bu, and Nianwen Xue. 2016. Annotating the little prince with Chinese AMRs. In *Proceedings of the 10th Linguistic Annotation Workshop held in conjunction with ACL 2016 (LAW-X 2016)*, pages 7–15, Berlin, Germany. Association for Computational Linguistics.

Matthias Lindemann, Jonas Groschwitz, and Alexander Koller. 2019. Compositional semantic parsing across graphbanks. In *Proceedings of the 57th Annual Meeting of the Association for Computational Linguistics*, pages 4576–4585, Florence, Italy. Association for Computational Linguistics.

Yinhan Liu, Myle Ott, Naman Goyal, Jingfei Du, Mandar Joshi, Danqi Chen, Omer Levy, Mike Lewis, Luke Zettlemoyer, and Veselin Stoyanov. 2019. RoBERTa: A robustly optimized bert pretraining approach. *arXiv preprint arXiv:1907.11692*.

Xuezhe Ma, Zecong Hu, Jingzhou Liu, Nanyun Peng, Graham Neubig, and Eduard Hovy. 2018. Stack-pointer networks for dependency parsing. In *Proceedings of the 56th Annual Meeting of the Association for Computational Linguistics (Volume 1: Long Papers)*, pages 1403–1414, Melbourne, Australia. Association for Computational Linguistics.

Christian Matthiessen and John A Bateman. 1991. *Text generation and systemic-functional linguistics: experiences from English and Japanese*. Pinter Publishers.

Ryan McDonald, Koby Crammer, and Fernando Pereira. 2005. Online large-margin training of dependency parsers. In *Proceedings of the 43rd Annual Meeting of the Association for Computational Linguistics (ACL'05)*, pages 91–98, Ann Arbor, Michigan. Association for Computational Linguistics.

Seung-Hoon Na and Jinwoo Min. 2020. JBNU at MRP 2020: AMR parsing using a joint state model for graph-sequence iterative inference. In *Proceedings of the CoNLL 2020 Shared Task: Cross-Framework Meaning Representation Parsing*, pages 83 – 87, Online.

Stephan Oepen, Omri Abend, Lasha Abzianidze, Johan Bos, Jan Hajič, Daniel Hershcovich, Bin Li, Tim O'Gorman, Nianwen Xue, and Daniel Zeman. 2020. MRP 2020: The Second Shared Task on Cross-framework and Cross-Lingual Meaning Representation Parsing. In *Proceedings of the CoNLL 2020 Shared Task: Cross-Framework Meaning Representation Parsing*, pages 1 – 22, Online.

Stephan Oepen, Omri Abend, Jan Hajic, Daniel Hershcovich, Marco Kuhlmann, Tim O'Gorman, and Nianwen Xue, editors. 2019. *Proceedings of the Shared Task on Cross-Framework Meaning Representation Parsing at the 2019 Conference on Natural Language Learning*. Association for Computational Linguistics, Hong Kong.

Stephan Oepen and Jan Tore Lønning. 2006. Discriminant-based MRS banking. In *Proceedings of the Fifth International Conference on Language Resources and Evaluation*.

Matthew Peters, Mark Neumann, Mohit Iyyer, Matt Gardner, Christopher Clark, Kenton Lee, and Luke Zettlemoyer. 2018. Deep contextualized word representations. In *Proceedings of the 2018 Conference of the North American Chapter of the Association for Computational Linguistics: Human Language Technologies, Volume 1 (Long Papers)*, pages 2227–2237, New Orleans, Louisiana. Association for Computational Linguistics.

David Samuel and Milan Straka. 2020. ÚFAL at MRP 2020: Permutation-invariant semantic parsing in PERIN. In *Proceedings of the CoNLL 2020 Shared Task: Cross-Framework Meaning Representation Parsing*, pages 53 – 64, Online.

Sainbayar Sukhbaatar, arthur szlam, Jason Weston, and Rob Fergus. 2015. End-to-end memory networks. In C. Cortes, N. D. Lawrence, D. D. Lee, M. Sugiyama, and R. Garnett, editors, *Advances in Neural Information Processing Systems 28*, pages 2440–2448. Curran Associates, Inc.

Rob A. Van Der Sandt. 1992. Presupposition Projection as Anaphora Resolution. *Journal of Semantics*, 9(4):333–377.

Ashish Vaswani, Noam Shazeer, Niki Parmar, Jakob Uszkoreit, Llion Jones, Aidan N Gomez, Ł ukasz Kaiser, and Illia Polosukhin. 2017. Attention is all you need. In I. Guyon, U. V. Luxburg, S. Bengio, H. Wallach, R. Fergus, S. Vishwanathan, and R. Garnett, editors, *Advances in Neural Information Processing Systems 30*, pages 5998–6008. Curran Associates, Inc.

David Vilares and Carlos Gómez-Rodríguez. 2018. A transition-based algorithm for unrestricted AMR parsing. In *Proceedings of the 2018 Conference of the North American Chapter of the Association for Computational Linguistics: Human Language Technologies, Volume 2 (Short Papers)*, pages 142–149, New Orleans, Louisiana. Association for Computational Linguistics.

Thomas Wolf, Lysandre Debut, Victor Sanh, Julien Chaumond, Clement Delangue, Anthony Moi, Pierric Cistac, Tim Rault, R'emi Louf, Morgan Funtowicz, and Jamie Brew. 2019. HuggingFace's transformers: State-of-the-art natural language processing. *ArXiv*, abs/1910.03771.

Hiroyasu Yamada and Yuji Matsumoto. 2003. Statistical dependency analysis with support vector machines. In *Proceedings of the Eighth International Conference on Parsing Technologies*, pages 195–206, Nancy, France.

Sheng Zhang, Xutai Ma, Kevin Duh, and Benjamin Van Durme. 2019a. AMR parsing as sequence-to-graph transduction. In *Proceedings of the 57th Annual Meeting of the Association for Computational Linguistics*, pages 80–94, Florence, Italy. Association for Computational Linguistics.

Sheng Zhang, Xutai Ma, Kevin Duh, and Benjamin Van Durme. 2019b. Broad-coverage semantic parsing as transduction. In *Proceedings of the 2019 Conference on Empirical Methods in Natural Language Processing and the 9th International Joint Conference on Natural Language Processing (EMNLP-IJCNLP)*, pages 3786–3798, Hong Kong, China. Association for Computational Linguistics.

Yue Zhang, Wei Jiang, Qingrong Xia, Junjie Cao, Rui Wang, Zhenghua Li, and Min Zhang. 2019c. SUDA-Alibaba at MRP 2019: Graph-based models with BERT. In *Proceedings of the Shared Task on Cross-Framework Meaning Representation Parsing at the 2019 Conference on Natural Language Learning*, pages 149–157, Hong Kong. Association for Computational Linguistics.

ÚFAL at MRP 2020: Permutation-invariant Semantic Parsing in PERIN

David Samuel and **Milan Straka**
Charles University
Faculty of Mathematics and Physics
Institute of Formal and Applied Linguistics
{samuel,straka}@ufal.mff.cuni.cz

Abstract

We present PERIN, a novel permutation-invariant approach to sentence-to-graph semantic parsing. PERIN is a versatile, cross-framework and language independent architecture for universal modeling of semantic structures. Our system participated in the CoNLL 2020 shared task, Cross-Framework Meaning Representation Parsing (MRP 2020), where it was evaluated on five different frameworks (AMR, DRG, EDS, PTG and UCCA) across four languages. PERIN was one of the winners of the shared task. The source code and pre-trained models are available at http://www.github.com/ufal/perin.

1 Introduction

The aim of the CoNLL 2020 shared task, Cross-Framework Meaning Representation Parsing (MRP 2020; Oepen et al., 2020), is to translate plain text sentences into their corresponding graph-structured meaning representation.[1] MRP 2020 features five formally and linguistically different frameworks with varying degrees of linguistic and structural complexity:

- **AMR:** Abstract Meaning Representation (Banarescu et al., 2013);

- **DRG:** Discourse Representation Graphs (Abzianidze et al., 2017) provide a graph encoding of Discourse Representation Structure (Van der Sandt, 1992);

- **EDS:** Elementary Dependency Structures (Oepen and Lønning, 2006);

- **PTG:** Prague Tectogrammatical Graphs (Hajic et al., 2012);

- **UCCA:** Universal Conceptual Cognitive Annotation (Abend and Rappoport, 2013).

These frameworks constitute the *cross-framework* track of MRP 2020, while the separate *cross-lingual* track introduces one additional language for four out of the five frameworks: Chinese AMR (Li et al., 2016), German DRG, Czech PTG and German UCCA (Hershcovich et al., 2019).

In agreement with the shared task objective to advance uniform meaning representation parsing across diverse semantic graph frameworks and languages, we propose a language and structure agnostic sentence-to-graph neural network architecture modeling semantic representations from input sequences.

The main characteristics of our approach are:

- **Permutation-invariant model:** PERIN is, to our best knowledge, the first graph-based semantic parser that predicts all nodes at once in parallel and trains them with a permutation-invariant loss function. Semantic graphs are naturally *orderless*, so constraining them to an artificial node ordering creates an unfounded restriction; furthermore, our approach is more expressive and more efficient than *order-based* auto-regressive models.

- **Relative encoding:** We present a substantial improvement of relative encodings of node labels, which map anchored tokens onto label strings (Straka and Straková, 2019). Our novel formulation allows using a richer set of encoding rules.

- **Universal architecture:** Our work presents a general sentence-to-graph pipeline adaptable for specific frameworks only by adjusting pre-processing and post-processing steps.

Our model was ranked among the two winning systems in both the *cross-framework* and the *cross-lingual* tracks of MRP 2020 and significantly advanced the accuracy of semantic parsing from the last year's MRP 2019.

---

[1]See http://mrp.nlpl.eu/2020/ for more details.

Proceedings of the CoNLL 2020 Shared Task: Cross-Framework Meaning Representation Parsing, pages 53–64
Online, Nov. 19-20, 2020. ©2020 Association for Computational Linguistics

2   Related Work

Examples of general, formalism-independent semantic parsers are scarce in the literature. Hershcovich et al. (2018) propose a universal transition-based parser for directed, acyclic graphs, capable of parsing multiple conceptually and formally different schemes. Furthermore, several participants of MRP 2019 presented universal parsers. Che et al. (2019) improved uniform transition-based parsing and used a different set of actions for each framework. Lai et al. (2019) submitted a transition-based parser with shared actions across treebanks, but failed to match the performance of the other parsers. Straka and Straková (2019) presented a general graph-based parser, where the meaning representation graphs are created by repeatedly adding nodes and edges.

Graph-based parsers (McDonald and Pereira, 2006; Peng et al., 2017; Dozat and Manning, 2018; Cai and Lam, 2020) usually predict nodes in a sequential, auto-regressive manner and then connect them with a biaffine classifier. Unlike these approaches, our model infers all nodes in parallel while allowing the creation of rich intermediate representations by node-to-node self-attention.

Machine learning tools able to efficiently process unordered sets are gaining more attention in recent years. Qi et al. (2017) and particularly Zhang et al. (2019b) proposed permutation-invariant neural networks for point clouds, which are of great relevance to our system. Our work was further inspired by Carion et al. (2020), who utilize permutation invariance for object detection in a similar fashion to our sentence-to-graph generation.

3   Methods

3.1   Graph Representation

All five semantic formalisms share the same representation via directed labeled multigraphs in the graph interchange format proposed by Kuhlmann and Oepen (2016). Universally, the semantic units are represented by nodes and the semantic relationships by labeled edges. Each node can be anchored to a (possibly empty) set of input characters, and can contain a (possibly empty) list of properties, each being an attribute-value pair.

We simplify this graph structure by turning the properties into graph nodes: every property {attribute : value} of node n is removed and a new node with label value is connected

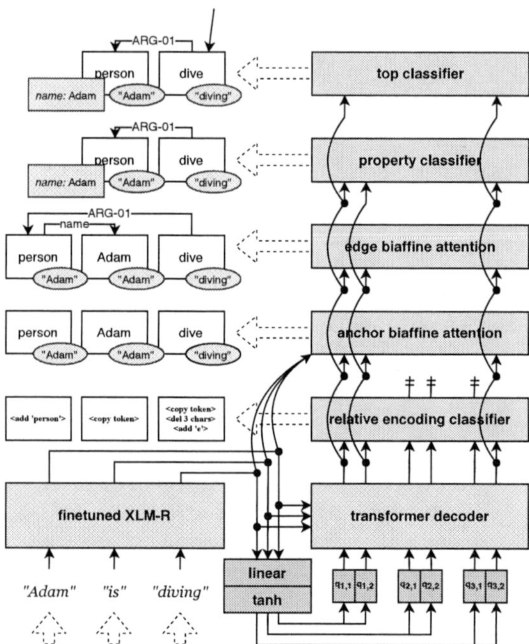

Figure 1: Data flow through PERIN during inference. Every input token is processed by an encoder and transformed into multiple queries, which are further refined by a decoder. Each query is either *denied* or *accepted*, and the accepted ones are then gradually processed into the final semantic graph.

to the parent node n by an edge labeled with attribute; the anchors of the new node are the same as of its parent.[2] Figure 4 illustrates this transformation together with other pre-processing steps (specific for each framework) explained in detail in Section 3.7.

Another change to the internal graph representation is the use of relative label encoding (discussed in Section 3.4), which substitutes the original node labels by lists of relative encoding rules.

3.2   Overall Architecture

A simplified illustration of the whole model can be seen in Figure 1. The input is tokenized, an encoder (Section 3.5) computes contextual embeddings of the tokens, and each embedded token $\mathbf{e}_i$ is then mapped onto Q queries by nonlinear transformations $\mathbf{q}_{i,t} = \tanh\left(\mathbf{W}_t\mathbf{e}_i + \mathbf{b}_t\right), t \in \{1, \ldots Q\}$, where $\mathbf{W}_t$ is a trainable weight matrix and $\mathbf{b}_t$

---

[2]"Nodeification" of properties was motivated by the nature of AMR graphs, where the properties are equivalent to instanced concepts/nodes (Banarescu et al., 2013). From a more practical viewpoint, it allows us to utilize a single classifier for both the node labels and the less-frequent properties, and to simplify the whole architecture.

is a trainable bias vector. After that, a decoder (Transformer with pre-norm residual connections (Nguyen and Salazar, 2019) and cross-attention into the contextual embeddings $\mathbf{e}_i$) processes the queries, obtaining their final feature vectors $\mathbf{h}_{i,t}$. These feature vectors are shared across all classification heads, each inferring specific aspects of the final meaning representation graph from them:

- **Relative encoding classifier** decides what node label should serve as the "answer" to each query; a query can also be *denied* (no node is created) when classified as "null". Relative label prediction is described in detail in Section 3.4.3.

- **Anchor biaffine classifier** uses deep biaffine attention (Dozat and Manning, 2017) to create anchors between nodes and surface tokens – to be more precise, the biaffine attention processes the latent vectors of queries $\mathbf{h}_{i,t}$ and tokens $\mathbf{e}_j$, and predicts the presence of an anchor between every pair of them as a binary classification task.

- **Edge biaffine classifier** uses three biaffine attention modules to predict whether an edge should exist between a pair of nodes (*presence* binary classification), what label(s) should it have (*label* multi-class or multi-label classification, depending on the framework) and what attribute should it have (*attribute* multi-class classification) – in essence, this module is a simple extension of the standard edge classifier by Dozat and Manning (2018).

- **Property classifier** uses a linear layer followed by a sigmoid nonlinearity to identify nodes that should be converted to properties.

- **Top classifier** uses a linear layer followed by a softmax nonlinearity (where the probabilities are normalized across nodes) to detect the *top* node.

This section described all modules capable of handling different characteristics of meaning representation graphs. Not all of them appear in each framework – for example, AMR graphs do not need edge attributes, while UCCA graphs do not contain any properties. More details about specific framework configurations are given in Section 3.7.

3.3 Permutation-invariant Graph Generation

Semantic graphs are *orderless*, so it is unnatural to constrain their generation by some artificial node ordering. Traditionally, graph nodes have been predicted by a sequence-to-sequence model (Peng et al., 2017), with the nodes being generated in some hardwired order (Zhang et al., 2019a). Demanding a fixed node ordering causes the *discontinuity issue* (Zhang et al., 2019b): even when correct items are predicted, they are viewed as completely wrong if not in the expected order. We avoid this issue by using such a loss function and such a model that produce the same outcome independently on the node ordering (Zaheer et al., 2017).

3.3.1 Permutation-equivariant Model

We transform the queries $\mathbf{q} = \{\mathbf{q}_i\}_{i=1}^N$ into hidden features $\mathbf{h} = \{\mathbf{h}_i\}_{i=1}^N$ in such manner that any permutation $\pi \in \mathfrak{G}_N$ of the input $\pi(\mathbf{q}) = \{\mathbf{q}_{\pi(i)}\}_{i=1}^N$ produces the same – but permuted – output $\pi(\mathbf{h}) = \{\mathbf{h}_{\pi(i)}\}_{i=1}^N$. The Transformer architecture (Vaswani et al., 2017) conveniently fulfills this requirement (assuming positional embeddings are not used). Furthermore, it can combine any pair of input items independently of their distance and in an efficient non-autoregressive way.

3.3.2 Permutation-invariant Loss

The hidden features $\mathbf{h}$ are further refined into predictions $\hat{\mathbf{y}} = f_\theta(\mathbf{h})$ by the classification heads. In order to create a permutation-invariant loss function, i.e., a function $\mathcal{L}(\pi(\hat{\mathbf{y}}), \mathbf{y})$ giving the same result for every $\pi \in \mathfrak{G}_N$, we find a permutation $\pi^* \in \mathfrak{G}_N$ assigning each query to its most similar node. After permuting the targets according to π^*, the standard losses can be computed, because they are no longer dependent on the original ordering of $\hat{\mathbf{y}}$ and $\mathbf{y}$.[3]

To find the minimizing permutation π^*, we start by extending the (multi)set of target nodes $\mathbf{y}$ by "null" nodes (denoted as $\varnothing$) in order to fulfill $|\hat{\mathbf{y}}| = |\mathbf{y}|$. When classified as "null" during inference, the query is *denied* and omitted from further processing. The permutation π^* is then defined as

$$\pi^* = \arg\max_{\pi \in \mathfrak{G}_N} \sum_{i=1}^N p_{\text{match}}(\hat{\mathbf{y}}_i, \mathbf{y}_{\pi(i)}), \qquad (1)$$

where the matching score p_{match} is composed of a *label score* and the geometric mean (GM) of

---

[3]Unfortunately, the uniqueness of π^* is not always guaranteed: given that the proposed matching depends only on labels and anchors, there might be multiple equivalent nodes (considering only labels and anchors). We break ties between such nodes by also minimizing the likelihood of their edges across all their permutations.

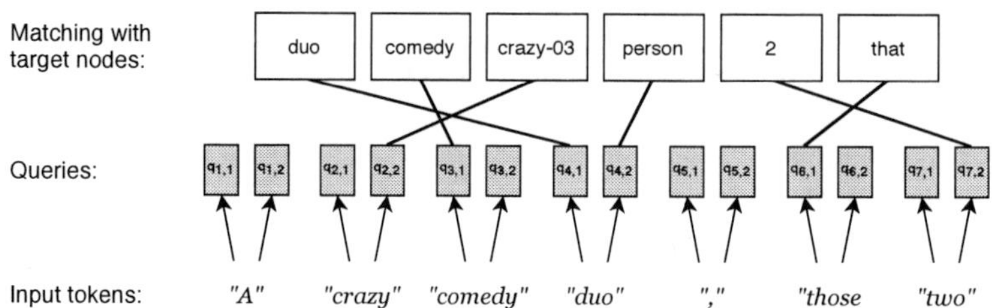

Figure 2: Example of a matching between queries and target nodes during training. Every input token is mapped onto Q (2 in this case) queries $\mathbf{q}_{i,j}$, which are decoded into node predictions $\hat{\mathbf{y}}_{i,j}$. These predictions are paired with the ground truth nodes $\mathbf{y}$, as in Equation 1. Then, the loss functions are computed with respect to the paired target nodes. Queries without any match should be classified as "null" nodes. When classified as "null" during inference, the query is not turned into any node (the query is *denied*).

anchor scores of all input tokens T. The *label score* of the ith query and the jth node is defined as the predicted probability of the target j^{th} label; the *anchor score* of the ith query, j^{th} node and a token $t \in T$ is defined as the predicted probability of the actual (non)existence of an anchor between t and the jth node:

$$p_{\text{match}} = p_{\text{label}} \cdot \bar{p}_{\text{anchor}}$$
$$p_{\text{label}}(\hat{\mathbf{y}}_i, \mathbf{y}_j) = \mathbb{1}_{\mathbf{y}_j^{\text{label}} \neq \varnothing} P(\mathbf{y}_j^{\text{label}} | \mathbf{h}_i; \boldsymbol{\theta})$$
$$\bar{p}_{\text{anchor}}(\hat{\mathbf{y}}_i, \mathbf{y}_j) = \underset{t \in \text{tokens}}{\text{GM}} P(\mathbb{1}_{t \in \mathbf{y}_j^{\text{anchors}}} | t, \mathbf{h}_i; \boldsymbol{\theta}).$$

We use the geometric mean to keep the anchor score $\bar{p}_{\text{anchor}}$ magnitude independent of the number of tokens, and therefore have a similar weight as the label score p_{label}.

The optimal matching π^* can be efficiently computed by the Hungarian algorithm (Kuhn, 1955) in $O(n^3)$. As a result, every query is assigned either to a regular node or to a "null" node $\varnothing$. An illustration of a matching between queries and target nodes is presented in Figure 2.

The loss functions for the queries are computed with respect to the matched nodes. After finding π^*, we permute all target nodes and compute the classification losses in the standard "order-based" way (i.e., by minimizing the cross-entropy between the predictions and the corresponding targets). The losses of queries matched to the "null" nodes are ignored, except for their relative label loss ℓ_{label}, which pushes these queries to predict $\varnothing$ as their label. The label loss is further altered by the focal loss factor (Lin et al., 2017) to mitigate the imbalance of labels introduced by extending the targets with the "null" nodes.

3.3.3 Anchor Masking

During the early experiments with this architecture, we noticed that nodes tend to be generated from their anchored tokens (or more precisely from the queries of their anchored tokens), after the outputs stabilize during first epochs. We employ this observation to create an inductive bias by limiting the possible pairings to occur only between target nodes and predictions from their anchored tokens. Formally, this is achieved by setting

$$\bar{p}_{\text{anchor}}(f_{\boldsymbol{\theta}}(\mathbf{h}_i), \mathbf{y}_j) = \varepsilon,$$

if the jth node is not anchored to the ith token, with ε being a small positive constant close to 0.

3.4 Relative Label Encoding

Similarly to Straka et al. (2019); Straka and Straková (2019), we use *relative encodings* for the prediction of node labels: instead of direct classification of label strings, we utilize rules specifying how to transform anchored surface tokens into the semantic labels. For example, in Figure 1, the anchored token *"diving"* is transformed into *"dive"* by using a relative encoding rule deleting its last three characters and appending a character *"e"*. Such a rule could be also employed for predicting a node anchored to *"taking"* or *"giving"*. Relative encoding of labels is thus able to reduce the number of classification targets and generalize outside of the set of "absolute" label strings seen during training. Alternatively, the relative encoding can be seen as an extension of the pointer networks (Gu et al., 2016), which also decides how to post-process the copied tokens. Table 1 demonstrates how the relative encoding rules reduce the number of targets that need to be classified.

framework	language	# labels strings	# encoding rules
AMR	English	27,049	4,385
	Chinese	30,949	2,560
DRG	English	5,715	684
	German	1,905	918
EDS	English	31,933	1,322
PTG	English	39,336	529
	Czech	38,448	1,321

Table 1: The numbers of absolutely and relatively encoded node labels. Relative encodings lead to a significant reduction of classification targets in an order of magnitude across all frameworks. Note that node labels are the union of labels and property values (except for PTG), as described in Section 3.1.

3.4.1 Minimal Encoding Rule Set

Naturally, a label can be generated from anchored tokens in multiple ways. Unlike previous works that needed some heuristic to select a single rule from all suitable ones (Straka and Straková, 2019), we do not constraint the space of the possible rules much. Instead, we construct the final set of encoding rules to be the smallest possible one capable of encoding all labels.

Formally, let $\mathcal{S}$ be an arbitrary class of functions transforming a list of text strings (anchored tokens) into another string (node label), and let N be the set of all nodes from the training set. For $n \in \mathsf{N}$, denote n_t the anchored surface tokens and n_ℓ the target label string. Then the set of applicable rules for the node n is $\mathcal{S}_n = \{r \in \mathcal{S} | r(n_t) = n_\ell\}$. Our goal is to find the smallest subclass $\mathcal{S}^* \subseteq \mathcal{S}$ capable of encoding all node labels, in other words a subclass $\mathcal{S}^*$ satisfying

$$\forall n \in \mathsf{N} : \mathcal{S}^* \cap \mathcal{S}_n \neq \emptyset.$$

This formulation is equivalent to the minimal hitting set problem. Therefore, we can find the optimal solution of our problem by reducing it to a weighted MaxSAT formula in CNF: every $\mathcal{S}_n = \{r_1, r_2, \ldots, r_k\}$ becomes a hard clause $(r_1 \vee r_2 \vee \ldots \vee r_k)$ and every $r \in \mathcal{S}$ becomes a soft clause $(\neg r)$. We then submit this formula to the RC2 solver (Ignatiev et al., 2019) to obtain the minimal set of rules. Note that although solving this problem can take up to several hours, it needs to be done only once and then cached for all the training runs.

3.4.2 Space of Relative Rules

Our space of relative rules $\mathcal{S}$ consists of four disjoint subclasses:

1. *token rules* are represented by seven-tuples $(d_l, d_r, s, r_l, r_r, a_l, a_r)$ and process a list of anchored tokens n_t by first deleting the first d_l and the last d_r tokens, then by concatenating the remaining ones into one text string with the separator s inserted between them, followed by removing the first r_l and last r_r characters and finally by adding the prefix a_l and suffix a_r;[4]

2. *lemma rules* are created similarly to the token rules, but use the provided lemmas instead of tokens;

3. *number rules* transform word numerals into digits – for example, tokens [*"forty"*, *"two"*] become *"42"*;

4. *absolute rules* use the original label string n_ℓ, without taking into account any anchored tokens n_t; they serve as the fallback rules when no relative encodings are applicable.

3.4.3 Prediction of Relative Rules

Even with the minimal set of rules $\mathcal{S}^*$, multiple rules may be applicable to a single node. Therefore, the prediction of relative rules is a multi-label classification problem. The target distribution for a node n over all $r \in \mathcal{S}^*$ is defined as follows:[5]

$$P(r|n) = \begin{cases} \dfrac{1}{|\mathcal{S}^* \cap \mathcal{S}_n|}, & \text{if } r \in \mathcal{S}_n; \\ 0, & \text{otherwise.} \end{cases}$$

The label loss ℓ_{label} is then calculated as the cross-entropy between the target and the predicted distributions.

We use mixture of softmaxes (MoS) to mitigate the softmax bottleneck (Yang et al., 2018) that arises when multiple hypotheses can be correctly applied to a single input. MoS allows the model to consider K different hypotheses at the same time and weight them relatively to their plausibility.

Formally, let $\mathbf{h}_q$ be the final latent vector for query q and let $\mathbf{W}_k, \mathbf{b}_k, \mathbf{w}_k, b_k, \mathbf{w}_r, b_r$ be the trainable weights. Then, the estimated MoS distribution

---

[4] To show a real example of a *token rule* from EDS, the rule (0, 1, +, 0, 0, _, _a_1) maps tokens ("at", "the", "very", "least", ",") into the label "_at+the+very+least_a_1".

[5] The target distribution is further modified by label smoothing (Szegedy et al., 2016) for better regularization.

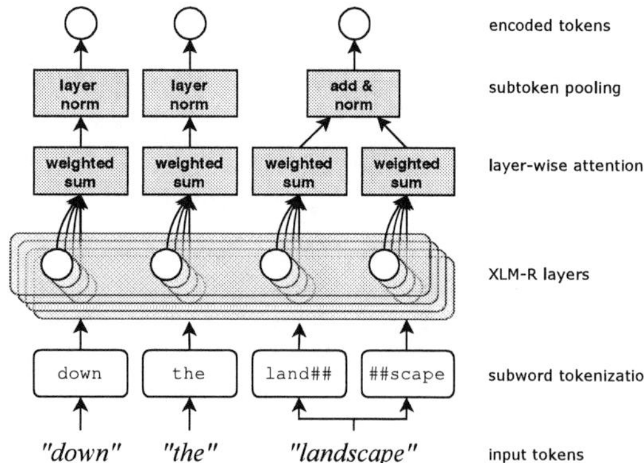

Figure 3: Architecture of the encoder with finetuned XLM-R. The input tokens are first tokenized into subwords, which are then processed into contextual embeddings by layer-wise attention on the XLM-R intermediate layers. Finally, the subword embeddings are pooled to obtain the encoded tokens.

of relative rules $P_{\boldsymbol{\theta}}(r|n)$ is defined as follows:

$$\mathbf{x}_k = \tanh(\mathbf{W}_k \mathbf{h}_q + \mathbf{b}_k)$$

$$\pi_k = \frac{\text{sigmoid}(\mathbf{h}_q^\top \mathbf{w}_k + b_k)}{\sum_{k'} \text{sigmoid}(\mathbf{h}_q^\top \mathbf{w}_{k'} + b_{k'})}$$

$$P_{\boldsymbol{\theta}}(r|n) = \sum_{k=1}^{K} \pi_k \, \text{softmax}(\mathbf{x}_k^\top \mathbf{w}_r + b_r).$$

3.5 Finetuning XLM-R

To obtain rich contextual embeddings for each input token, we finetune the pretrained multilingual model XLM-R (Conneau et al., 2020). The architecture of the encoder is presented in Figure 3.

3.5.1 Contextual Embedding Extraction

Different layers in BERT-like models represent varying levels of syntactic and semantic knowledge (van Aken et al., 2019), raising a question of which layer (or layers) should be used to extract the embeddings from. Following Kondratyuk and Straka (2019), we solve this problem by a purely data-driven approach and compute the weighted sum of all layers. Formally, let $\mathbf{e}_l$ be the intermediate output from the lth layer and let w_l be a trainable scalar weight. The final contextual embedding is then calculated as

$$\mathbf{e} = \sum_{l=1}^{L} \text{softmax}(w_l)\mathbf{e}_l.$$

Note that each input token can be divided into multiple subwords by the XLM-R tokenizer. To obtain

a single embedding for every token, we sum the embeddings of all its subwords. Finally, the contextual embeddings are normalized with layer normalization (Ba et al., 2016) to stabilize the training.[6]

3.5.2 Finetuning Stabilization

Given the large number of parameters in the pretrained XLM-R model, we employ several stabilization and regularization techniques in attempt to avoid overfitting.

We start by dividing the model parameters into two groups: the finetuned XLM-R and the rest of the network. Both groups are updated with AdamW optimizer (Loshchilov and Hutter, 2019) , and their learning rate follows the inverse square root schedule with warmup (Vaswani et al., 2017). The learning rate of the finetuned encoder is frozen for the first 2000 steps before the warmup phase starts (Howard and Ruder, 2018). The warmup is set to 6000 steps for both groups, while the learning rate peak is $6 \cdot 10^{-5}$ for the XLM-R and $6 \cdot 10^{-4}$ for the rest of the network. The weight decay for XLM-R, 10^{-2}, is considerably higher compared to $1.2 \cdot 10^{-6}$ used in the rest of the network (Devlin et al., 2019).

Dropout of entire intermediate XLM-R layers results in additional regularization – we drop each layer with 10% probability by replacing w_l with $-\infty$ during the final contextual embedding computation (Section 3.5.1). Inter-layer and attention dropout rates are the same as during the XLM-R pretraining.[7]

3.6 Balanced Loss Weights

Semantic parsing is an instance of multi-task learning, where each task $t \in \mathsf{T}$ can have conflicting needs and where the task losses ℓ_t can have different magnitudes. The overall loss function $\mathcal{L}$ to be optimized therefore consists of the weighted sum of partial losses ℓ_t:

$$\mathcal{L}(f_{\boldsymbol{\theta}}(\mathbf{x}), y) = \sum_{t \in \mathsf{T}} w_t \ell_t(f_{\boldsymbol{\theta}}(\mathbf{x}), y).$$

Finding optimal values for the loss weights w_t is extremely complicated. This issue is usually resolved either by (suboptimally) setting all weights equally to 1 or by a thorough grid search. However, the

---

[6]A side effect of the normalization step is that the subword summation is equal to the more common subword average (Zhang et al., 2019a).

[7]Due to the space constrains, all hyperparameters for each training configuration (together with the source code and pretrained models) are published at `https://github.com/ufal/perin`.

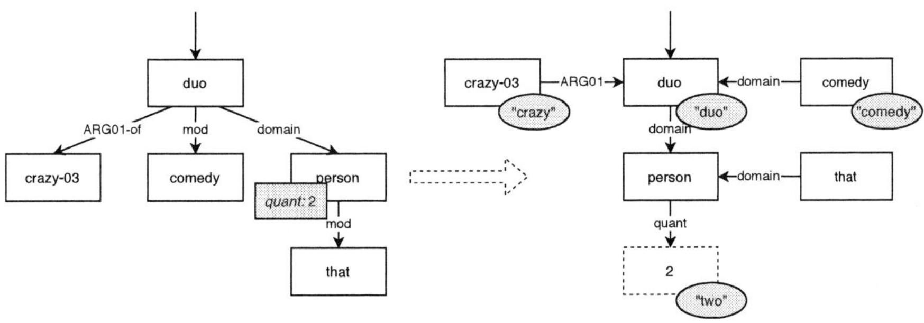

"a crazy comedy duo, those two"

Figure 4: Visualization of AMR pre-processing (Section 3.7.1) for the sentence *"a crazy comedy duo, those two"*. The original graph is on the left and the transformed graph is shown on the right. Notice that the property `quant:2` of `person` is converted into a standalone node. The graph is normalized by reversing three inverted edges (note that `mod` is in fact `domain-of`) and some nodes get artificial anchors. Relative encoding rules are not included in this illustration for the sake of clarity, but it is worthwhile noting that nodes `person` and `that` contain only absolute label rules and are therefore not anchored.

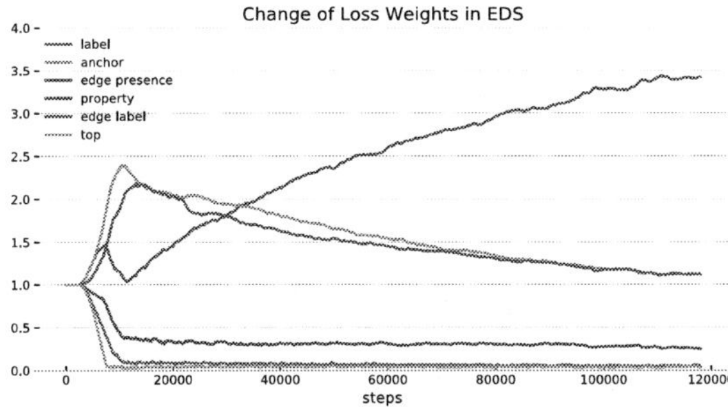

Figure 5: Change of the loss weights throughout the training of an EDS parser. The relative difficulty of edge and anchor predictions seems to be higher at the beginning of the training, but then gradually decreases, allowing the model to concentrate primarily on label prediction.

complexity of the grid search grows exponentially with $|T|$ and would need to be performed independently for all nine combinations of frameworks and languages.

A more feasible solution is to set the weights adaptively according to a data-driven metric as in Kendall et al. (2018). We follow Chen et al. (2018), who balance the magnitudes of gradients $\|\nabla_{\boldsymbol{\theta}_s} w_i \ell_i\|_2$, where $\boldsymbol{\theta}_s$ are the weights of the shared part of the network. That magnitude is made proportional to the ratio of the current loss and its initial value: when ℓ_i decreases relatively quickly, its strength gets reduced to leave more space for the other tasks. Consequently, the loss weights w_t are not static, but change throughout the training to balance the individual gradient norms. Figure 5 shows an example of the balancing dynamics.

3.7 Framework Specifics

3.7.1 AMR

AMR is a *Flavor 2* framework, which means its nodes are not anchored to the surface forms. We instead exploit the general algorithm for the minimal encoding rule set (Section 3.4.1) to create artificial anchors: considering all possible one-to-one anchors $a \in A_n$ for each node n, we infer all compatible rules $\mathcal{S}_n = \bigcup_{a \in A_n} \mathcal{S}_n^a$, and find the minimal set of rules $\mathcal{S}^*$. The artificial anchors of a node n are then defined as $\{a \in A_n | \mathcal{S}_n^a \cap \mathcal{S}^* \neq \emptyset\}$. Consequently, our parser does not need any approximate anchoring (because we instead compute an anchoring minimizing the number of relative rules).

On the other hand, Chinese AMR graphs contain anchors (they are actually of *Flavor 1*), therefore, the described procedure is applied only on English AMR.

AMR graphs also contains inverted edges that transform them into tree-like structures. The inverted edges are marked by modified edge labels (for example, `ARG0` becomes `ARG0-of`). We normalize the graphs back into their original non-inverted form, making them more uniform, simplifying edge prediction to become more local and independent of the global graph structure. An example of AMR pre-processing is shown in Figure 4.

Considering the fact that every node is artificially anchored to at most a single token, the anchor classifier is not needed, if anchor masking is used (Section 3.3.3). Finally, AMR parsing does not employ the edge attribute classifier.

System	AMR^{eng}	DRG^{eng}	EDS^{eng}	PTG^{eng}	UCCA^{eng}	Average
HUJI-KU (Arviv et al., 2020)	52.36%	62.75%	79.68%	53.76%	72.91%	64.29%
Hitachi (Ozaki et al., 2020)	**81.54%**	93.19%	**93.56%**	88.73%	75.07%	86.42%
HIT-SCIR (Dou et al., 2020)	69.80%	89.07%	87.40%	84.26%	74.76%	81.06%
ÚFAL PERIN	80.23%	**94.16%**	92.73%	88.44%	**76.40%**	86.39%
ÚFAL PERIN*	80.23%	**94.16%**	92.73%	**89.19%**	**76.40%**	**86.54%**

System	AMR^{zho}	DRG^{deu}	——	PTG^{ces}	UCCA^{deu}	Average
HUJI-KU (Arviv et al., 2020)	44.92%	62.33%	——	58.49%	74.72%	60.11%
Hitachi (Ozaki et al., 2020)	80.44%	**93.36%**	——	87.35%	79.04%	85.05%
HIT-SCIR (Dou et al., 2020)	49.39%	68.31%	——	77.93%	80.02%	68.91%
ÚFAL PERIN	78.17%	89.83%	——	91.27%	**81.01%**	85.07%
ÚFAL PERIN*	**80.52%**	89.83%	——	**92.24%**	**81.01%**	**85.90%**

Table 2: The **all** F1 scores and a macro-average total score of the shared task systems. PERIN is our official shared task submission and PERIN* is a post-competition submission with a fixed bug. The best results are typeset in **bold**. The top table contains the *cross-framework* scores on English treebanks, while the bottom table presents the *cross-lingual* ones.

3.7.2 DRG

Since the DRG graphs are also of *Flavor 2*, they are pre-processed similarly to English AMR. Additionally, we reduce all nodes representing binary relations into labeled edges between the corresponding discourse elements.

Nodes in German DRG graphs are labeled in English, which decreases the applicability of relative encoding. Therefore, we employ the `opus-mt-de-en` (Tiedemann and Thottingal, 2020) machine translation model from Huggingface's transformers package (Wolf et al., 2019) to translate the provided lemmas from German to English, before computing the relative encoding rules.

DRG parsing does not make use of anchor and edge attribute classifiers, just like AMR parsing.

3.7.3 EDS

EDS graphs are post-processed to contain a single continuous anchor for every node. The EDS parser contains all the classification modules described in Section 3.2, except for the edge attribute classifier.

3.7.4 PTG

Properties in PTG graphs are not converted into nodes as in other frameworks, but are directly predicted from latent vectors $\mathbf{h}_q$ by multi-class classifiers (one for each property type). Additionally, the `frame` properties are selected only from frames listed in CzEngVallex (Urešová et al., 2015).

We utilize all classification heads except for the top node classification, because PTG graphs contain special `<TOP>` nodes, which make the separate top prediction redundant.

3.7.5 UCCA

We augment the UCCA nodes by assigning them `leaf` and `inner` labels. Additionally, the `inner` nodes are anchored to the union of anchors of their children. Therefore, the nodes can be differentiated by the permutation-invariant loss (Section 3.3.2).

The UCCA parser does not have the property classifier and the top classifier, where the latter is not needed, because the top node can be inferred from the structure of the rooted UCCA graphs.

4 Results

We present the overall results of our system in Table 2 and Table 3. Both tables contain F1 scores obtained using the official MRP metric.[8] Table 2 shows the **all** F1 scores for the individual frameworks together with the overall averages for the *cross-framework* and *cross-lingual* tracks. Macro-averaged results (across all nine frameworks) for the different MRP metrics are displayed in Table 3.

Note that our original submission (denoted as PERIN) contained a bug in anchor prediction for Chinese AMR and both PTG frameworks. The bug caused the nodes to get anchored to at least one token. We submitted a fixed version called PERIN* in the post-competition evaluation and compare it with the original one in Table 2.

According to the official whole-percent-only **all** F1 score, our competition submission reached tied first place in both the *cross-lingual* and the *cross-framework* track, with its performance virtually

---

[8] Fine-grained results for each framework are available in the task overview by Oepen et al. (2020).

System	Tops	Labels	Properties	Anchors	Edges	Attributes	Average
HUJI-KU (Arviv et al., 2020)	85.85%	22.80%	29.48%	46.79%	61.35%	7.67%	62.43%
Hitachi (Ozaki et al., 2020)	**95.67%**	68.93%	48.89%	61.95%	**80.14%**	24.93%	85.81%
HIT-SCIR (Dou et al., 2020)	94.37%	61.84%	30.80%	52.18%	71.41%	22.51%	75.66%
ÚFAL PERIN*	94.20%	**70.36%**	**49.34%**	**63.45%**	79.68%	**27.07%**	**86.26%**

Table 3: Overall results for different MRP metrics, macro-averaged over all frameworks and languages. The best results are typeset in **bold**.

Configuration	Tops	Labels	Properties	Anchors	Edges	Average
ÚFAL PERIN*	89.53%	93.45%	94.34%	93.40%	90.74%	92.73%
w/o MoS	88.04%	93.39%	93.79%	93.48%	90.76%	92.65%
w/o focal loss	89.08%	93.33%	93.59%	93.21%	90.46%	92.46%
BERT encoder	89.95%	92.97%	94.74%	92.92%	89.84%	92.27%
w/o balanced losses	89.23%	92.28%	94.46%	92.12%	89.19%	91.60%

Table 4: Ablation study showing MRP scores of different configurations on EDS. The top row contains the submitted configuration without any changes; then we report the results for 1) label classifier without the mixture of softmaxes (MoS); 2) label loss not multiplied by the focal loss coefficient; 3) encoder with finetuned BERT-large (English) instead of multilingual XLM-R and 4) constant loss weights, equally set to 1.0.

System	AMR[eng]	EDS[eng]	UCCA[eng]
best from MRP 2019	73.11%	92.55%	82.61%
ÚFAL PERIN*	**78.43%**	**95.17%**	**82.71%**

Table 5: The last year's shared task had three frameworks – English AMR, EDS and UCCA – in common with MRP 2020. All parsers were evaluated on *The Little Prince* dataset, the first row shows the F1 scores of the best performing parser for each framework (Oepen et al., 2019).

identical to the system by Hitachi (Ozaki et al., 2020). Our bugfixed submission reached the first rank in both tracks, improving the *cross-lingual* score by nearly one percent point. Our system excels in label prediction, which might suggest the effectiveness of the relative label encoding. Furthermore, our system surpasses the best systems from the last year's semantic shared task, MRP 2019 (Oepen et al., 2019), by a wide margin – as can be seen in Table 5.

PERIN falls short in AMR[eng] parsing by 1.31 %. On closer inspection, this follows from the inferior edge accuracy on this framework – the difference to Hitachi is 4.56 % on AMR[eng] and 2.78 % on AMR[zho]. Furthermore, Hitachi is better in all aspects of EDS[eng] and DRG[deu]. On the other hand PERIN consistently beats Hitachi in both PTG and both UCCA frameworks. We hope that combining the strengths of these two parsers will help to further advance the state of meaning representation parsing.

4.1 Ablation Experiments

We conducted several additional experiments to evaluate the effects of various components of our architecture. The results are summarized in Table 4. We have decided to use EDS for these experiments because – in our eyes – it represents the "average" framework without any significant irregularities.

The experiments show that using the mixture of softmaxes for label prediction does not have a substantial effect and can be potentially omitted to reduce the parameter count. On the other hand, the inferior results of the model with constant equal loss weights demonstrate the importance of balancing them.

5 Conclusion

We introduced a novel permutation-invariant sentence-to-graph semantic parser called PERIN. Given its state-of-the-art performance across a number of frameworks, we believe permutation-invariant node prediction might be the first step in a promising direction of semantic parsing and generally of graph generation.

Acknowledgments

This work has been supported by the Grant Agency of the Czech Republic, project EXPRO LUSyD (GX20-16819X). It has also been supported by the Ministry of Education, Youth and Sports of the Czech Republic, Project No. LM2018101 LINDAT/CLARIAH-CZ.

References

Omri Abend and Ari Rappoport. 2013. Universal Conceptual Cognitive Annotation (UCCA). In *Proceedings of the 51st Annual Meeting of the Association for Computational Linguistics (Volume 1: Long Papers)*, pages 228–238, Sofia, Bulgaria. Association for Computational Linguistics.

Lasha Abzianidze, Johannes Bjerva, Kilian Evang, Hessel Haagsma, Rik van Noord, Pierre Ludmann, Duc-Duy Nguyen, and Johan Bos. 2017. The Parallel Meaning Bank: Towards a Multilingual Corpus of Translations Annotated with Compositional Meaning Representations. In *Proceedings of the 15th Conference of the European Chapter of the Association for Computational Linguistics: Volume 2, Short Papers*, pages 242–247, Valencia, Spain. Association for Computational Linguistics.

Betty van Aken, Benjamin Winter, Alexander Löser, and Felix A Gers. 2019. How does bert answer questions? a layer-wise analysis of transformer representations. In *Proceedings of the 28th ACM International Conference on Information and Knowledge Management*, pages 1823–1832.

Ofir Arviv, Ruixiang Cui, and Daniel Hershcovich. 2020. HUJI-KU at MRP 2020: Two Transition-based Neural Parsers. In *Proceedings of the CoNLL 2020 Shared Task: Cross-Framework Meaning Representation Parsing*, pages 73–82, Online.

Jimmy Lei Ba, Jamie Ryan Kiros, and Geoffrey E Hinton. 2016. Layer normalization. *arXiv preprint arXiv:1607.06450*.

Laura Banarescu, Claire Bonial, Shu Cai, Madalina Georgescu, Kira Griffitt, Ulf Hermjakob, Kevin Knight, Philipp Koehn, Martha Palmer, and Nathan Schneider. 2013. Abstract Meaning Representation for Sembanking. In *Proceedings of the 7th Linguistic Annotation Workshop and Interoperability with Discourse*, pages 178–186, Sofia, Bulgaria. Association for Computational Linguistics.

Deng Cai and Wai Lam. 2020. AMR Parsing via Graph-Sequence Iterative Inference. In *Proceedings of the 58th Annual Meeting of the Association for Computational Linguistics*, pages 1290–1301, Online. Association for Computational Linguistics.

Nicolas Carion, Francisco Massa, Gabriel Synnaeve, Nicolas Usunier, Alexander Kirillov, and Sergey Zagoruyko. 2020. End-to-End Object Detection with Transformers. *CoRR*, abs/2005.12872.

Wanxiang Che, Longxu Dou, Yang Xu, Yuxuan Wang, Yijia Liu, and Ting Liu. 2019. HIT-SCIR at MRP 2019: A Unified Pipeline for Meaning Representation Parsing via Efficient Training and Effective Encoding. In *Proceedings of the Shared Task on Cross-Framework Meaning Representation Parsing at the 2019 Conference on Computational Natural Language Learning*, pages 76–85, Hong Kong, China.

Zhao Chen, Vijay Badrinarayanan, Chen-Yu Lee, and Andrew Rabinovich. 2018. Gradnorm: Gradient normalization for adaptive loss balancing in deep multitask networks. In *International Conference on Machine Learning*, pages 794–803.

Alexis Conneau, Kartikay Khandelwal, Naman Goyal, Vishrav Chaudhary, Guillaume Wenzek, Francisco Guzmán, Edouard Grave, Myle Ott, Luke Zettlemoyer, and Veselin Stoyanov. 2020. Unsupervised Cross-lingual Representation Learning at Scale. In *Proceedings of the 58th Annual Meeting of the Association for Computational Linguistics*, pages 8440–8451, Online. Association for Computational Linguistics.

Jacob Devlin, Ming-Wei Chang, Kenton Lee, and Kristina Toutanova. 2019. BERT: Pre-training of Deep Bidirectional Transformers for Language Understanding. In *Proceedings of the 2019 Conference of the North American Chapter of the Association for Computational Linguistics: Human Language Technologies, Volume 1 (Long and Short Papers)*, pages 4171–4186, Minneapolis, Minnesota. Association for Computational Linguistics.

Longxu Dou, Yunlong Feng, Yuqiu Ji, Wanxiang Che, and Ting Liu. 2020. HIT-SCIR at MRP 2020: Transition-Based Parser and Iterative Inference Parser. In *Proceedings of the CoNLL 2020 Shared Task: Cross-Framework Meaning Representation Parsing*, pages 65–72, Online.

Timothy Dozat and Christopher D. Manning. 2017. Deep Biaffine Attention for Neural Dependency Parsing. In *5th International Conference on Learning Representations, ICLR 2017, Toulon, France, April 24-26, 2017, Conference Track Proceedings*. OpenReview.net.

Timothy Dozat and Christopher D. Manning. 2018. Simpler but More Accurate Semantic Dependency Parsing. In *Proceedings of the 56th Annual Meeting of the Association for Computational Linguistics (Volume 2: Short Papers)*, pages 484–490, Melbourne, Australia. Association for Computational Linguistics.

Jiatao Gu, Zhengdong Lu, Hang Li, and Victor O.K. Li. 2016. Incorporating Copying Mechanism in Sequence-to-Sequence Learning. In *Proceedings of the 54th Annual Meeting of the Association for Computational Linguistics (Volume 1: Long Papers)*, pages 1631–1640, Berlin, Germany. Association for Computational Linguistics.

Jan Hajic, Eva Hajicová, Jarmila Panevová, Petr Sgall, Ondrej Bojar, Silvie Cinková, Eva Fucíková, Marie Mikulová, Petr Pajas, Jan Popelka, et al. 2012. Announcing Prague Czech-English Dependency Treebank 2.0. In *LREC*, pages 3153–3160.

Daniel Hershcovich, Omri Abend, and Ari Rappoport. 2018. Multitask Parsing Across Semantic Representations. In *Proceedings of the 56th Annual Meeting of the Association for Computational Linguistics (Volume 1: Long Papers)*, pages 373–385, Melbourne, Australia. Association for Computational Linguistics.

Daniel Hershcovich, Zohar Aizenbud, Leshem Choshen, Elior Sulem, Ari Rappoport, and Omri Abend. 2019. SemEval-2019 Task 1: Cross-lingual Semantic Parsing with UCCA. In *Proceedings of the 13th International Workshop on Semantic Evaluation*, pages 1–10, Minneapolis, Minnesota, USA. Association for Computational Linguistics.

Jeremy Howard and Sebastian Ruder. 2018. Universal Language Model Fine-tuning for Text Classification. In *Proceedings of the 56th Annual Meeting of the Association for Computational Linguistics (Volume 1: Long Papers)*, pages 328–339, Melbourne, Australia. Association for Computational Linguistics.

Alexey Ignatiev, Antonio Morgado, and Joao Marques-Silva. 2019. RC2: An efficient MaxSAT solver. *Journal on Satisfiability, Boolean Modeling and Computation*, 11(1):53–64.

Alex Kendall, Yarin Gal, and Roberto Cipolla. 2018. Multi-task learning using uncertainty to weigh losses for scene geometry and semantics. In *Proceedings of the IEEE conference on computer vision and pattern recognition*, pages 7482–7491.

Dan Kondratyuk and Milan Straka. 2019. 75 Languages, 1 Model: Parsing Universal Dependencies Universally. In *Proceedings of the 2019 Conference on Empirical Methods in Natural Language Processing and the 9th International Joint Conference on Natural Language Processing (EMNLP-IJCNLP)*, pages 2779–2795, Hong Kong, China. Association for Computational Linguistics.

Marco Kuhlmann and Stephan Oepen. 2016. Towards a catalogue of linguistic graph banks. *Computational Linguistics*, 42(4):819–827.

Harold W Kuhn. 1955. The Hungarian method for the assignment problem. *Naval research logistics quarterly*, 2(1-2):83–97.

Sunny Lai, Chun Hei Lo, Kwong Sak Leung, and Yee Leung. 2019. CUHK at MRP 2019: Transition-Based Parser with Cross-Framework Variable-Arity Resolve Action. In *Proceedings of the Shared Task on Cross-Framework Meaning Representation Parsing at the 2019 Conference on Computational Natural Language Learning*, pages 104–113, Hong Kong, China.

Bin Li, Yuan Wen, Weiguang Qu, Lijun Bu, and Nianwen Xue. 2016. Annotating the little prince with chinese amrs. In *Proceedings of the 10th Linguistic Annotation Workshop held in conjunction with ACL 2016 (LAW-X 2016)*, pages 7–15.

Tsung-Yi Lin, Priya Goyal, Ross Girshick, Kaiming He, and Piotr Dollár. 2017. Focal loss for dense object detection. In *Proceedings of the IEEE international conference on computer vision*, pages 2980–2988.

Ilya Loshchilov and Frank Hutter. 2019. Decoupled Weight Decay Regularization. In *7th International Conference on Learning Representations, ICLR 2019, New Orleans, LA, USA, May 6-9, 2019*. OpenReview.net.

Ryan McDonald and Fernando Pereira. 2006. Online learning of approximate dependency parsing algorithms. In *11th Conference of the European Chapter of the Association for Computational Linguistics*.

Toan Q. Nguyen and Julian Salazar. 2019. Transformers without Tears: Improving the Normalization of Self-Attention. In *Proc. Workshop on Spoken Language Translation*.

Stephan Oepen, Omri Abend, Lasha Abzianidze, Johan Bos, Jan Hajič, Daniel Hershcovich, Bin Li, Tim O'Gorman, Nianwen Xue, and Daniel Zeman. 2020. MRP 2020: The Second Shared Task on Cross-Framework and Cross-Lingual Meaning Representation Parsing. In *Proceedings of the CoNLL 2020 Shared Task: Cross-Framework Meaning Representation Parsing*, pages 1–22, Online.

Stephan Oepen, Omri Abend, Jan Hajič, Daniel Hershcovich, Marco Kuhlmann, Tim O'Gorman, Nianwen Xue, Jayeol Chun, Milan Straka, and Zdeňka Urešová. 2019. MRP 2019: Cross-Framework Meaning Representation Parsing. In *Proceedings of the Shared Task on Cross-Framework Meaning Representation Parsing at the 2019 Conference on Computational Natural Language Learning*, pages 1–27, Hong Kong, China.

Stephan Oepen and Jan Tore Lønning. 2006. Discriminant-Based MRS Banking. In *LREC*, pages 1250–1255.

Hiroaki Ozaki, Gaku Morio, Yuta Koreeda, Terufumi Morishita, and Toshinori Miyoshi. 2020. Hitachi at MRP 2020: Text-to-Graph-Notation Transducer. In *Proceedings of the CoNLL 2020 Shared Task: Cross-Framework Meaning Representation Parsing*, pages 40–52, Online.

Xiaochang Peng, Chuan Wang, Daniel Gildea, and Nianwen Xue. 2017. Addressing the Data Sparsity Issue in Neural AMR Parsing. In *Proceedings of the 15th Conference of the European Chapter of the Association for Computational Linguistics: Volume 1, Long Papers*, pages 366–375, Valencia, Spain. Association for Computational Linguistics.

Charles R Qi, Hao Su, Kaichun Mo, and Leonidas J Guibas. 2017. Pointnet: Deep learning on point sets for 3d classification and segmentation. In *Proceedings of the IEEE conference on computer vision and pattern recognition*, pages 652–660.

Rob A Van der Sandt. 1992. Presupposition projection as anaphora resolution. *Journal of semantics*, 9(4):333–377.

Milan Straka and Jana Straková. 2019. ÚFAL MRPipe at MRP 2019: UDPipe Goes Semantic in the Meaning Representation Parsing Shared Task. In *Proceedings of the Shared Task on Cross-Framework Meaning Representation Parsing at the 2019 Conference on Computational Natural Language Learning*, pages 127–137, Hong Kong, China.

Milan Straka, Jana Straková, and Jan Hajic. 2019. UDPipe at SIGMORPHON 2019: Contextualized Embeddings, Regularization with Morphological Categories, Corpora Merging. In *Proceedings of the 16th Workshop on Computational Research in Phonetics, Phonology, and Morphology*, pages 95–103, Florence, Italy. Association for Computational Linguistics.

Christian Szegedy, Vincent Vanhoucke, Sergey Ioffe, Jon Shlens, and Zbigniew Wojna. 2016. Rethinking the inception architecture for computer vision. In *Proceedings of the IEEE conference on computer vision and pattern recognition*, pages 2818–2826.

Jörg Tiedemann and Santhosh Thottingal. 2020. OPUS-MT — Building open translation services for the World. In *Proceedings of the 22nd Annual Conferenec of the European Association for Machine Translation (EAMT)*, Lisbon, Portugal.

Zdeňka Urešová, Eva Fučíková, Jan Hajič, and Jana Šindlerová. 2015. CzEngVallex. LINDAT/CLARIAH-CZ digital library at the Institute of Formal and Applied Linguistics (ÚFAL), Faculty of Mathematics and Physics, Charles University.

Ashish Vaswani, Noam Shazeer, Niki Parmar, Jakob Uszkoreit, Llion Jones, Aidan N Gomez, Łukasz Kaiser, and Illia Polosukhin. 2017. Attention is all you need. In *Advances in neural information processing systems*, pages 5998–6008.

Thomas Wolf, Lysandre Debut, Victor Sanh, Julien Chaumond, Clement Delangue, Anthony Moi, Pierric Cistac, Tim Rault, Rémi Louf, Morgan Funtowicz, Joe Davison, Sam Shleifer, Patrick von Platen, Clara Ma, Yacine Jernite, Julien Plu, Canwen Xu, Teven Le Scao, Sylvain Gugger, Mariama Drame, Quentin Lhoest, and Alexander M. Rush. 2019. HuggingFace's Transformers: State-of-the-art Natural Language Processing. *ArXiv*, abs/1910.03771.

Zhilin Yang, Zihang Dai, Ruslan Salakhutdinov, and William W. Cohen. 2018. Breaking the Softmax Bottleneck: A High-Rank RNN Language Model. In *International Conference on Learning Representations*.

Manzil Zaheer, Satwik Kottur, Siamak Ravanbakhsh, Barnabas Poczos, Russ R Salakhutdinov, and Alexander J Smola. 2017. Deep sets. In *Advances in neural information processing systems*, pages 3391–3401.

Sheng Zhang, Xutai Ma, Kevin Duh, and Benjamin Van Durme. 2019a. AMR Parsing as Sequence-to-Graph Transduction. In *Proceedings of the 57th Annual Meeting of the Association for Computational Linguistics*, pages 80–94, Florence, Italy. Association for Computational Linguistics.

Yan Zhang, Jonathon Hare, and Adam Prugel-Bennett. 2019b. Deep set prediction networks. In *Advances in Neural Information Processing Systems*, pages 3212–3222.

HIT-SCIR at MRP 2020:
Transition-based Parser and Iterative Inference Parser

Longxu Dou, Yunlong Feng, Yuqiu Ji, Wanxiang Che, Ting Liu
Research Center for Social Computing and Information Retrieval
Harbin Institute of Technology, China
{lxdou,ylfeng,yqji,car,tliu}@ir.hit.edu.cn

Abstract

This paper describes our submission system (HIT-SCIR) for the *CoNLL 2020 shared task: Cross-Framework and Cross-Lingual Meaning Representation Parsing*. The task includes five frameworks for graph-based meaning representations, *i.e.*, UCCA, EDS, PTG, AMR, and DRG. Our solution consists of two subsystems: transition-based parser for Flavor (1) frameworks (UCCA, EDS, PTG) and iterative inference parser for Flavor (2) frameworks (DRG, AMR). In the final evaluation, our system is ranked 3rd among the seven team both in Cross-Framework Track and Cross-Lingual Track, with the macro-averaged MRP F1 score of 0.81/0.69.

1 Introduction

The goal of the CoNLL 2020 shared task (Oepen et al., 2020) is to develop a unified parsing system to process all five semantic graph banks across different languages. This task combines five frameworks for graph-based meaning representation, each with its specific formal and linguistic assumptions, including UCCA, EDS, PTG, AMR, and DRG. [1]

In the context of the shared task, the organizers distinguish different flavors of semantic graphs based on the nature of the relationship they assume between the linguistic surface string and the nodes of the graph. They call this relation *anchoring*. Therefore, the involved five frameworks could be divided into two classes: (a) **Flavor (1)**, including UCCA, EDS, and PTG, allowing arbitrary parts of the sentence as node anchors, as well as multiple nodes anchored to overlapping sub-strings, and (b) **Flavor (2)**, including AMR and DRG, not considering the correspondence between nodes and the surface tokens.

---

[1] See http://mrp.nlpl.eu/ for further technical details, information on how to obtain the data, and official results.

Our submitted system could be summarized in the following:

- **Transition-based Parser for Flavor (1)**

  Following Che et al. (2019), the top system in CoNLL 2019 shared task (Oepen et al., 2019), we employ the transition-based parser for Flavor (1) frameworks since it's very flexible in predicting the anchor information. We directly use their parser for UCCA and EDS. And we design a new parser for PTG.

- **Iterative Inference Parser for Flavor (2)**

  Recently, Cai and Lam (2020) proposed Graph⇔Sequence Iterative Inference system for AMR parsing, which treats parsing as a series of dual decisions on the input sequence and the incrementally constructed graph, achieving state-of-the-art results. We adopt their model for Flavor (2) frameworks (AMR, DRG).

- **Pretrained Language Model**

  Our systems benefit a lot from the pretrained language models, *i.e.*, BERT (Devlin et al., 2019), ELECTRA (Clark et al., 2020) and XLM-RoBERTa (Conneau et al., 2020).

2 Background

In the following, we will give a brief introduction to these frameworks and our corresponding solutions.

Universal Conceptual Cognitive Annotation (UCCA) is a multi-layer linguistic framework (Flavor (1)) firstly proposed by Abend and Rappoport (2013), which treats input words as terminal nodes. The non-terminal node might govern one or more nodes, which may be discontinuous. Moreover, one node can have multiple governing (parent) nodes through multiple edges, consisting of a single primary edge and other remote edges. Relationships

Proceedings of the CoNLL 2020 Shared Task: Cross-Framework Meaning Representation Parsing, pages 65–72
Online, Nov. 19-20, 2020. ©2020 Association for Computational Linguistics

between nodes are represented by edge labels. The primary edges form a tree structure, whereas the remote edges introduce reentrancy, forming directed acyclic graphs (DAGs). We directly employ the system of Che et al. (2019), which achieves the 1st at CoNLL 2019 shared task.

Elementary Dependency Structure (EDS) is a graph-structured semantic representation formalism (Flavor (1)) proposed by Oepen and Lønning (2006). Che et al. (2019) introduce a neural encoder-decoder transition-based parser for the EDS graph, which extracts the node alignment (or anchoring) information effectively.

Prague Tectogrammatical Graphs (PTG) are graph-structured multi-layered semantic representation formalism (Flavor (1)) proposed by Zeman and Hajič (2020). PTG graphs essentially recast core predicate–argument structure in the form of mostly anchored dependency graphs, albeit introducing 'empty' (or generated, in FGD terminology) nodes, for which there is no corresponding surface token. We didn't find any existing parser for PTG. Thus we design a list-based arc-eager transition-based parser for PTG.

Abstract Meaning Representation (AMR), proposed by Banarescu et al. (2013), is a broad-coverage sentence-level semantic formalism (Flavor (2)) used to encode the meaning of natural language sentences. AMR can be regarded as a rooted labeled directed acyclic graph. Nodes in AMR graphs represent concepts and labeled directed edges are relations between the concepts. We directly employ state-of-the-art parser of Cai and Lam (2020).

Discourse Representation Graphs (DRG) are proposed by Abzianidze et al. (2020) (Flavor (2)), which are derived from the DRS annotations in the Parallel Meaning Bank (Bos et al., 2017; Abzianidze et al., 2017). Its concepts are represented by WordNet 3.0 (Fellbaum, 1998) senses and semantic roles by the adapted version of VerbNet (Schuler, 2006) roles. Similar to PTG, we don't find any existing parser for DRG, thus we modify the AMR parser to process the DRG.

3 Transition-based Parser for Flavor (1)

3.1 Background

A tuple (S, L, B, E, V) is used to represent the parsing state, where S is a stack holding processed words, L is a list holding words popped out of S that will be pushed back in the future, and B is a buffer holding unprocessed words. E is a set of labeled dependency arcs. V is a set of graph nodes including concept nodes and surface tokens. The initial state is $([0], [\,], [1, \cdots, n], [\,], V)$, where V only contains surface tokens, whereas the concept nodes will be generated during parsing. And the terminal state is $([0], [\,], [\,], E, V')$. We model the S, L, B and action history with Stack-LSTM, which supports PUSH and POP operations. [2]

3.2 Transition Systems

For brevity, we omit the descriptions of the transition system for UCCA and EDS (Che et al., 2019). As for PTG, we propose a new arc-eager transition-based parser. To illustrate the transition-set and configuration more clearly, we list the transition process in Table 1 (UCCA), Table 2 (EDS) and Table 3 (PTG).

3.2.1 PTG

We are not aware of any parser specifically designed for PTG. But we found it is highly related to UCCA and EDS. Thus, based on the transition systems of UCCA and EDS and the definition of PTG (Čmejrek et al., 2004), we design a new system for PTG as shown in Table 3. x is the top element in the buffer and y is the top element in the stack. Moreover, y could only be a concept node (stack and list only contain concept nodes), and x could be a concept node or a surface token.

LEFT-EDGE$_X$, RIGHT-EDGE$_X$, SHIFT, DROP, REDUCE, PASS and FINISH are the same as EDS.

- SELF-EDGE$_X$ adds an arc with label X between x and itself.

- TERMINAL-NOLABEL creates new non-terminal nodes without label. These nodes have corresponding surface token(s) and their labels will be determined by rule, which will be introduced in Section 5.

- TERMINAL$_X$ creates new non-terminal nodes with label X.

- NODE$_X$ creates a new node on the buffer as a parent of the first element on the stack, with X as its label.

- NODE-ROOT$_X$ creates a new node on the buffer as a child of the root with X as its label.

---

[2]We recommend reading Dyer et al. (2015) for more details.

Before Transition				Transition	After Transition				Condition
Stack	**Buffer**	**Nodes**	**Edges**		**Stack**	**Buffer**	**Nodes**	**Edges**	
S	$x \mid B$	V	E	SHIFT	$S \mid x$	B	V	E	
$S \mid x$	B	V	E	REDUCE	S	B	V	E	
$S \mid x$	B	V	E	NODE$_X$	$S \mid x$	$y \mid B$	$V \cup \{y\}$	$E \cup \{(y,x)_X\}$	$x \neq$ root
$S \mid y,x$	B	V	E	LEFT-EDGE$_X$	$S \mid y,x$	B	V	$E \cup \{(x,y)_X\}$	
$S \mid x,y$	B	V	E	RIGHT-EDGE$_X$	$S \mid x,y$	B	V	$E \cup \{(x,y)_X\}$	$\begin{cases} x \notin w_{1:n}, \\ y \neq \text{root}, \\ y \not\rightsquigarrow_G x \end{cases}$
$S \mid y,x$	B	V	E	LEFT-REMOTE$_X$	$S \mid y,x$	B	V	$E \cup \{(x,y)_X^*\}$	
$S \mid x,y$	B	V	E	RIGHT-REMOTE$_X$	$S \mid x,y$	B	V	$E \cup \{(x,y)_X^*\}$	
$S \mid x,y$	B	V	E	SWAP	$S \mid y$	$x \mid B$	V	E	$\mathrm{i}(x) < \mathrm{i}(y)$
[root]	$\emptyset$	V	E	FINISH	$\emptyset$	$\emptyset$	V	E	

Table 1: The transition set of UCCA parser. We write the **Stack** with its top to the right and the **Buffer** with its head to the left. $(\cdot,\cdot)_X$ denotes a primary X-labeled edge, and $(\cdot,\cdot)_X^*$ a remote X-labeled edge. $\mathrm{i}(x)$ is a running index for the created nodes. In addition to the specified conditions, the prospective child in an EDGE transition must not already have a primary parent. From (Hershcovich et al., 2017).

Before Transition					Transition	After Transition					Condition
Stack	**List**	**Buffer**	**Nodes**	**Edges**		**Stack**	**List**	**Buffer**	**Nodes**	**Edges**	
S	L	$x \mid B$	V	E	SHIFT	$S \mid L \mid x$	$\emptyset$	B	V	E	concept(x)
$S \mid x$	L	B	V	E	REDUCE	S	L	B	V	E	
$S \mid x$	L	$y \mid B$	V	E	RIGHT-EDGE$_X$	$S \mid x$	L	$y \mid B$	V	$E \cup \{(x,y)_X\}$	concept(x) $\wedge$ concept(y)
$S \mid y$	L	$x \mid B$	V	E	LEFT-EDGE$_X$	$S \mid y$	L	$x \mid B$	V	$E \cup \{(x,y)_X\}$	concept(x) $\wedge$ concept(y)
$S \mid x$	L	B	V	E	PASS	S	$x \mid L$	B	V	E	
S	L	$x \mid B$	V	E	DROP	$S \mid L$	$\emptyset$	B	V	E	token(x)
S	L	$x \mid B$	V	E	TOP	S	L	$x \mid B$	$V \cup \mathrm{Top}(x)$	E	concept(x)
S	L	$x \mid B$	V	E	NODE-START$_X$	$S \mid y$	L	$x \mid B$	$V \cup \{y_{start=x,label=X}\}$	E	token(x)
$S \mid y$	L	$x \mid B$	V	E	NODE-END	$S \mid y$	L	$x \mid B$	$V \cup \{y_{end=x}\}$	E	token(x)
[root]	$\emptyset$	$\emptyset$	V	E	FINISH	$\emptyset$	$\emptyset$	$\emptyset$	V	E	

Table 2: The transition set of EDS parser. We write the **Stack** with its top to the right, the **Buffer** with its head to the left and the **List** with its head to the left. The elements in **Stack** and **List** are all concept nodes. Indicator function token(x) means x is a token of the sentence, while concept(x) means it's a concept node. Top(x) indicates x is the top node. $y_{start=w_i,label=X,end=w_j}$ indicates the alignments of concept node y is starting at token w_i, ending at token w_j and its label is X.

Before Transition					Transition	After Transition					Condition
Stack	**List**	**Buffer**	**Nodes**	**Edges**		**Stack**	**List**	**Buffer**	**Nodes**	**Edges**	
S	L	$x \mid B$	V	E	SHIFT	$S \mid L \mid x$	$\emptyset$	B	V	E	concept(x)
$S \mid x$	L	B	V	E	REDUCE	S	L	B	V	E	
$S \mid x$	L	$y \mid B$	V	E	RIGHT-EDGE$_X$	$S \mid x$	L	$y \mid B$	V	$E \cup \{(x,y)_X\}$	
$S \mid y$	L	$x \mid B$	V	E	LEFT-EDGE$_X$	$S \mid y$	L	$x \mid B$	V	$E \cup \{(x,y)_X\}$	
$S \mid y$	L	$x \mid B$	V	E	SELF-EDGE$_X$	$S \mid y$	L	$x \mid B$	V	$E \cup \{(x,x)_X\}$	
$S \mid x$	L	B	V	E	PASS	S	$x \mid L$	B	V	E	
S	L	$x \mid B$	V	E	DROP	$S \mid L$	$\emptyset$	B	V	E	token(x)
S	L	$x \mid B$	V	E	NODE$_X$	S	L	$y \mid x \mid B$	$V \cup \{y_{label=X}\}$	E	token(x)
S	L	$x \mid B$	V	E	NODE-ROOT$_X$	S	L	$y \mid x \mid B$	$V \cup \{y_{label=X}\}$	E	root(x)
S	L	$x \mid B$	V	E	TERMINAL-NOLABEL	S	L	$y \mid x \mid B$	$V \cup \{y\}$	E	
S	L	$x \mid B$	V	E	TERMINAL$_X$	S	L	$y \mid x \mid B$	$V \cup \{y_{label=X}\}$	E	
[root]	$\emptyset$	$\emptyset$	V	E	FINISH	$\emptyset$	$\emptyset$	$\emptyset$	V	E	

Table 3: The transition set of PTG parser. We write the **Stack** with its top to the right, the **Buffer** with its head to the left and the **List** with its head to the left. The elements in **Stack** and **List** are all concept nodes. Indicator function token(x) means x is a token of the sentence, while concept(x) means it's a concept node. root(x) indicates x is the top node.

The differences between TERMINAL and NODE are (a) TERMINAL generates the node ahead of NODE in the oracle transition sequence, which means the nodes generated by TERMINAL are more closer to the surface tokens, and (b) TERMINAL could generate the concept node that aligns to surface tokens(s) while NODE could only generates the node with the particular label.

4 Iterative Inference Parser for Flavor (2)

4.1 Overview

We adopt the Graph⇔Sequence Iterative Inference system proposed by Cai and Lam (2020) to parse the Flavor (2) graphs. We name it iterative inference parser in this paper. At each time step, the model performs multiple rounds of attention, reasoning, and composition that aim to answer two critical questions: (a) which part of the input sequence to abstract, and (b) where in the output graph to construct the new concept.

4.2 Implementation

This model consists of four modules:

- **Sentence Encoder** encodes the input sequence and generates a set of text memories to provide grounding for concept node generation.

- **Graph Encoder** encodes the partial graph and generate a set of graph memories to provide grounding for relation prediction.

- **Concept Solver** uses the graph hypothesis for concept node generation.

- **Graph Solver** uses the concept node hypothesis for relation prediction.

The last two components correspond to the reasoning functions $g(\cdot)$ and $f(\cdot)$ respectively.

More specifically, at the beginning of parsing, Sentence Encoder computes the text memories, while Graph Encoder constructs the graph memories incrementally.[3] During the iterative inference, a semantic representation of the current state is used to attend to both graph and text memories to locate the new concept and obtain its relations to the existing graph, both of which subsequently refine each other. Then in each step, Concept Solver generates the concept node and Relation Solver predicts the relation between the concept node with other node(s) through attention.[4]

This process could be described as follows:

$$y_t^i = g(G^i, x_t^i),$$
$$x_{t+1}^i = f(W, y_t^i),$$

where W and G^i are the input sentence and the current semantic graph respectively. $g(\cdot)$ looks for where to construct (edge prediction) and $f(\cdot)$ seeks what to abstract (node prediction) respectively. The x_t^i, y_t^i are the $t-$th graph hypothesis and the $t-$th sequence hypothesis for the $i-$th expansion step respectively.

In summary, Iterative Inference Parser uses a sentence encoder to encode the input sequence and a graph encoder to build the graph iteratively. In each step, the parser uses the graph state and the sentence representation to generate a new concept node and build the relation between the concept node and other parts of the graph.[5]

5 Pre-processing and Post-processing

In this session, we introduce the pre-processing and post-processing work. The MRP graph can be broken down into seven component pieces: top nodes, node labels, node properties, node anchoring, directed edges, edge labels, and edge attributes.

The directed edges, edge labels, and node id form the standard input of our system. For node anchoring, we directly derive the anchoring information through segmentation from companion data. For other elements, such as top nodes, are a bit different among the frameworks. We will introduce these framework-specific work in the following.

5.1 UCCA

Top Nodes There is only one top node for each sentence in UCCA, which is used to initialize the stack. Meanwhile, the top node is the protected symbol of the stack (which will never be popped out).

Edge Properties The edge property in UCCA is used as the sign for remote edges. We treat remote edges in the same way as primary edges, except for those with a special star (*) symbol.

---

[3]In the beginning, we represent the empty graph with a special symbol: BOG (begin of graph).

[4]The iterative process between concept node generation and relation prediction will last until the concept solver predicts a special symbol: EOG (end of graph).

[5]More details could be found in the original paper (Cai and Lam, 2020).

Node Anchoring Referring to the original UCCA framework design, we link the node in the foundational layer to the surface token with the edge label 'Terminal'. In post-processing, we combine surface tokens and foundational layer nodes via collapsing 'Terminal' edge to extract the anchor information.

5.2 EDS

Top Nodes The TOP operation will set the first concept node in the buffer as top node.

Node Labels We train a tagger to predict the node labels. The tagger is directly adopted from AllenNLP. Although there are thousands of node labels, the result shows our system performs well on this.

Node Properties We count the co-occurrence of node_label, upos, dep and property value in the training dataset, and select the property based on the co-occurrence statistics in the predicting procedure. If the triple (node_label, upos, dep) is not found, we backoff to the tuple (upos, dep).[6]

Node Anchoring We obtain alignment information through NODE_START and NODE_END operation.

5.3 PTG

The original PTG is not a directed acyclic graph (DAG). We find that all the cycles are caused by *coref.gram* edges. Thus we reverse these edges to convert PTG to DAG to avoid this problem.

Top Nodes The top node of PTG is the root of the stack, which is used to initialize the stack.

Node Labels We obtain the node label through a rule-based method: (1) collecting the tokens that node aligns to, and (2) setting the node label as the lemma of one of the tokens. Which token to be chosen is determined by a rule considering the pos-tag, dependency tree.

Node Properties Similar to EDS, we used the statistic-based method to compute the properties.

Node Anchoring We obtain alignment information through NODE or TERMINAL operation.

5.4 AMR

The original definition of AMR consists of TOP NODES, NODE LABELS and NODE PROPERTIES. Thus we directly used the system's output.

5.5 DRG

The DRG parsing system is based on the parser of AMR (Cai and Lam, 2020). Before training, we need to convert DRG to AMR. After prediction, we recover it reversely. More specifically, we attach the *unreal* label to the unlabeled node of DRG to satisfy the requirement of AMR that all nodes must have a label. The labeled node of DRG can be divided into three types:

- **Abstract Node** Such nodes are representing comparison relations, *e.g.*, EQU, which is usually uppercased.

- **Labeled Node with property**: We split the node into the label part and property parts. For example, impossible.a.01 could be spilt into label part (impossible) and property parts (a and 01). Then we add two edges with the label 'op' from label part to property parts.

- **Labeled Node without property**: Such node are covered by double quotes, like "now". We simply copy the node label to the AMR graph ignoring the double quotes. We will add them back during post-processing.

6 Experiments

In this section, we will show the basic model setup and overall evaluation results.

6.1 Model Setup

Transition-based Parser Based on the system of Che et al. (2019), we build the transition-based parser for UCCA, EDS, and PTG. We split parameters into two groups, *i.e.*, BERT parameters and other parameters (base parameters). The two parameter groups differ in the learning rate. For training, we use the Adam optimizer (Kingma and Ba, 2015).

Iterative Inference Parser Based on the system of Cai and Lam (2020), we build the parser for AMR and DRG.[7]

Code for our parser and model weights are available at https://github.com/DreamerDeo/HIT-SCIR-CoNLL2020.

---

[6]The 'upos' and 'dep' are obtained from corresponding companion data, which refers to the upos-tag of the token(s) that the concept node aligns to, and the label of the edge between the token(s) and its parents in the dependency tree.

[7]https://github.com/jcyk/AMR-gs

System	UCCA	EDS	PTG	AMR	DRG	ALL
Hitachi	0.75	0.94	0.89	0.82	0.93	0.86
UFAL	0.76	0.93	0.88	0.80	0.94	0.86
HIT-SCIR	0.75	0.87	0.84	0.70	0.89	0.81
HUJI-KU	0.73	0.80	0.54	0.52	0.63	0.64
ISCAS	0.06	0.86	0.18	0.61	0.69	0.48
TJU-BLCU	0.10	0.49	0.21	0.3	0.40	0.30

Table 4: Evaluation results on Cross-Framework Track upon MRP F1.

System	UCCA	PTG	AMR	DRG	ALL
UFAL	0.81	0.91	0.78	0.90	0.85
Hitachi	0.79	0.87	0.80	0.93	0.85
HIT-SCIR	0.80	0.78	0.49	0.68	0.69
HUJI-KU	0.75	0.58	0.45	0.62	0.60

Table 5: Evaluation results on Cross-Lingual Track upon MRP F1.

6.2 Fine-Tuning BERT with Parser

Based on Devlin et al. (2019), fine-tuning BERT with supervised downstream task will receive the most benefit. So we choose to fine-tune BERT model together with the original parser. In our preliminary study, gradual unfreezing and slanted triangular learning rate scheduler is essential for BERT fine-tuning model.

We find it beneficial to warm up the learning rate at beginning of training progress and cool down after. With the slanted triangular learning rate scheduler, the learning rate increases linearly from $lr/ratio$ to lr during the first $num\_step \times cut\_frac$ steps and decreases linearly back to $lr/ratio$ during the left steps.

Gradual unfreezing is also used during training so in the first few $(1 \sim 5)$ epochs BERT parameters are frozen. While being gradually unfrozen, the learning rate experiences a full warm-up and cool-down cycle per epoch. And then a full cycle is performed during the rest training progress once all parameters are unfrozen. Batch normalization (Sergey and Christian, 2015) is useful when avoiding the gradient exploding during training UCCA and EDS.

6.3 Hyperparameters

Pretrained Language Model The model choices for each framework across two tracks, are listed in Table 6.

Transition-based Parser Following Che et al. (2019), we adopt the hyper-parameters listed in Table 7.

Iterative Inference Parser Following Cai and Lam (2020), we perform $N = 4$ steps of iterative inference. Other hyper-parameter settings can be found in the Table 8.

6.4 Overall Evaluation Results and Analysis

We list the evaluation results on Table 4 and Table 5, which is ranked by the cross-framework metric, named macro-averaged MRP F1.[8]

For Flavor (1) framework, our transition-based parser is a local-decision model. Thus, our parser cannot effectively use global information when predicting the attributes of graph nodes, resulting in some more complex structures that can not be effectively generated. On another hand, our system in UCCA achieves nearly state-of-the-art performance but falls behind in EDS and PTG. We argue that the main reason is that we obtain the properties by the statistic-based way instead of training a specific model, which lower the overall performance in EDS and PTG.

For Flavor (2) framework, we suppose that the main reason for the performance degradation in AMR is the entity vocabulary, which is obtained in AMR2.0 from Cai and Lam (2020) and doesn't match the MRP2020-AMR very well. Based on our experience, the AMR parser will benefit a lot from a high-quality entity vocabulary.

7 Conclusion

In this paper, we describe our submission system for the CoNLL 2020 shared task. We separate

---

[8]Evaluation results of CoNLL 2020 shared task are available at `http://bit.ly/cfmrp20`.

Track	Cross-Framework	Cross-Lingual
UCCA	BERT-Base	BERT-Base German
EDS	BERT-Base	-
PTG	BERT-Base	BERT-Base Multilingual
AMR	ELECTRA-Large	ELECTRA-Large Chinese
DRG	ELECTRA-Large	XLM-RoBERTa-Large

Table 6: The pretrained language model used in each track .

HYPERPARAMETER	VALUE
Hidden dimension	200
Action dimension	50
Optimizer	Adam
β_1, β_2	0.9, 0.99
Dropout	0.5
Layer dropout	0.2
Recurrent dropout	0.2
Input dropout	0.2
Batch size	16
Epochs	50
Base learning rate	1×10^{-3}
BERT learning rate	5×10^{-5}
Gradient clipping	5.0
Gradient norm	5.0
Learning rate scheduler	slanted triangular
Gradual Unfreezing	True
Cut Frac	0.1
Ratio	32

Table 7: Transition-based parser hyper-parameters settings.

HYPERPARAMETER	VALUE
lemma dimension	300
NER dimension	16
POS dimension	32
concept dimension	300
char dimension	32
CNN	
filters	256
filter size	3
output size	128
Transformer	
heads	8
hidden size	512
feed-forward hidden size	1024
Sentence Encoder transformer layers	4
Graph Encoder transformer layers	2
Concept Solver feed-forward hidden size	1024
Releation Solver feed-forward hidden size	1024
Releation Solver feed-forward heads	8
Deep biaffine classifier hidden size	100

Table 8: Iterative Inference parser hyper-parameters settings.

our solutions into two classes based on the flavor of the framework: (a) transition-based parser for Flavor (1) (UCCA, EDS, PTG), and (b) iterative inference parser for Flavor (2) (AMR, DRG). Especially, we propose a new transition-based parser for the PTG framework, which achieves comparable performance. In the final evaluation, our system positions at 3rd in both tracks.

Acknowledgments

We thank the reviewers for their insightful comments and the HIT-SCIR colleagues for the coordination on the machine usage. This work was supported by the National Natural Science Foundation of China (NSFC) via grant 61976072, 61632011 and 61772153.

References

Omri Abend and Ari Rappoport. 2013. Universal conceptual cognitive annotation (UCCA). In *ACL*, pages 228–238.

Lasha Abzianidze, Johannes Bjerva, Kilian Evang, Hessel Haagsma, Rik van Noord, Pierre Ludmann, Duc-Duy Nguyen, and Johan Bos. 2017. The parallel meaning bank: Towards a multilingual corpus of translations annotated with compositional meaning representations. In *EACL*, pages 242–247.

Lasha Abzianidze, Johan Bos, and Stephan Oepen. 2020. DRS at MRP 2020: Dressing up Discourse Representation Structures as graphs. In *Proceedings of the CoNLL 2020 Shared Task: Cross-Framework Meaning Representation Parsing*, pages 23 – 32, Online.

Laura Banarescu, Claire Bonial, Shu Cai, Madalina Georgescu, Kira Griffitt, Ulf Hermjakob, Kevin Knight, Philipp Koehn, Martha Palmer, and Nathan Schneider. 2013. Abstract meaning representation for sembanking. In *Proceedings of the 7th Linguistic Annotation Workshop and Interoperability with Discourse*, pages 178–186.

Johan Bos, Valerio Basile, Kilian Evang, Noortje J. Venhuizen, and Johannes Bjerva. 2017. *The Groningen Meaning Bank*, pages 463–496.

Deng Cai and Wai Lam. 2020. AMR parsing via graph-sequence iterative inference. In *ACL*, pages 1290–1301.

Wanxiang Che, Longxu Dou, Yang Xu, Yuxuan Wang, Yijia Liu, and Ting Liu. 2019. HIT-SCIR at MRP 2019: A unified pipeline for meaning representation parsing via efficient training and effective encoding. In *Proceedings of the Shared Task on Cross-Framework Meaning Representation Parsing at the 2019 Conference on Computational Natural Language Learning*, pages 76 – 85, Hong Kong, China.

Kevin Clark, Minh-Thang Luong, Quoc V. Le, and Christopher D. Manning. 2020. ELECTRA: Pre-training text encoders as discriminators rather than generators. In *ICLR*.

Martin Čmejrek, Jan Cuřín, and Jiří Havelka. 2004. Prague Czech-English dependency treebank: Any hopes for a common annotation scheme? In *HLT-NAACL*, pages 47–54.

Alexis Conneau, Kartikay Khandelwal, Naman Goyal, Vishrav Chaudhary, Guillaume Wenzek, Francisco Guzmán, Edouard Grave, Myle Ott, Luke Zettlemoyer, and Veselin Stoyanov. 2020. Unsupervised cross-lingual representation learning at scale. In *ACL*, pages 8440–8451.

Jacob Devlin, Ming-Wei Chang, Kenton Lee, and Kristina Toutanova. 2019. BERT: Pre-training of deep bidirectional transformers for language understanding. In *NAACL-HLT*, pages 4171–4186.

Chris Dyer, Miguel Ballesteros, Wang Ling, Austin Matthews, and Noah A. Smith. 2015. Transition-based dependency parsing with stack long short-term memory. In *ACL and IJCNLP*, pages 334–343.

Christiane Fellbaum. 1998. *WordNet: An Electronic Lexical Database*. Bradford Books.

Daniel Hershcovich, Omri Abend, and Ari Rappoport. 2017. A transition-based directed acyclic graph parser for UCCA. In *ACL*, pages 1127–1138.

Diederik P. Kingma and Jimmy Ba. 2015. Adam: A method for stochastic optimization. In *ICLR*.

Stephan Oepen, Omri Abend, Lasha Abzianidze, Johan Bos, Jan Hajič, Daniel Hershcovich, Bin Li, Tim O'Gorman, Nianwen Xue, and Daniel Zeman. 2020. MRP 2020: The Second Shared Task on Cross-framework and Cross-Lingual Meaning Representation Parsing. In *Proceedings of the CoNLL 2020 Shared Task: Cross-Framework Meaning Representation Parsing*, pages 1 – 22, Online.

Stephan Oepen, Omri Abend, Jan Hajič, Daniel Hershcovich, Marco Kuhlmann, Tim O'Gorman, Nianwen Xue, Jayeol Chun, Milan Straka, and Zdeňka Urešová. 2019. MRP 2019: Cross-framework Meaning Representation Parsing. In *Proceedings of the Shared Task on Cross-Framework Meaning Representation Parsing at the 2019 Conference on Computational Natural Language Learning*, pages 1 – 27, Hong Kong, China.

Stephan Oepen and Jan Tore Lønning. 2006. Discriminant-based MRS banking. In *Proceedings of the Fifth International Conference on Language Resources and Evaluation (LREC'06)*.

Karin Kipper Schuler. 2006. *VerbNet: A Broad-Coverage, Comprehensive Verb Lexicon*. Ph.D. thesis.

Ioffe Sergey and Szegedy Christian. 2015. Batch normalization: Accelerating deep network training by reducing internal covariate shift. In *ICML*.

Daniel Zeman and Jan Hajič. 2020. FGD at MRP 2020: Prague Tectogrammatical Graphs. In *Proceedings of the CoNLL 2020 Shared Task: Cross-Framework Meaning Representation Parsing*, pages 33 – 39, Online.

HUJI-KU at MRP 2020: Two Transition-based Neural Parsers

Ofir Arviv[*], **Ruixiang Cui**[**], and **Daniel Hershcovich**[**]

[*]Hebrew University of Jerusalem, School of Computer Science and Engineering
[**]University of Copenhagen, Department of Computer Science
`ofir.arviv@mail.huji.ac.il`, `{rc,dh}@di.ku.dk`

Abstract

This paper describes the HUJI-KU system submission to the shared task on Cross-Framework Meaning Representation Parsing (MRP) at the 2020 Conference for Computational Language Learning (CoNLL), employing TUPA and the HIT-SCIR parser, which were, respectively, the baseline system and winning system in the 2019 MRP shared task. Both are transition-based parsers using BERT contextualized embeddings. We generalized TUPA to support the newly-added MRP frameworks and languages, and experimented with multitask learning with the HIT-SCIR parser. We reached 4th place in both the cross-framework and cross-lingual tracks.

1 Introduction

The CoNLL 2020 MRP Shared Task (Oepen et al., 2020) combines five frameworks for graph-based meaning representation: EDS, PTG, UCCA, AMR and DRG. It further includes evaluations in English, Czech, German and Chinese. While EDS, UCCA and AMR participated in the 2019 MRP shared task (Oepen et al., 2019), which focused only on English, PTG and DRG are newly-added frameworks to the MRP uniform format.

For this shared task, we extended TUPA (Hershcovich et al., 2017), which was adapted as the baseline system in the 2019 MRP shared task (Hershcovich and Arviv, 2019), to support the two new frameworks and the different languages. In order to add this support, only minimal changes were needed, demonstrating TUPA's strength in parsing a wide array of representations. TUPA is a general transition-based parser for directed acyclic graphs (DAGs), originally designed for parsing UCCA (Abend and Rappoport, 2013). It was previously used as the baseline system in SemEval 2019 Task 1 (Hershcovich et al., 2019), and generalized to support other frameworks (Hershcovich

et al., 2018a,b).

We also experimented with the HIT-SCIR parser (Che et al., 2019). This was the parser with the highest average score across frameworks in the 2019 MRP shared task, and has also since been applied to other frameworks (Hershcovich et al., 2020).

2 TUPA-MRP

TUPA (Hershcovich et al., 2017) is a transition-based parser supporting general DAG parsing. The parser state is composed of a buffer B of tokens and nodes to be processed, a stack S of nodes currently being processed, and an incrementally constructed graph G. The input to the parser is a sequence of tokens: $w_1, \ldots, w_n$. A classifier is trained using an oracle to select the next transition based on features encoding the parser's current state, where the training objective is to maximize the sum of log-likelihoods of all gold transitions at each step.

The MRP variant (Hershcovich and Arviv, 2019) supports node and edge labels, as well as node properties and edge attributes. The code is publicly available.[1]

2.1 Transition set

The TUPA-MRP transition set, shown in Figure 1, is the same as the one used by Hershcovich and Arviv (2019). It includes the transitions SHIFT and REDUCE to manipulate the stack, NODE$_X$ to create nodes compositionally, CHILD$_X$ to create unanchored children, LABEL$_X$ to label nodes, PROPERTY$_X$ to set node properties, LEFT-EDGE$_X$ and RIGHT-EDGE$_X$ to create edges, ATTRIBUTE$_X$ to set edge attributes, SWAP to allow non-planar graphs and FINISH to terminate the sequence.

---

[1] `https://github.com/danielhers/tupa/tree/mrp`

Proceedings of the CoNLL 2020 Shared Task: Cross-Framework Meaning Representation Parsing, pages 73–82
Online, Nov. 19-20, 2020. ©2020 Association for Computational Linguistics

Before Transition				Transition	After Transition				
Stack	Buffer	N.	Edges		Stack	Buffer	Nodes	Edges	Extra Effect
S	$x \mid B$	V	E	SHIFT	$S \mid x$	B	V	E	
$S \mid x$	B	V	E	REDUCE	S	B	V	E	
$S \mid x$	B	V	E	NODE$_X$	$S \mid x$	$y \mid B$	$V \cup \{y\}$	$E \mid (y,x)$	$\ell_E(y,x) \leftarrow X$
$S \mid x$	B	V	E	CHILD$_X$	$S \mid x$	$y \mid B$	$V \cup \{y\}$	$E \mid (x,y)$	$\ell_E(x,y) \leftarrow X$
$S \mid x$	B	V	E	LABEL$_X$	$S \mid x$	B	V	E	$\ell_V(x) \leftarrow X$
$S \mid x$	B	V	E	PROPERTY$_X$	$S \mid x$	B	V	E	$p(x) \leftarrow p(x) \cup \{X\}$
$S \mid y,x$	B	V	E	LEFT-EDGE$_X$	$S \mid y,x$	B	V	$E \mid (x,y)$	$\ell_E(x,y) \leftarrow X$
$S \mid x,y$	B	V	E	RIGHT-EDGE$_X$	$S \mid x,y$	B	V	$E \mid (x,y)$	$\ell_E(x,y) \leftarrow X$
S	B	V	$E \mid (x,y)$	ATTRIBUTE$_X$	S	B	V	$E \mid (x,y)$	$a(x,y) \leftarrow a(x,y) \cup \{X\}$
$S \mid x,y$	B	V	E	SWAP	$S \mid y$	$x \mid B$	V	E	
[root]	$\emptyset$	V	E	FINISH	$\emptyset$	$\emptyset$	V	E	terminal state

Figure 1: The TUPA-MRP transition set, from Hershcovich and Arviv (2019). We write the stack with its top to the right and the buffer with its head to the left; the set of edges is also ordered with the latest edge on the right. NODE, LABEL, PROPERTY and ATTRIBUTE require that $x \neq$ root; CHILD, LABEL, PROPERTY, LEFT-EDGE and RIGHT-EDGE require that $x \notin w_{1:n}$; ATTRIBUTE requires that $y \notin w_{1:n}$; LEFT-EDGE and RIGHT-EDGE require that $y \neq$ root and that there is no directed path from y to x; and SWAP requires that i$(x) <$ i(y), where i(x) is a running index for nodes. ℓ_E and ℓ_V are respectively the edge and node labeling functions. $p(x)$ is the set of node x's properties, and $a(x,y)$ is the set of edge (x,y)'s attributes.

2.2 Transition Classifier

To predict the next transition at each step, TUPA uses a BiLSTM module followed by an MLP and a softmax layer for classification (Kiperwasser and Goldberg, 2016). The BiLSTM module is applied before the transition sequence starts, running over the input tokenized sequence. It consists of a pre-BiLSTM MLP with feature embeddings (§2.3) and pre-trained contextualized BERT (Devlin et al., 2019) embeddings concatenated as inputs, followed by (multiple layers of) a bidirectional recurrent neural network (Schuster and Paliwal, 1997; Graves, 2008) with a long short-term memory cell (Hochreiter and Schmidhuber, 1997).

Whenever a LABEL$_X$/PROPERTY$_X$/ATTRIBUTE$_X$ transition is selected, an additional classifier is evoked with the set of possible label/property/attribute values for the currently parsed framework, respectively, as possible outputs. This hard separation is made due to the large number of node labels and properties in the MRP frameworks.

2.3 Features

In both training and testing, we use vector embeddings representing the lemmas, coarse POS tags (UPOS) and fine-grained POS tags (XPOS). These feature values are provided by UDPipe as companion data by the task organizers. In addition, we use punctuation and gap type features (Maier and Lichte, 2016), and previously predicted node and edge labels, node properties, edge attributes and parser actions. These embeddings are initialized randomly (Glorot and Bengio, 2010).

To the feature embeddings, we concatenate numeric features representing the node height, number of parents and children, and the ratio between the number of terminals to total number of nodes in the graph G (Hershcovich et al., 2017). Numeric features are taken as they are, whereas categorical features are mapped to real-valued embedding vectors. For each non-terminal node, we select a *head terminal* for feature extraction, by traversing down the graph, selecting the first outgoing edge each time according to alphabetical order of labels.

2.4 Intermediate Graph Representation

We mostly reuse Hershcovich and Arviv (2019)'s internal representation of MRP graphs in TUPA, where top nodes and anchoring are combined into the graph by adding a virtual root node and virtual terminal nodes, respectively, during preprocessing. Similarly, we introduce placeholders in the node labels and properties matching the tokens they are aligned to, and collapse AMR name properties. In the case of DRG and PTG, the newly added frameworks, where graphs may contains cycles, we break those cycles in order for them to be parseable by TUPA, which supports general DAG parsing. Only 0.27% of the DRG graphs in the provided dataset are cyclic. In the case of PTG, 33.97% are cyclic. Figure 2 shows an example PTG graph, and Figure 3 the graph in TUPA's intermediate representation. As the latter demon-

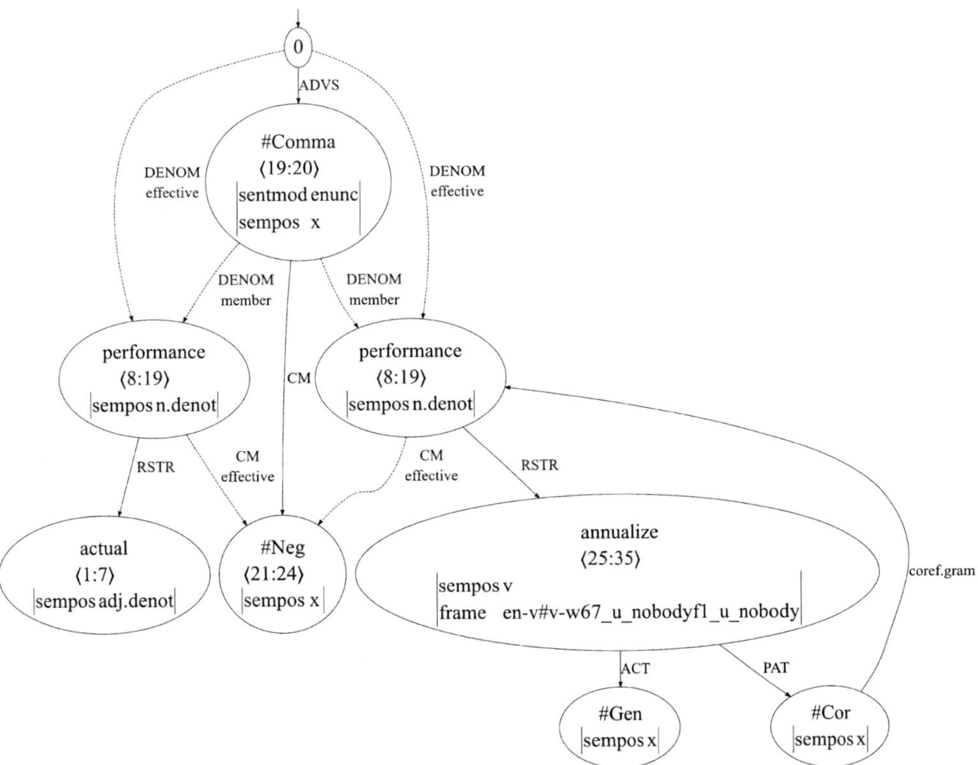

Figure 2: PTG graph, in the MRP formalism, for the sentence "*Actual performance, not annualized". Edge labels are shown on the edges. Node labels are shown inside the nodes, along with any node properties (in the form `|property value|`). Anchoring is also provided for PTG.

strates, cycles are broken by removing an arbitrary edge in the cycle (the `coref.gram` edge in this case).

2.5 Constraints

As each framework has different constraints on the allowed graph structures, we apply these constraints separately for each one. During training and parsing, the relevant constraint set rules out some of the transitions according to the parser state.

Some constraints are task-specific, others are generic. For the new frameworks, DRG and PTG, all the constraints, except for one (PTG being multigraph), are derived from the graph properties as defined by their component pieces.[2] For example, both require node labels, but only PTG requires node properties. No new types of constraints were needed to be added to TUPA to support these frameworks.

2.6 Training details

The model is implemented using DyNet v2.1 (Neubig et al., 2017).[3] Unless otherwise noted, we use the default values provided by the package. We use the same hyperparameters as Hershcovich and Arviv (2019), without any hyperparameter tuning on the CoNLL 2020 data.

We use the weighted sum of last four hidden layers of a BERT (Devlin et al., 2019) pre-trained model[4] as extra input features, summing over wordpiece vectors to get word representations.

2.7 Cross-framework track

In the cross-framework track, we use the English `bert-large-cased` pre-trained encoder, and train separate TUPA models for each of the PTG, UCCA, AMR and DRG frameworks. Table 1 shows the number of training epochs per framework, as well as validation and evaluation results.

[2]`http://mrp.nlpl.eu/2020/index.php?page=15`

[3]`http://dynet.io`
[4]`https://github.com/huggingface/pytorch-transformers`

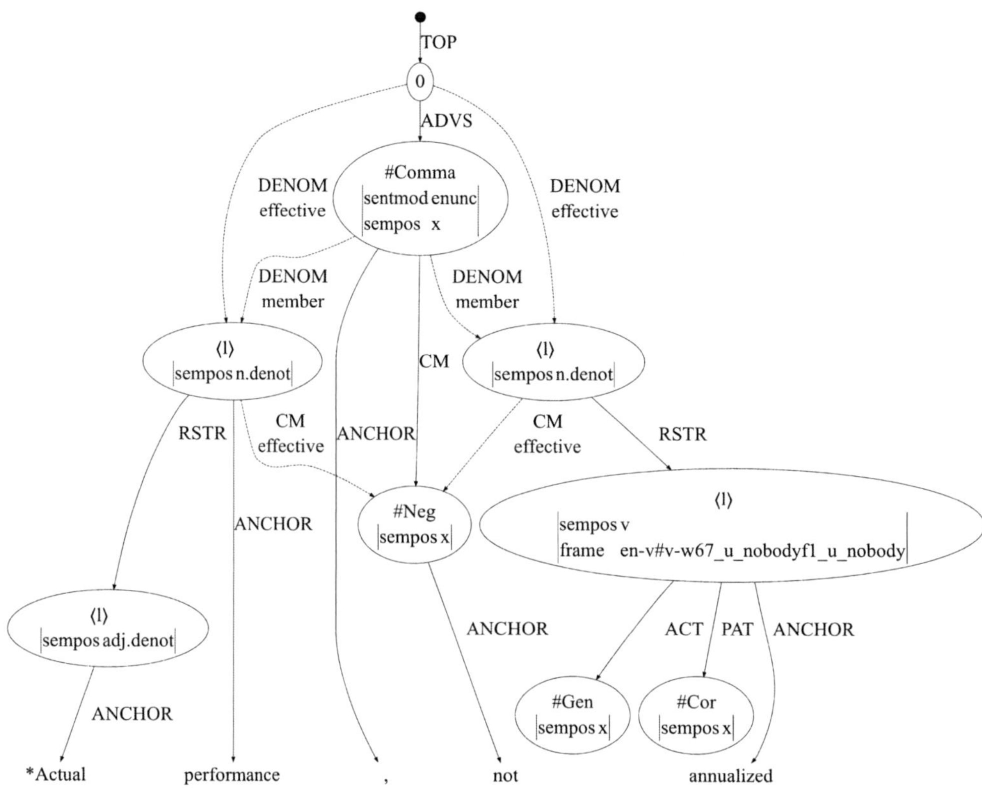

Figure 3: Converted PTG graph in the TUPA intermediate graph representation. Same as in the intermediate graph representation for all frameworks, it contains a virtual root node attached to the graph's top node with a TOP edge, and virtual terminal nodes corresponding to text tokens, attached according to the anchoring with ANCHOR edges. Same as for all frameworks with node labels and properties (i.e., all but UCCA), labels and properties are replaced with placeholders corresponding to anchored tokens, where possible. The placeholder ⟨ℓ⟩ corresponds to the concatenated lemmas of anchored tokens. For graphs containing cycles, like this one, the cycles are broken by removing an arbitrary edge in the cycle (the `coref.gram` edge in this case).

2.8   Cross-lingual track

For the cross-lingual track, as a generic contextualized encoder that supports many languages, we use multilingual BERT (`bert-base-multilingual-cased`) and train the models exactly the same as in the cross-framework track (separate model for each framework's respective monolingual dataset from the cross-lingual track), for Czech PTG and Chinese AMR.

For German DRG, as the provided dataset contains a relatively small amount of examples, 1575 as opposed to 6606 in English DRG (from the cross-framework track), we first pre-train a model on the DRG data in English and then fine-tune it on the DRG German dataset, in this case using mBERT to facilitate cross-lingual transfer. Surprisingly, this improves our validation F1 score only by 0.013 points as opposed to training on the German dataset only, showing that the contribution of cross-lingual transfer is limited (but at least not detrimental) with this architecture and data sizes.

3   HIT-SCIR Parser

The HIT-SCIR parser (Che et al., 2019) is a transition-based parser, which extended previous parsers by employing stack LSTM (Dyer et al., 2015) to allow computing homogeneous operation within a batch efficiently, and by adopting and fine-tuning BERT (Devlin et al., 2019) embedding for effectively encoding contextual information. The parser is implemented in the AllenNLP framework (Gardner et al., 2018). It supports parsing DM, PSD, UCCA, EDS and AMR, all included in the 2019 MRP shared task. The official dataset would be pre-processed for system input and post-processed for output.

In our experiment, we modified the HIT-SCIR

Track	Framework	System	# Epochs	Best Epoch	Validation F1	Eval F1	Rank	Best System
CF	EDS	HIT-SCIR	6	2	0.82	0.80	5	0.94 (H)
CF	PTG	TUPA	32	19	0.53	0.54	4	0.89 (H)
CF	UCCA	TUPA	99	66	0.79	0.73	4	0.76 (Ú)
CF	UCCA	HIT-SCIR	6	3	0.78			
CF	AMR	TUPA	8	2	0.44	0.52	5	0.82 (H)
CF	DRG	TUPA	200	99	0.52	0.63	5	0.94 (Ú)
CL	PTG	TUPA	20	13	0.60	0.58	4	0.91 (Ú)
CL	UCCA	HIT-SCIR	13	6	0.77	0.75	4	0.81 (Ú)
CL	UCCA	TUPA	100	95	0.43			
CL	AMR	TUPA	21	12	0.44	0.45	4	0.80 (H)
CL	DRG	TUPA	100	(*) 68	0.52	0.62	4	0.93 (H)
CL	DRG	TUPA	100	81	0.51			
CF	Overall					0.64	4	0.86 (H&Ú)
CL	Overall					0.60	4	0.85 (H&Ú)

Table 1: Training details and official evaluation MRP F-scores. For comparison, the highest score achieved for each framework and evaluation set is shown: H stands for Hitachi (Ozaki et al., 2020) and Ú for ÚFAL (Na and Min, 2020). HIT-SCIR for English UCCA (CF) and TUPA for German UCCA (CL), both in gray, were not used in the submission, since their validation F1 were lower than the other system. For German DRG (CL) we trained 2 parsers: one on only the CL DRG dataset (in grey), not used in the submission, and another (*) trained on the English DRG dataset in per-training. The number of epochs does not include pre-training on English DRG.

MRP 2019 parser to support the 2020 data for English EDS (for the cross-framework track) and German UCCA (for the cross-lingual track). We also explored the possibilities of employing multi-task learning with the parser (§5). A repository containing our modified version of the parser is publicly available.[5]

3.1 Transition set

Che et al. (2019) defined a different transition set per framework, according to framework's characteristics. As UCCA and EDS are already targets of 2019 MRP shared task, we inherit the existing transition sets for both frameworks. For UCCA, the transition system was modelled after that of the UCCA-specific (not MRP generic) TUPA (Hershcovich et al., 2017), which includes SHIFT, RE-DUCE, NODE$_X$, LEFT-EDGE$_X$, RIGHT-EDGE$_X$, LEFT-REMOTE$_X$, RIGHT-REMOTE$_X$ and SWAP.

The parser's EDS transition set is based on Buys and Blunsom (2017)'s work, from which NODE-START$_X$ and NODE-END are two steps to create concept nodes and form node alignment. Apart from these two, SHIFT, REDUCE, LEFT-EDGE$_X$, RIGHT-EDGE$_X$, DROP, PASS and FINISH are also used to represent EDS transition process.

[5] https://github.com/ruixiangcui/hit-scir-mrp2020

3.2 Transition Classifier

The parser state is represented by (S, L, B, E, V), where S is a stack holding processed words, L is a list holding words popped out of S that will be pushed back in the future, and B is a buffer holding unprocessed words. E is a set of labeled dependency arcs. V is a set of graph nodes include concept nodes and surface tokens. Transition classifier takes S, L, B and also the action history as input, all are modeled with stack LSTM, and outputs an action. The input to the parser is a sequence of BERT embedding. A transition classifier takes S, L, B and the action history as inputs and maximizes the log-likeihood of the correct action given the current state using an oracle to get the correct action.

3.3 Preprocessing

MRP 2019 provided companion data (containing the results of syntactic preprocessing) in both `CoNLL-U` and `mrp` formats. However, this year's task only provides `mrp`-formatted companion data. Since the HIT-SCIR 2019 parser can only take `CoNLL-U`-formatted companion data, we update it to allow converting companion data provided by 2020 MRP shared task from `mrp` format to `CoNLL-U` format.

3.4 Anchoring

The parser itself is also modified to support the MRP 2020 task. For EDS parsing specifically, in this year's task's provided data, anchoring for a token containing spaces, such as an integer number followed by a fraction number (e.g., "3 1/2") is treated as one token, while the original parser's node anchoring treats the two parts separately. Another example would be: "x-Year-to-date 1988 figure includes Volkswagen domestic-production through July." In this sentence, "x-Year-to-date 1988" is marked as a node anchored from characters 2 to 26, but the provided companion data treats "x-Year-to-date" as anchored from characters 0 to 14 as the corresponding token anchor. To handle these cases, we allow the parsing system to perform partial node alignment regardless of overlapping token anchors.

3.5 Constraints

The second problem we encounter when parsing EDS is that there are a few instances that are too short, and no valid actions can be performed according to the existing transition system. In this case, we allow the FINISH action, adding it directly to the allowed action set when no valid action exists, with the effect that the transition sequence is terminated and the current graph is returned.

3.6 Training

We train the modified HIT-SCIR parser on English and German UCCA (in the cross-framework and cross-lingual tracks, respectively) and English EDS (in the cross-lingual track). The training time is 2 days 1 hour for English UCCA, 22 hours for German UCCA, and 4 days 6 hours for English EDS. The training details are shown in Table 1. Since HIT-SCIR parser's validation score on cross-framework UCCA is 0.01 lower than TUPA, we opt for TUPA in that category. Hyperparameters are taken directly from Che et al. (2019).

4 Results

Table 1 presents the averaged scores on the test sets in the official evaluation, for our submission and for the best-performing system in each framework and evaluation set.

Validation vs. evaluation scores. The validation scores of 5 out of the 9 parsers is lower than their evaluation score: CF PTG by 0.01 F1 points, CF AMR by 0.08, CF DRG by 0.11, CL AMR by 0.01 and CL DRG by 0.1. We hypothesize it is due to the randomness in the evaluation metric: the MRP scorer uses a search algorithm to find a correspondence relation between the gold-standard and system graphs that maximizes tuple overlap. This search algorithm runs for a limited number of iterations. In order to decrease its running time, we used a lower limit on its parameters (10 random restarts, 5,000 iterations) than the default (20 random restarts, 50,000 iterations), which may have affected the accuracy of our validation score and potentially our system performance.

CF vs. CL tracks. Surprisingly, the CL track scores are mostly on-par with the CF tack ones, even though the CL parsers were often trained on significantly less examples. While the CF UCCA training dataset contains 6,872 examples and the CL UCCA contains only 3,713, both parsers gained similar scores. Similarly, the CF DRG dataset contains 6,606 example, while the the CL DRG contains only 1,575. TUPA trained only on the 1,575 examples gained a similar score to the CF one, while training on less then a fourth of the examples. The CF PTG dataset contains 42,024 examples. And while the CL PTG contains a lower, however similar, amount (39,560), it got a higher score (0.07 F1 point in validation, and 0.04 in evaluation). And while the CL AMR dataset is only a third of the CF AMR datsaet (16,529 and 57,885 examples respectively), both parser gained the same validation score. However, the evaluation score of the CF AMR is higher by 0.07 F1 points. This could be possibly attributed to our MRP scorer low iteration limit.

5 Multitask Cross-Framework Parsing

In addition to training separate models per framework and language, we also experiment with training multitask cross-framework parsers, using a neural architecture with parameter sharing (Peng et al., 2017, 2018; Hershcovich et al., 2018a; Lindemann et al., 2019; Hershcovich and Arviv, 2019). We use the HIT-SCIR parser as a basis, with different variations of shared architecture on top of it. For our experiments we choose the UCCA and EDS frameworks. The code is pub-

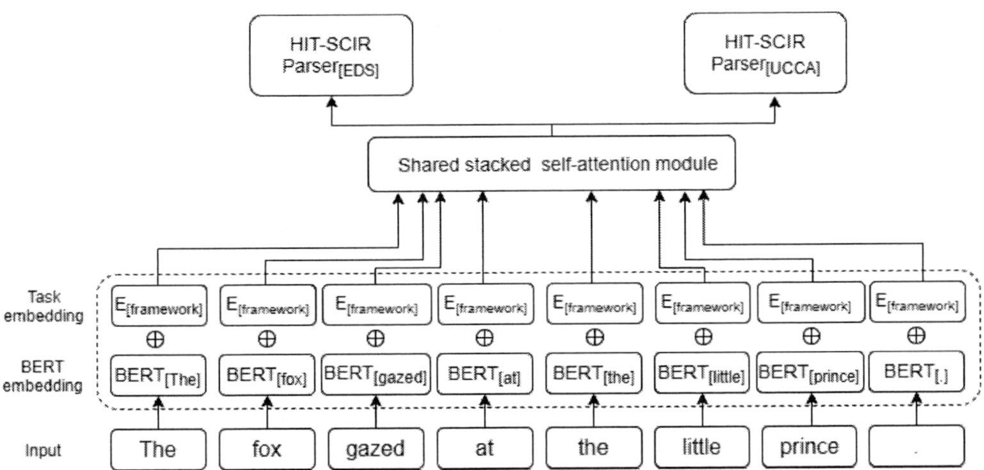

Figure 4: Illustration of the first variant of the HIT-SCIR multitask model, parsing the sentence "The fox gazed at the little prince." Top: Dedicated HIT-SCIR parsers for each framework. Bottom: Encoder architecture. BERT embeddings are extracted for each token and are concatenated with framework-specific learned embedding. Vector representations for the input tokens are then computed by a shared stacked self-attention encoder. The encoded vectors are then fed to a framework-specific HIT-SCIR parsers as input tokens.

Hyperparameter	Value
Task embedding dim	20
Shared encoder	
Input dim	1024
Framework-specific encoder	
Input dim	768
Both encoders	
Input dim	768
Projection dim	512
Feedforward hidden dim	512
# layers	3
# attention heads	8

Table 2: HIT-SCIR multitask model hyperparameters.

licly available.[6]

5.1 Model

We try two different sharing architectures. In both architectures, both frameworks share a stacked self-attention encoder (see Table 2 for details). In the first variation, we additionally use task embeddings; in the second, we use task-specific encoders instead.

Task embedding. In the first sharing architecture, both frameworks share a stacked self-attention encoder whose input is a BERT embedding concatenated with a learned task embedding of dimension 20. This has been shown to help in shared architecture multitask models (Sun et al., 2020), as well as cross-lingual parsing models, where a language embedding is used (Ammar et al., 2016; de Lhoneux et al., 2018). In our case, the "task" has two possible values, namely UCCA and EDS. The output of the shared encoder is then fed into two separate "decoders", which are HIT-SCIR parser transition classifiers. We use one for each framework, whose architecture and hyperparameters are the same as in the single task setting. Figure 4 illustrates this architecture.

Task-specific encoders. In the second architectures, both frameworks share a stacked self-attention encoder whose input is a BERT embedding, and in addition each framework has another stacked self-attention encoder of it own, similar in concept to Peng et al. (2017, 2018)'s FREDA1 architecture (which, however, used BiLSTMs), also employed by Hershcovich et al. (2018a); Lindemann et al. (2019). The outputs of these encoders are processed the same as in the first variation (task-specific decoders). Figure 5 illustrates this architecture.

5.2 Training details

Each training batch contains examples from a single framework, while the model is alternating between the different batch types. As the EDS training dataset is much larger than the UCCA one,

---

[6]https://github.com/OfirArviv/
hit-scir-mrp2020/tree/multitask

Sharing architecture	# Epochs	Best Epoch	Validation Average F1	Validation UCCA F1	Validation EDS F1
Shared encoder					
+ task embedding	13	2	0.55	0.68	0.43
+ task specific encoders	13	4	0.38	0.49	0.27

Table 3: HIT-SCIR multitask model training details and scores.

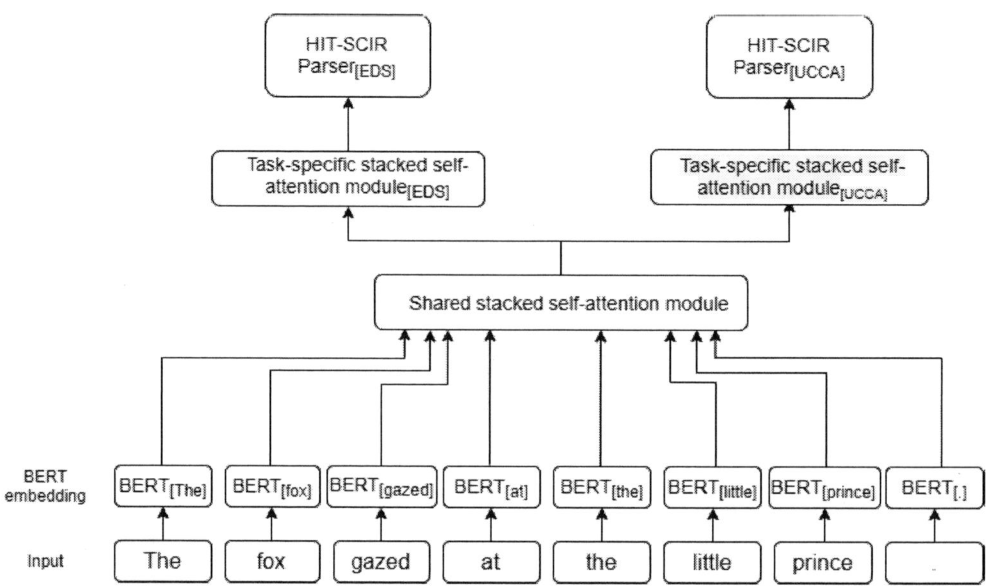

Figure 5: Illustration of the second variant of the HIT-SCIR multitask model, parsing the sentence "The fox gazed at the little prince." Top: Dedicated HIT-SCIR parsers for each framework. Bottom: Encoder architecture. BERT embeddings are extracted for each token. Vector representations for the input tokens are then computed by a shared stacked self-attention encoder and by a framework-specific self-attention encoder. The encoded vectors are then fed to a framework-specific HIT-SCIR parsers as input tokens.

we balance them out by training the same number of examples from each framework in each epoch. Due to time constraints we tried out only a single set of hyperparameters, chosen arbitrarily without tuning. We select the epoch with the best average MRP F-score on a validation set, which is the union of both validation sets of EDS and UCCA.

5.3 Results

Table 3 presents the average scores on the validation sets for multitask trained models. The multitask HIT-SCIR consistently falls behind the single-task one, for each framework separately and in the overall scores; but it is clear that our first multitask architecture (with task embedding) outperforms the second one (with task-specific encoders).

5.4 Discussion

Previous results on multitask MRP showed mixed results, some showing improved performances (Peng et al., 2017; Hershcovich et al., 2018a; Lindemann et al., 2019). Others failed to show improvements (Hershcovich and Arviv, 2019), and argued that the large multitask models were underfitting due to insufficient training. In our case, however, the multitask models underperform despite reaching convergence.

We hypothesize that with better hyperparameters or different sharing architectures, more favorable results could be obtained. However, it is possible that multitask learning would be more helpful in a factorization-based parser (Peng et al., 2017; Lindemann et al., 2019), where inference is global and more uniform across frameworks. A transition-based parser may be less suited for utilizing information from different tasks that have different transition systems, as in the HIT-SCIR parser. Adapting it to have a more uniform transition system, like TUPA does, could facilitate cross-framework sharing. Alternatively, improving TUPA's training efficiency would also enable such experimentation.

6 Conclusion

We have presented TUPA-MRP and a modified HIT-SCIR parser, which constitute the HUJI-KU submission in the CoNLL 2020 shared task on Cross-Framework Meaning Representation. TUPA is a general transition-based DAG parser with a uniform transition system, which is easily adaptable for multiple frameworks. We used it for parsing in both the cross-framework and the cross-lingual tracks, adapting it for the newly introduced frameworks, PTG and DRG. HIT-SCIR is a transition-based parser with framework-specific transition systems, which we adapted for this year's shared task and used for English EDS and UCCA parsing in the cross-framework track. The HIT-SCIR parser was additionally used in experimenting on multitask learning, with negative results for that approach.

Future work will tackle the MRP task with more modern transition-based-like parser architectures, such as pointer networks (Ma et al., 2018), which have so far only been applied to bilexical framworks, i.e., flavor-0 SDP (Fernández-González and Gómez-Rodríguez, 2020).

Acknowledgments

We are grateful for the valuable feedback from the anonymous reviewers.

References

Omri Abend and Ari Rappoport. 2013. Universal Conceptual Cognitive Annotation (UCCA). In *Proc. of ACL*, pages 228–238.

Waleed Ammar, George Mulcaire, Miguel Ballesteros, Chris Dyer, and Noah A. Smith. 2016. Many languages, one parser. *Transactions of the Association for Computational Linguistics*, 4:431–444.

Jan Buys and Phil Blunsom. 2017. Robust incremental neural semantic graph parsing. In *Proceedings of the 55th Annual Meeting of the Association for Computational Linguistics (Volume 1: Long Papers)*, pages 1215–1226, Vancouver, Canada. Association for Computational Linguistics.

Wanxiang Che, Longxu Dou, Yang Xu, Yuxuan Wang, Yijia Liu, and Ting Liu. 2019. HIT-SCIR at MRP 2019: A unified pipeline for meaning representation parsing via efficient training and effective encoding. In *Proceedings of the Shared Task on Cross-Framework Meaning Representation Parsing at the 2019 Conference on Natural Language Learning*, pages 76–85, Hong Kong. Association for Computational Linguistics.

Jacob Devlin, Ming-Wei Chang, Kenton Lee, and Kristina Toutanova. 2019. BERT: Pre-training of deep bidirectional transformers for language understanding. In *Proc. of NAACL*, pages 4171–4186.

Chris Dyer, Miguel Ballesteros, Wang Ling, Austin Matthews, and Noah A. Smith. 2015. Transition-based dependeny parsing with stack long short-term memory. In *Proc. of ACL*, pages 334–343.

Daniel Fernández-González and Carlos Gómez-Rodríguez. 2020. Transition-based semantic dependency parsing with pointer networks. In *Proceedings of the 58th Annual Meeting of the Association for Computational Linguistics*, pages 7035–7046, Online. Association for Computational Linguistics.

Matt Gardner, Joel Grus, Mark Neumann, Oyvind Tafjord, Pradeep Dasigi, Nelson F. Liu, Matthew Peters, Michael Schmitz, and Luke S. Zettlemoyer. 2018. AllenNLP: A deep semantic natural language processing platform. *arXiv preprint arXiv:1803.07640*.

Xavier Glorot and Yoshua Bengio. 2010. Understanding the difficulty of training deep feedforward neural networks. In *Proceedings of the thirteenth international conference on artificial intelligence and statistics*, pages 249–256.

Alex Graves. 2008. Supervised sequence labelling with recurrent neural networks. *Ph. D. thesis*.

Daniel Hershcovich, Omri Abend, and Ari Rappoport. 2017. A transition-based directed acyclic graph parser for UCCA. In *Proc. of ACL*, pages 1127–1138.

Daniel Hershcovich, Omri Abend, and Ari Rappoport. 2018a. Multitask parsing across semantic representations. In *Proceedings of the 56th Meeting of the Association for Computational Linguistics*, pages 373 – 385, Melbourne, Australia.

Daniel Hershcovich, Omri Abend, and Ari Rappoport. 2018b. Universal dependency parsing with a general transition-based DAG parser. In *Proc. of CoNLL UD Shared Task*, pages 103–112.

Daniel Hershcovich, Zohar Aizenbud, Leshem Choshen, Elior Sulem, Ari Rappoport, and Omri Abend. 2019. SemEval-2019 task 1: Cross-lingual semantic parsing with UCCA. In *Proc. of SemEval*, pages 1–10.

Daniel Hershcovich and Ofir Arviv. 2019. TUPA at MRP 2019: A multi-task baseline system. In *Proceedings of the Shared Task on Cross-Framework Meaning Representation Parsing at the 2019 Conference on Natural Language Learning*, pages 28–39, Hong Kong. Association for Computational Linguistics.

Daniel Hershcovich, Miryam de Lhoneux, Artur Kulmizev, Elham Pejhan, and Joakim Nivre. 2020. Køpsala: Transition-based graph parsing via efficient training and effective encoding. In *Proceedings of the 16th International Conference on Parsing Technologies and the IWPT 2020 Shared Task on Parsing into Enhanced Universal Dependencies*, pages 236–244, Online. Association for Computational Linguistics.

Sepp Hochreiter and Jürgen Schmidhuber. 1997. Long short-term memory. *Neural computation*, 9(8):1735–1780.

Eliyahu Kiperwasser and Yoav Goldberg. 2016. Simple and accurate dependency parsing using bidirectional LSTM feature representations. *TACL*, 4:313–327.

Miryam de Lhoneux, Johannes Bjerva, Isabelle Augenstein, and Anders Søgaard. 2018. Parameter sharing between dependency parsers for related languages. In *Proceedings of the 2018 Conference on Empirical Methods in Natural Language Processing*, pages 4992–4997, Brussels, Belgium. Association for Computational Linguistics.

Matthias Lindemann, Jonas Groschwitz, and Alexander Koller. 2019. Compositional semantic parsing across graphbanks. In *Proceedings of the 57th Annual Meeting of the Association for Computational Linguistics*, pages 4576–4585, Florence, Italy. Association for Computational Linguistics.

Xuezhe Ma, Zecong Hu, Jingzhou Liu, Nanyun Peng, Graham Neubig, and Eduard Hovy. 2018. Stack-pointer networks for dependency parsing. In *Proceedings of the 56th Annual Meeting of the Association for Computational Linguistics (Volume 1: Long Papers)*, pages 1403–1414, Melbourne, Australia. Association for Computational Linguistics.

Wolfgang Maier and Timm Lichte. 2016. Discontinuous parsing with continuous trees. In *Proc. of Workshop on Discontinuous Structures in NLP*, pages 47–57.

Seung-Hoon Na and Jinwoo Min. 2020. JBNU at MRP 2020: AMR parsing using a joint state model for graph-sequence iterative inference. In *Proceedings of the CoNLL 2020 Shared Task: Cross-Framework Meaning Representation Parsing*, pages 83–87, Online.

Graham Neubig, Chris Dyer, Yoav Goldberg, Austin Matthews, Waleed Ammar, Antonios Anastasopoulos, Miguel Ballesteros, David Chiang, Daniel Clothiaux, Trevor Cohn, Kevin Duh, Manaal Faruqui, Cynthia Gan, Dan Garrette, Yangfeng Ji, Lingpeng Kong, Adhiguna Kuncoro, Gaurav Kumar, Chaitanya Malaviya, Paul Michel, Yusuke Oda, Matthew Richardson, Naomi Saphra, Swabha Swayamdipta, and Pengcheng Yin. 2017. DyNet: The dynamic neural network toolkit. *CoRR*, abs/1701.03980.

Stephan Oepen, Omri Abend, Lasha Abzianidze, Johan Bos, Jan Hajič, Daniel Hershcovich, Bin Li, Tim O'Gorman, Nianwen Xue, and Daniel Zeman. 2020. MRP 2020: The Second Shared Task on Cross-framework and Cross-Lingual Meaning Representation Parsing. In *Proceedings of the CoNLL 2020 Shared Task: Cross-Framework Meaning Representation Parsing*, pages 1–22, Online.

Stephan Oepen, Omri Abend, Jan Hajič, Daniel Hershcovich, Marco Kuhlmann, Tim O'Gorman, Nianwen Xue, Jayeol Chun, Milan Straka, and Zdeňka Urešová. 2019. MRP 2019: Cross-framework Meaning Representation Parsing. In *Proceedings of the Shared Task on Cross-Framework Meaning Representation Parsing at the 2019 Conference on Computational Natural Language Learning*, pages 1–27, Hong Kong, China.

Hiroaki Ozaki, Gaku Morio, Yuta Koreeda, Terufumi Morishita, and Toshinori Miyoshi. 2020. Hitachi at MRP 2020: Text-to-graph-notation transducer. In *Proceedings of the CoNLL 2020 Shared Task: Cross-Framework Meaning Representation Parsing*, pages 40–52, Online.

Hao Peng, Sam Thomson, and Noah A. Smith. 2017. Deep multitask learning for semantic dependency parsing. In *Proceedings of the 55th Annual Meeting of the Association for Computational Linguistics (Volume 1: Long Papers)*, pages 2037–2048, Vancouver, Canada. Association for Computational Linguistics.

Hao Peng, Sam Thomson, Swabha Swayamdipta, and Noah A. Smith. 2018. Learning joint semantic parsers from disjoint data. In *Proc. of NAACL-HLT*.

Mike Schuster and Kuldip K Paliwal. 1997. Bidirectional recurrent neural networks. *IEEE Transactions on Signal Processing*, 45(11):2673–2681.

Y. Sun, Shuohuan Wang, Yukun Li, Shikun Feng, Hao Tian, H. Wu, and Haifeng Wang. 2020. Ernie 2.0: A continual pre-training framework for language understanding. In *AAAI*.

JBNU at MRP 2020: AMR Parsing Using a Joint State Model for Graph-Sequence Iterative Inference

Jinwoo Min[†], Seung-Hoon Na[†], Jong-Hun Shin[‡] and **Young-Kil Kim[‡]**
[†]Computer Science and Engineering, Jeonbuk National University, South Korea
[‡]Electronics and Telecommunication Research Institute (ETRI), South Korea
`jinwoomin4488@gmail.com, nash@jbnu.ac.kr`
`{jhshin82,kimyk}@etri.re.kr`

Abstract

This paper describes the Jeonbuk National University (JBNU) system for the 2020 shared task on Cross-Framework Meaning Representation Parsing at the Conference on Computational Natural Language Learning. Among the five frameworks, we address only the abstract meaning representation framework and propose a *joint state* model for the graph-sequence iterative inference of (Cai and Lam, 2020) for a simplified graph-sequence inference. In our joint state model, we update only a single joint state vector during the graph-sequence inference process instead of keeping the dual state vectors, and all other components are exactly the same as in (Cai and Lam, 2020).

1 Introduction

Recent studies on meaning representation parsing (MRP) have focused on different semantic graph frameworks (Oepen et al., 2019) such as bilexical semantic dependency graphs (Peng et al., 2017; Wang et al., 2018; Peng et al., 2018; Dozat and Manning, 2018; Na et al., 2019), a universal conceptual cognitive annotation (Hershcovich et al., 2017, 2018), abstract meaning representation (Wang and Xue, 2017; Guo and Lu, 2018; Song et al., 2019; Zhang et al., 2019; Cai and Lam, 2019, 2020; Zhou et al., 2020), and a discourse representation structure (Abzianidze et al., 2019; Liu et al., 2018; van Noord et al., 2018; Liu et al., 2019; Evang, 2019; Liu et al., 2020). To jointly address various semantic graphs, the aim of the Cross-Framework MRP task at the 2020 Conference (MRP 2020) on Computational Natural Language Learning (CoNLL) is to develop semantic graph parsing across the following five frameworks (Oepen et al., 2020): 1) **EDS**: Elementary Dependency Structures (Oepen and Lønning, 2006), 2) **PTG**: Prague Tectogrammatical Graphs

(Hajič et al., 2012), 3) **UCCA**: Universal Conceptual Cognitive Annotation (Abend and Rappoport, 2013), 4) **AMR**: Abstract Meaning Representation (Banarescu et al., 2013), and 5) **DRG**: Discourse Representation Graphs (Abzianidze et al., 2017).

For MRP 2020, we address only the AMR framework and present a *joint state* model for graph-sequence iterative inference, as a simple extension of (Cai and Lam, 2020). The graph-sequence iterative model of (Cai and Lam, 2020) incrementally constructs an AMR graph starting from an empty graph G_0 by alternatively applying two modules: 1) *Concept Solver*, which uses a previous graph hypothesis G_i to predict a new concept, and 2) *Relation Solver*, which uses a previous concept hypothesis to predict relations for the new concept.

The *dual-state* model of (Cai and Lam, 2020) deploys two state vectors x_t and y_t for the graph-sequence iterative inference, which refers to the t-th sequence hypothesis and t-th graph hypothesis, respectively. Unlike the dual state model, we instead maintain a *joint state* vector z_t, which encodes both sequence and graph hypotheses to apply a graph-sequence iterative inference in a simple and unified manner. During the iterative inference stage, we take the current joint state vector as a query vector and update the next joint state vector by applying attention mechanisms both to the text (i.e., sequence memory) and graph (i.e., graph memory) parts separately. The final joint state vector is then passed to the concept and relation solvers, which predict new concepts and their relations, respectively, as with the dual state model by (Cai and Lam, 2020).

We submitted the results of our AMR parsing model during the post-evaluation stage and ranked between 3rd and 4th place among the participants in the official results under the cross-framework

83

Proceedings of the CoNLL 2020 Shared Task: Cross-Framework Meaning Representation Parsing, pages 83–87
Online, Nov. 19-20, 2020. ©2020 Association for Computational Linguistics

metric [1].

The remainder of this paper is organized as follows: Section 2 presents the detailed architecture of our system. Section 3 describes the detailed process used for training biaffine attention models. Section 4 provides the official results of MRP 2020. Finally, some concluding remarks and a description of future research are given in Section 5.

2 Model

Figure 1 shows the neural architecture based on the joint state model for a graph-sequence iterative inference.

The neural architecture consists of five components: a 1) *sequence encoder*, 2) *graph encoder*, 3) *concept solver*, 4) *relation solver*, and 5) *joint state model* for a graph-sequence iterative inference.

In the following, we briefly summarize the first four components of our model, which are almost the same as those of (Cai and Lam, 2020), where only the joint state vector is used as the unified query vector for the concept and relation solvers. We then present our joint state model in more details.

2.1 Sequence encoder: Multi-layer transformer

Following the notations of (Cai and Lam, 2020), let W be the input sentence consisting of $w_1, \cdots, w_n$. The sequence encoder is based on a multi-layer transformer architecture (Vaswani et al., 2017), where inputs at the bottom layer combine the character-level features, POS tag, named entity tags, and BERT-based features. Roughly, the sequence encoder takes W as input and generates the sequence of hidden states as follows:

$$h_0, h_1, \cdots, h_n =$$
$$\text{SequenceEncoder}((BOS, w_1, \cdots, w_N))$$

where h_0 corresponds to the special token BOS.

2.2 Graph encoder: Multi-layer Transformer

Suppose that G_i is the current graph consisting of i nodes, $c_1, \cdots, c_i$. The graph encoder is based on a multi-layer transformer encoder with masked self-attention and source-attention. Roughly, the

graph encoder takes G and produces the following hidden states of the concept nodes:

$$s_0, s_1, \cdots, s_i = \text{GraphEncoder}(G = \{c_1, \cdots, c_i\})$$

where s_0 corresponds to the special token BOG.

2.3 Concept solver: Attention over words

Suppose that z_t is the current joint state vector that encodes the t-th sequence and graph hypotheses. The concept solver takes z_t and generates a new concept.

$$
\begin{aligned}
q_t &= W^Q z_t \\
k_{1:n} &= W^K h_{1:n} \\
v_{1:n} &= W^V h_{1:n} \\
[\alpha_t, r_t] &= Attention(q_t, k_{1:n}, v_{1:n}) \\
z'_t &= z_t + r_t
\end{aligned}
$$

$$(1)$$

where $Attention(q, k, v)$ is the attention module that takes q, k, and v as the query vector, keys, and values, respectively, and returns the attention probabilities α_t and attentive representation r_t. Given z'_t, the concept generation process equipped with the copying mechanism generates a new concept as follows:

$$
\begin{aligned}
P^{(vocab)} &= softmax\left(W^{(vocab)} z'_t + b^{(vocab)}\right) \\
[p_1, p_2, p_3] &= softmax\left(W^{(switch)} z'_t\right) \\
P(c) &= p_0 \cdot P^{(vocab)}(c) + \\
&\quad p_1 \cdot \left(\sum_{i \in L(c)} \alpha_t[i]\right) + \\
&\quad p_2 \cdot \left(\sum_{i \in T(c)} \alpha_t[i]\right)
\end{aligned}
$$

where $L(c)$ and $T(c)$ are index sets of lemmas and tokens respectively, which have the surface form as a concept c defined by (Cai and Lam, 2020).

2.4 Relation solver: Multi-head attention over graph nodes

The relation solver is based on the multi-head attention over graph nodes. Suppose that z_t is the current joint state vector, G_i is the current graph, and H is the number of heads for the multi-head attention. For each head h, the relation solver first

---

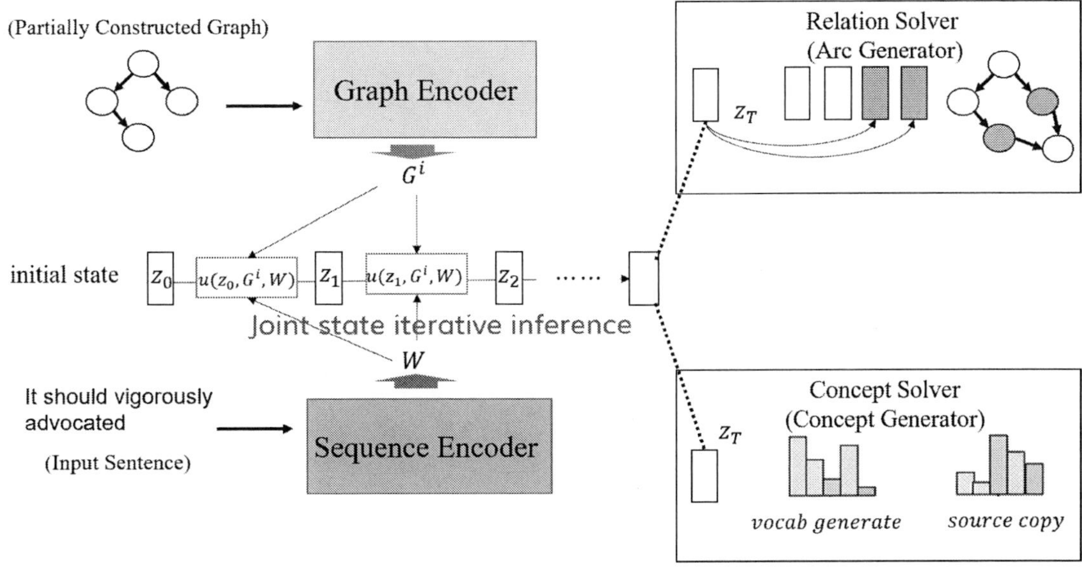

Figure 1: The neural architecture of the joint state model for a graph-sequence iterative inference.

applies the attention over graph nodes $s_0, \cdots, s_i$.

$$
\begin{aligned}
q_t^h &= W_h^Q z_t \\
k_{0:i}^h &= W_h^K s_{0:i} \\
v_{0:i}^h &= W_h^V s_{0:i} \\
\left[\beta_t^h, r_t^h\right] &= Attention(q_t^h, k_{0:i}^h, v_{0:i}^h)
\end{aligned}
\tag{2}
$$

The final edge probabilities are obtained by taking the maximum over the multi-attention probabilities:

$$
\beta_t[i] = max_{h=1}^{H}\beta_t^h[i]
\tag{3}
$$

2.5 Iterative inference: Joint state model

The remaining part is to obtain the new joint state vector z_{t+1} from z_t. Suppose again that z_t is the current joint state vector and G_i is the current graph. The joint state model for an iterative inference is formulated as follows:

$$
\begin{aligned}
z_0 &= fusion(h_0, s_i) \\
g_t &= \sigma(W_g z_t + b_g) \\
\left[\_, z_t^{seq}\right] &= Attention(z_t, h_{1:n}, h_{1:n}) \\
\left[\_, z_t^{graph}\right] &= Attention(z_t, s_{0:i}, s_{0:i}) \\
z_{t+1} &= z_t + (1 - g_t)z_t^{seq} + g_t z_t^{graph}
\end{aligned}
$$

where W_g and b_g are the parameters for the affine transformation of z_t and $fusion(\mathbf{x}, \mathbf{y})$ is the fusion

Encoder	
lemma emb dim	300
char emb dim	50
cnn filter size	100
pos emb dim	50
ner emb dim	50
encoder layers	3
encoder dropout	0.33
Decoder	
concept emb dim	300
concept char emb dim	50
cnn filter size	100
decoder layers	3
decoder dropout	0.33

Table 1: Hyper-parameter settings

function defined by (Hu et al., 2018) [2].

3 Training

3.1 Hyperparameters

We used the Adam optimizer (Kingma and Ba, 2015) to train our AMR parsing model. Table 1 summarizes the hyper-parameters used for training these models

4 Official Results

The official results of our AMR parsing based on the joint state model, referred to as "Graph-Sequence+Joint", are summarized in Table 2,

---

[2]For simplicity, we obtain z_0 based on a function of h_0 and s_i. More generally, however, z_0 could be initialized as a function of $h_{1:n}$ and $s_{0:i}$.

which compares the results of the top-2 systems (Hitachi and ÚFAL). Overall, our system ranks between 3rd and 4th place among all participants which submitted to the AMR framework.

5 Summary and Conclusion

In this paper, we presented the Jeonbuk National University system based on a joint state model for a graph-sequence iterative inference on the AMR framework at MRP 2020 task. However, one limitation of the current joint state model is that the iterative inference process is separately formulated from the concept and relation solvers, without a tight coupling. In a future study, we plan to further elaborate the joint state models by reformulating an iterative inference based on attention results from the concept and relation solvers.

Acknowledgments

This work was supported by Institute of Information & communications Technology Planning & Evaluation (IITP) grant funded by the Korea government(MSIT) (R7119-16-1001, Core technology development of the real-time simultaneous speech translation based on knowledge enhancement)

References

Omri Abend and Ari Rappoport. 2013. Universal conceptual cognitive annotation (UCCA). In *Proceedings of the 51st Annual Meeting of the Association for Computational Linguistics*, ACL '13, pages 228–238. Association for Computational Linguistics.

Lasha Abzianidze, Johannes Bjerva, Kilian Evang, Hessel Haagsma, Rik van Noord, Pierre Ludmann, Duc-Duy Nguyen, and Johan Bos. 2017. The Parallel Meaning Bank: Towards a multilingual corpus of translations annotated with compositional meaning representations. In *Proceedings of the 15th Conference of the European Chapter of the Association for Computational Linguistics*, pages 242–247.

Lasha Abzianidze, Rik van Noord, Hessel Haagsma, and Johan Bos. 2019. The first shared task on discourse representation structure parsing. In *Proceedings of the IWCS Shared Task on Semantic Parsing*.

Laura Banarescu, Claire Bonial, Shu Cai, Madalina Georgescu, Kira Griffitt, Ulf Hermjakob, Kevin Knight, Philipp Koehn, Martha Palmer, and Nathan Schneider. 2013. Abstract meaning representation for sembanking. In *Proceedings of the 7th Linguistic Annotation Workshop and Interoperability with Discourse*, pages 178–186.

Deng Cai and Wai Lam. 2019. Core semantic first: A top-down approach for AMR parsing. In *Proceedings of the 2019 Conference on Empirical Methods in Natural Language Processing and the 9th International Joint Conference on Natural Language Processing (EMNLP-IJCNLP)*, pages 3799–3809.

Deng Cai and Wai Lam. 2020. AMR parsing via graph-sequence iterative inference. In *Proceedings of the 58th Annual Meeting of the Association for Computational Linguistics*, pages 1290–1301.

Timothy Dozat and Christopher D. Manning. 2018. Simpler but more accurate semantic dependency parsing. In *Proceedings of the 56th Annual Meeting of the Association for Computational Linguistics*, ACL '18, pages 484–490.

Kilian Evang. 2019. Transition-based DRS parsing using stack-LSTMs. In *Proceedings of the IWCS Shared Task on Semantic Parsing*.

Zhijiang Guo and Wei Lu. 2018. Better transition-based AMR parsing with a refined search space. In *Proceedings of the 2018 Conference on Empirical Methods in Natural Language Processing*, EMNLP '18, pages 1712–1722.

Jan Hajič, Eva Hajičová, Jarmila Panevová, Petr Sgall, Ondřej Bojar, Silvie Cinková, Eva Fučíková, Marie Mikulová, Petr Pajas, Jan Popelka, Jiří Semecký, Jana Šindlerová, Jan Štěpánek, Josef Toman, Zdeňka Urešová, and Zdeněk Žabokrtský. 2012. Announcing Prague Czech-English dependency treebank 2.0. In *Proceedings of the Eighth International Conference on Language Resources and Evaluation (LREC-2012)*, LREC-2012, pages 3153–3160.

Daniel Hershcovich, Omri Abend, and Ari Rappoport. 2017. A transition-based directed acyclic graph parser for UCCA. In *Proceedings of the 55th Annual Meeting of the Association for Computational Linguistics*, ACL '17, pages 1127–1138.

Daniel Hershcovich, Omri Abend, and Ari Rappoport. 2018. Multitask parsing across semantic representations. In *Proceedings of the 56th Annual Meeting of the Association for Computational Linguistics*, pages 373–385.

Minghao Hu, Yuxing Peng, Zhen Huang, Xipeng Qiu, Furu Wei, and Ming Zhou. 2018. Reinforced mnemonic reader for machine reading comprehension. In *Proceedings of the Twenty-Seventh International Joint Conference on Artificial Intelligence*, IJCAI '18, pages 4099–4106.

Diederick P Kingma and Jimmy Ba. 2015. Adam: A method for stochastic optimization. In *International Conference on Learning Representations*, ICLR '13.

Jiangming Liu, Shay B. Cohen, and Mirella Lapata. 2018. Discourse representation structure parsing. In *Proceedings of the 56th Annual Meeting of the Association for Computational Linguistics (Volume 1: Long Papers)*, pages 429–439.

Jiangming Liu, Shay B. Cohen, and Mirella Lapata. 2019. Discourse representation parsing for sentences and documents. In *Proceedings of the 57th Annual Meeting of the Association for Computational Linguistics*, pages 6248–6262.

Jiangming Liu, Shay B. Cohen, and Mirella Lapata. 2020. Dscorer: A fast evaluation metric for discourse representation structure parsing. In *Proceedings of the 58th Annual Meeting of the Association for Computational Linguistics*, pages 4547–4554. Association for Computational Linguistics.

Seung-Hoon Na, Jinwoo Min, Kwanghyeon Park, Jong-Hun Shin, and Young-Kil Kim. 2019. Jbnu at MRP 2019: Multi-level biaffine attention for semantic dependency parsing. In *Proceedings of the Shared Task on Cross-Framework*

method		tops			labels			properties			edges			all		
		P	R	F	P	R	F	P	R	F	P	R	F	P	R	F
Hitachi	lpps	0.84	0.84	0.84	0.83	0.85	0.84	0.86	0.77	0.81	0.71	0.73	0.72	0.78	0.79	0.79
	all	0.86	0.86	0.86	0.88	0.86	0.87	0.83	0.81	0.82	0.77	0.74	0.76	0.83	0.80	0.82
ÚFAL	lpps	0.86	0.86	0.86	0.85	0.87	0.86	0.78	0.71	0.75	0.69	0.71	0.70	0.77	0.79	0.78
	all	0.84	0.84	0.84	0.88	0.87	0.87	0.86	0.85	0.85	0.73	0.70	0.71	0.81	0.79	0.80
Graph-Sequence+Joint	lpps	0.86	0.86	0.86	0.79	0.80	0.79	0.54	0.45	0.49	0.68	0.67	0.68	0.74	0.73	0.74
	all	0.84	0.84	0.84	0.79	0.73	0.76	0.68	0.39	0.50	0.61	0.54	0.57	0.71	0.62	0.66

Table 2: The official results of the MRP metrics on the AMR framework, comparing the top-2 systems (Hitachi and ÚFAL) with our system using the joint state iterative inference (Graph-Sequence+Joint).

Meaning Representation Parsing at the 2019 Conference on Computational Natural Language Learning, pages 95 – 103, Hong Kong, China.

Rik van Noord, Lasha Abzianidze, Antonio Toral, and Johan Bos. 2018. Exploring neural methods for parsing discourse representation structures. *Transactions of the Association for Computational Linguistics*, 6:619–633.

Stephan Oepen, Omri Abend, Lasha Abzianidze, Johan Bos, Jan Hajič, Daniel Hershcovich, Bin Li, Tim O'Gorman, Nianwen Xue, and Daniel Zeman. 2020. MRP 2020: The Second Shared Task on Cross-framework and Cross-Lingual Meaning Representation Parsing. In *Proceedings of the CoNLL 2020 Shared Task: Cross-Framework Meaning Representation Parsing*, pages 1 – 22, Online.

Stephan Oepen, Omri Abend, Jan Hajič, Daniel Hershcovich, Marco Kuhlmann, Tim O'Gorman, Nianwen Xue, Jayeol Chun, Milan Straka, and Zdeňka Urešová. 2019. MRP 2019: Cross-framework Meaning Representation Parsing. In *Proceedings of the Shared Task on Cross-Framework Meaning Representation Parsing at the 2019 Conference on Computational Natural Language Learning*, pages 1 – 27, Hong Kong, China.

Stephan Oepen and Jan Tore Lønning. 2006. Discriminant-based MRS banking. In *Proceedings of the Fifth International Conference on Language Resources and Evaluation*, LREC'06.

Hao Peng, Sam Thomson, and Noah A. Smith. 2017. Deep multitask learning for semantic dependency parsing. In *Proceedings of the 55th Annual Meeting of the Association for Computational Linguistics*, ACL '17, pages 2037–2048.

Hao Peng, Sam Thomson, Swabha Swayamdipta, and Noah A. Smith. 2018. Learning joint semantic parsers from disjoint data. In *Proceedings of the 2018 Conference of the North American Chapter of the Association for Computational Linguistics: Human Language Technologies*, NAACL '18, pages 1492–1502.

Linfeng Song, Daniel Gildea, Yue Zhang, Zhiguo Wang, and Jinsong Su. 2019. Semantic neural machine translation using AMR. *Transactions of the Association for Computational Linguistics*, 7:19–31.

Ashish Vaswani, Noam Shazeer, Niki Parmar, Jakob Uszkoreit, Llion Jones, Aidan N Gomez, Ł ukasz Kaiser, and Illia Polosukhin. 2017. Attention is all you need. In *Advances in Neural Information Processing Systems 30*, pages 5998–6008.

Chuan Wang and Nianwen Xue. 2017. Getting the most out of AMR parsing. In *Proceedings of the 2017 Conference on Empirical Methods in Natural Language Processing*, EMNLP '17, pages 1257–1268.

Yuxuan Wang, Wanxiang Che, Jiang Guo, and Ting Liu. 2018. A neural transition-based approach for semantic dependency graph parsing. In *Proceedings of the Thirty-Second AAAI Conference on Artificial Intelligence*, AAAI '18, pages 5561–5568.

Sheng Zhang, Xutai Ma, Kevin Duh, and Benjamin Van Durme. 2019. AMR parsing as sequence-to-graph transduction. In *Proceedings of the 57th Annual Meeting of the Association for Computational Linguistics*, ACL '19, pages 80–94.

Qiji Zhou, Yue Zhang, Donghong Ji, and Hao Tang. 2020. AMR parsing with latent structural information. In *Proceedings of the 58th Annual Meeting of the Association for Computational Linguistics*, pages 4306–4319. Association for Computational Linguistics.